Betty Crocker

the big book of bread

Houghton Mifflin Harcourt

Boston • New York

General Mills

Food Content and Relationship
Marketing Director: Geoff Johnson

Food Content Marketing Manager:
Susan Klobuchar

Editor: Grace Wells

Food Editor: Andrea Bidwell

Kitchen Manager: Ann Stuart

Recipe Development and Testing:
Betty Crocker Kitchens

Photography: General Mills Photography
Studios and Image Library

Photographers: Andy Swarbrick and
Erin Smith

Food Stylists: Carol Grones and
Karen Linden

Houghton Mifflin Harcourt

Publisher: Natalie Chapman

Editorial Director: Cindy Kitchel

Executive Editor: Anne Ficklen

Associate Editor: Heather Dabah

Managing Editor: Marina Padakis

Production Editor: Jamie Selzer

Art Director: Tai Blanche

Cover Design: Suzanne Sunwoo

Interior Design and Layout:
Holly Wittenberg

Manufacturing Manager: Kevin Watt

For information about permission to reproduce selections from this book, write to
Permissions, Houghton Mifflin Harcourt Publishing Company, 215 Park Avenue South,
New York, New York 10003.

www.hmhbooks.com

Library of Congress Cataloging-in-Publication Data is available upon request.
ISBN: 978-1-118-45345-2 (pbk.); 978-0-544-17831-1 (ebk.)

Manufactured in the United States of America

DOC 10   9   8   7   6   5   4   3   2

Cover Photos: Top (left to right): Snickerdoodle Mini Doughnuts (page 183); Oatmeal-Streusel
Bread (page 106); Strawberry-Buttermilk Muffins (page 33); Whole-Grain Artisan Bread (page 215)

Bottom (left to right): Cheddar-Chiles Cornbread Scones (page 65); Chocolate-Cherry Bread
(page 93)

dear friends,

There's something magical about homemade bread, fresh from the oven—and it doesn't matter what kind of bread it is. It might be a sweet quick bread loaf for brunch or savory muffins that you've made to serve with a meal. You may be looking for a bakery-style no-knead artisan loaf or a simple old-fashioned batter bread. Whatever you crave, you'll find it here in this fabulous book.

This *Big Book of Bread* is filled with more than 200 delicious recipes plus beautiful photos to inspire you. There are traditional favorites like Banana Bread (page 84) and French Bread (page 219). But you'll also discover new trendy recipes including Apple-Fig Bread with Honey Glaze (page 102) and treats like Snickerdoodle Mini Doughnuts (page 183). And be sure to look for the colorful "rainbow" frosted Cake Doughnuts (page 139)—they're really fun to make for a party. Each recipe is kitchen tested and includes complete easy-to-understand instructions so you can be sure of great results. Plus, there are easy-to-follow how-to photos showing many techniques throughout the book.

There's even a special feature on how to use up bread that is left over from a meal—included are creative ways to transform bread into a variety of recipes. What a great idea!

You'll refer to *The Big Book of Bread* again and again for recipes and ideas to please your family and friends. With complete instructions for an incredible variety of breads and lots of great baking tips, easy bread baking is at your fingertips—so let's start baking!

sincerely,
Betty Crocker

contents

the world of bread!

Making any kind of bread is certainly not difficult—many types are fairly simple, but some loaves require just a bit more effort and patience to get to the final result. But with the information here, you'll be mastering the art of bread baking in no time! And there's a whole array of breads to sample—from easy quick breads to more complicated yeast breads made the traditional way or in the bread machine. There's even an assortment of coffee cakes and doughnuts to round out the choices.

Quick breads include loaves, muffins, scones and biscuits. Because they are leavened with baking powder or baking soda instead of yeast, these are probably the quickest, simplest type of bread to make—they are mixed up quickly and can be baked right after mixing. Novice and accomplished bakers alike can offer fresh-from-the-oven goodies in no time with these bread choices.

Yeast breads can take just a bit more time and practice to make—but the aroma and fresh-baked results are worth all of the effort and wait! Types of yeast bread include traditional kneaded breads, no-knead artisan-style breads and batter breads. Yeast is the leavening agent in these breads, so proper rising time and technique are important for good results.

be bread smart

For all types of bread, use shiny pans and cookie sheets, which reflect heat, for the best results. If you are using dark or nonstick pans, reduce the oven temperature by 25°F. These darker pans absorb heat more easily than shiny ones, causing baked goods to brown more quickly. Insulated pans offer a different challenge—they often require slightly longer bake times and result in bread that may be less brown.

Bake bread in the center of the oven and allow at least 2 inches of space around pans for heat circulation. Follow baking directions in the recipe carefully for time and doneness. Cut cooled bread with a serrated knife, using a light sawing motion.

tips for perfect quick breads

+ For the best results, use butter. If you choose to use margarine, be sure the product has at least 65% fat. Do not use reduced-fat butter or whipped products.

+ Overmixing makes quick breads tough. Mix the batter for loaves and muffins with a spoon, not an electric mixer, just until the dry ingredients are moistened. For biscuits and scones, mix or knead lightly for as long as indicated in the recipe.

+ To prevent loaves from becoming gummy or soggy, do not increase the amount of fruit or vegetables called for in a recipe.

+ Grease the bottom only of loaf or muffin pans unless directed otherwise. This prevents a lip or dry, hard edge from forming.

+ Cracks will often form on the top of quick breads. This is caused by leavening action during baking and is normal.

+ Cool loaves completely (about 2 hours) to help prevent crumbling when slicing.

muffin success

The best muffins are golden brown, slightly rounded with bumpy tops, tender, moist, even textured and easy to remove from the pan. Here are some things that can happen, with solutions to help.

Pale—oven was not hot enough

Peaked or smooth top—too much mixing

Tough and heavy—too much flour or mixing

Dry—too much flour, oven too hot or baked too long

Tunnels (holes inside muffin)—too much mixing

Sticks to pan—pan not greased correctly

Perfect Muffin: This muffin is slightly rounded with a bumpy top.

Overmixed Muffin: This muffin has a peaked, smooth top.

Overbaked Muffin: This muffin is dry with a rough top and is too brown.

tips for perfect yeast breads

✛ Use the type of flour called for in the recipe—all-purpose and bread flour are generally interchangeable, so you can often use either one.

✛ Check the expiration date on the package of yeast to ensure it is fresh. Too much heat will kill the yeast and too little prevents growth. Follow directions in the recipe for activating the yeast—use a thermometer to check for the correct liquid temperature.

✛ Follow directions for kneading times in the recipe. Use just enough flour for kneading so that the dough is not sticky. Knead until it is smooth and springy. Too much flour will make the bread dry and crumbly.

✛ Let the dough rise in a warm, draft-free area until doubled in size. The dough is ready when you can press two fingertips into the dough and indentations remain.

✛ When you remove the bread from the oven, immediately remove the loaf from the pan (unless directed otherwise in the recipe) to prevent a soggy crust.

✛ Cool loaves at least 30 minutes before slicing. Warm bread is wonderful, but if too warm it will be difficult to cut and the slices won't hold their shape.

yeast bread success

The best yeast breads are high and evenly shaped, are golden or dark brown and have an even texture. Here are some things that can happen, with solutions to help.

Not high—water too hot for yeast, too little flour, not enough kneading or pan too large

Coarse texture—rose too long, too little flour, not enough kneading or oven too cool

Yeasty flavor—rose too long or temperature too high during rise time

Large air pockets—dough not rolled tightly when loaf was shaped

Dry and crumbly—too much flour or not enough kneading

Perfect Yeast Bread: This loaf is high, evenly shaped and golden brown with an even texture.

Under-Risen Yeast Bread: This loaf did not rise because the yeast got too hot and the dough was not kneaded enough.

Over-Risen Yeast Bread: This loaf was kneaded too much and contained too much flour.

types of yeast bread

Traditional Kneaded Breads: These loaves and rolls require hands-on work, and individual recipes will provide specific kneading times.

Artisan Breads: These breads are made with few ingredients and known for their crusty exterior and firm but moist interior. They often don't require kneading.

Batter Breads: Just mix and bake to make these easy breads. They don't require kneading and their texture will be coarser than traditional kneaded breads.

yeast bread ingredients

Flour: All-purpose and bread flours are both high-gluten flours and can be used interchangeably in these recipes. The gluten (an elastic protein) is developed when dough is kneaded, making these two flours ideal for bread baking. Whole wheat and rye flours have less gluten and should be combined with all-purpose or bread flour. Up to half of a recipe's all-purpose or bread flour can be replaced with whole wheat or rye flour.

Yeast: Yeast is temperature sensitive—too high will kill it while too low will prevent it from growing. Always check the package expiration date to ensure it is fresh. With fast-acting dry yeast, rising times may be shorter, so be sure to check the package for best results. Follow the directions given in the recipe for activating the yeast.

Liquid: Water gives bread a crisp crust, while milk results in a softer crust.

Sweetener: Sugar, honey or molasses feed yeast to help it grow, add flavor and help brown crust. Don't use artificial sweeteners because they won't feed the yeast.

Salt: Salt enhances flavor, provides structure to dough and controls yeast growth. Don't omit the salt from a yeast bread recipe.

Fat: Butter, margarine, shortening and oil make bread tender and moist, plus they add flavor.

Eggs: Eggs add flavor, richness and color, plus they promote a fine texture and tender crust.

Classic White Bread
(page 216)

Maple-Nut-Raisin Muffins
(page 21)

chapter one

muffins, scones and biscuits

blueberry pie muffins

prep time: 30 minutes ✛ start to finish: 1 hour ✛ 12 MUFFINS

filling

⅔ cup blueberry pie filling (from 21-oz can)

⅓ cup fresh blueberries

streusel

½ cup old-fashioned or quick-cooking oats

¼ cup all-purpose flour

¼ cup packed brown sugar

¼ teaspoon ground cinnamon

2 tablespoons cold butter, cut into small pieces

muffins

¾ cup milk

¼ cup vegetable oil

1 egg

1 tablespoon grated lemon peel

2 cups all-purpose flour

½ cup granulated sugar

2 teaspoons baking powder

½ teaspoon salt

1 Heat oven to 400°F. Place paper baking cup in each of 12 regular-size muffin cups or grease with shortening or cooking spray.

2 In small bowl, mix filling ingredients; set aside. In medium bowl, mix all streusel ingredients with fork until crumbly; set aside.

3 In large bowl, beat milk, oil, egg and lemon peel with fork or whisk until blended. Stir in remaining muffin ingredients all at once just until flour is moistened (batter will be lumpy).

4 Spoon about 1 tablespoon batter in bottom of each muffin cup (spread, if necessary, to cover most of bottom of cup). Alternately drop rounded ½ teaspoon blueberry mixture and 1 teaspoon remaining muffin batter in different areas in each muffin cup, layering as necessary. (Cups will be three-fourths full.)

5 Sprinkle streusel evenly over batter and blueberry mixture in each cup.

6 Bake 20 to 25 minutes or until golden brown and toothpick inserted in center comes out clean. Cool 5 minutes. Remove from pan to cooling rack. Serve warm if desired.

1 Muffin: Calories 230 (Calories from Fat 70); Total Fat 8g (Saturated Fat 2.5g; Trans Fat 0g); Cholesterol 25mg; Sodium 210mg; Total Carbohydrate 37g (Dietary Fiber 1g); Protein 4g **Exchanges:** 1½ Starch, 1 Other Carbohydrate, 1½ Fat **Carbohydrate Choices:** 2½

bake smart For the prettiest muffins, drop the blueberry mixture near the center, allowing only some of it to go toward the edge of the muffin cup.

Adding fresh blueberries to the pie filling gives a burst of fresh fruit flavor. But if blueberries are not in season, simply use 1 cup pie filling.

whole wheat blueberry muffins

prep time: 15 minutes ✛ start to finish: 35 minutes ✛ 12 MUFFINS

2 tablespoons packed brown sugar

¼ teaspoon ground cinnamon

¾ cup fat-free (skim) milk

¼ cup vegetable oil

¼ cup honey

1 egg

1 cup all-purpose flour

1 cup whole wheat flour

3 teaspoons baking powder

½ teaspoon salt

1 cup frozen (do not thaw) blueberries (from 8-oz bag)

1 Heat oven to 400°F. Spray 12 regular-size muffin cups with cooking spray or place paper baking cup in each muffin cup. In small bowl, mix brown sugar and cinnamon; set aside.

2 In large bowl, beat milk, oil, honey and egg with spoon. Stir in flours, baking powder and salt just until moistened (batter will be lumpy). Gently fold in blueberries. Divide batter evenly among muffin cups (cups will be full). Sprinkle with brown sugar mixture.

3 Bake 20 minutes or until golden brown. Immediately remove from pan to cooling rack. Serve warm.

1 Muffin: Calories 170 (Calories from Fat 50); Total Fat 5g (Saturated Fat 1g; Trans Fat 0g); Cholesterol 20mg; Sodium 230mg; Total Carbohydrate 27g (Dietary Fiber 2g); Protein 3g **Exchanges:** 1 Starch, 1 Other Carbohydrate, 1 Fat **Carbohydrate Choices:** 2

bake smart For a twist on this classic muffin recipe, substitute frozen raspberries for the blueberries.

If you like, use apple pie spice or pumpkin pie spice instead of cinnamon in the brown sugar topper.

golden harvest muffins

prop timo: 20 minutes + start to finish: 50 minutes + 18 MUFFINS

2 eggs
¾ cup vegetable oil
¼ cup milk
2 teaspoons vanilla
2 cups all-purpose flour
1 cup packed brown sugar
2 teaspoons baking soda
2 teaspoons ground cinnamon
½ teaspoon salt
1½ cups shredded carrots (2 to 3 medium)
1 cup shredded peeled apple (1 medium)
½ cup coconut
½ cup raisins
¾ cup sliced almonds

1 Heat oven to 350°F. Place paper baking cup in each of 18 regular-size muffin cups or grease with shortening or cooking spray.

2 In large bowl, beat eggs, oil, milk and vanilla with whisk until well blended. Add flour, brown sugar, baking soda, cinnamon and salt; stir just until dry ingredients are moistened. Stir in carrots, apple, coconut, raisins and ½ cup of the almonds. Divide batter evenly among muffin cups. Sprinkle remaining ¼ cup almonds over batter.

3 Bake 20 to 25 minutes or until toothpick inserted in center comes out clean. Cool 5 minutes. Remove from pan to cooling rack. Serve warm if desired.

1 Muffin: Calories 250 (Calories from Fat 110); Total Fat 13g (Saturated Fat 2.5g; Trans Fat 0g); Cholesterol 25mg; Sodium 230mg; Total Carbohydrate 29g (Dietary Fiber 2g); Protein 3g **Exchanges:** 1 Starch, 1 Other Carbohydrate, 2½ Fat **Carbohydrate Choices:** 2

bran muffins

prep time: 15 minutes ✛ start to finish: 50 minutes ✛ 12 MUFFINS

1¼ cups Fiber One® original bran cereal or 2 cups bran cereal flakes, crushed

1⅓ cups milk

½ cup raisins, dried cherries or sweetened dried cranberries, if desired

½ teaspoon vanilla

¼ cup vegetable oil

1 egg

1¼ cups all-purpose or whole wheat flour

½ cup packed brown sugar

3 teaspoons baking powder

¼ teaspoon salt

¼ teaspoon ground cinnamon, if desired

1 Heat oven to 400°F. Grease bottoms only of 12 regular-size muffin cups with shortening or cooking spray, or place paper baking cup in each muffin cup.

2 In medium bowl, stir cereal, milk, raisins and vanilla until well mixed. Let stand about 5 minutes or until cereal has softened. Beat in oil and egg with fork.

3 In another medium bowl, stir remaining ingredients until well mixed; stir into cereal mixture just until moistened. Divide batter evenly among muffin cups.

4 Bake 18 to 25 minutes or until toothpick inserted in center comes out clean. If baked in greased pan, let stand about 5 minutes in pan, then remove from pan to cooling rack; if baked in paper baking cups, immediately remove from pan to cooling rack. Serve warm if desired.

1 Muffin: Calories 170 (Calories from Fat 50); Total Fat 6g (Saturated Fat 1g; Trans Fat 0g); Cholesterol 20mg; Sodium 220mg; Total Carbohydrate 26g (Dietary Fiber 3g); Protein 3g **Exchanges:** 1½ Starch, 1 Fat **Carbohydrate Choices:** 2

bake smart For extra flavor, stir in 1 cup chopped dates with the remaining ingredients in step 3. Bake as directed.

To crush the cereal, place it in a plastic bag or between sheets of waxed paper or plastic wrap and crush with a rolling pin. Or crush it in a blender or food processor.

streusel-pumpkin muffins

prep time: 20 minutes ✛ start to finish: 45 minutes ✛ 12 MUFFINS

1½ cups all-purpose flour

1 cup packed brown sugar

1 teaspoon baking soda

1 teaspoon pumpkin pie spice

¼ teaspoon salt

1 cup canned pumpkin (not pumpkin pie mix)

½ cup buttermilk

2 tablespoons vegetable oil

1 egg

¾ cup crushed gingersnaps (about 13 cookies)

3 tablespoons all-purpose flour

3 tablespoons packed brown sugar

3 tablespoons butter, softened

Sliced almonds, if desired

1 Heat oven to 350°F. Place paper baking cup in each of 12 regular-size muffin cups; spray baking cups with cooking spray.

2 In large bowl, mix 1½ cups flour, 1 cup brown sugar, the baking soda, pumpkin pie spice and salt. Stir in pumpkin, buttermilk, oil and egg just until moistened. Divide batter evenly among muffin cups.

3 In small bowl, mix gingersnaps, 3 tablespoons flour, 3 tablespoons brown sugar and the butter with fork until crumbly. Sprinkle evenly over batter in each cup.

4 Bake 24 minutes or until toothpick inserted in center comes out clean. Remove muffins from pan to cooling rack. Sprinkle with sliced almonds. Serve warm.

1 Muffin: Calories 250 (Calories from Fat 60); Total Fat 7g (Saturated Fat 2.5g; Trans Fat 0g); Cholesterol 25mg; Sodium 250mg; Total Carbohydrate 43g (Dietary Fiber 1g); Protein 3g **Exchanges:** 1 Starch, 2 Other Carbohydrate, 1½ Fat **Carbohydrate Choices:** 3

maple-nut-raisin muffins

prep time: 20 minutes + start to finish: 45 minutes + 12 MUFFINS

topping

- 2 tablespoons packed brown sugar
- 1 tablespoon Original Bisquick® mix
- 1 teaspoon butter, softened

muffins

- 2 cups Original Bisquick mix
- ⅓ cup raisins
- ⅓ cup chopped pecans
- ¼ cup packed brown sugar
- ⅔ cup milk
- 2 tablespoons vegetable oil
- 1 teaspoon maple flavor
- 1 egg

1 Heat oven to 400°F. Grease bottoms only of 12 regular-size muffin cups with shortening or cooking spray, or place paper baking cup in each muffin cup.

2 In small bowl, stir all topping ingredients until crumbly. In large bowl, stir all muffin ingredients just until moistened. Divide batter evenly among muffin cups. Sprinkle evenly with topping.

3 Bake 15 to 18 minutes or until golden brown. Cool slightly; remove muffins from pan to cooling rack. Serve warm.

1 Muffin: Calories 180 (Calories from Fat 70); Total Fat 8g (Saturated Fat 2g; Trans Fat 1g); Cholesterol 20mg; Sodium 270mg; Total Carbohydrate 24g (Dietary Fiber 1g); Protein 3g **Exchanges:** 1 Starch, ½ Other Carbohydrate, 1½ Fat **Carbohydrate Choices:** 1½

bake smart Jazz up these muffins by using brightly colored or patterned paper liners. Visit www.fancyflours.com for examples.

To avoid soggy muffins, take them out of the pan immediately after removing them from the oven.

almond–poppy seed muffins

prep time: 15 minutes ✛ start to finish: 30 minutes ✛ 12 MUFFINS

½ cup sugar

⅓ cup vegetable oil

1 egg

½ teaspoon almond extract

½ cup sour cream

¼ cup milk

1⅓ cups all-purpose flour

½ teaspoon baking powder

½ teaspoon salt

¼ teaspoon baking soda

2 tablespoons poppy seed

1 tablespoon sugar

2 tablespoons sliced almonds

1 Heat oven to 375°F. Place paper baking cup in each of 12 regular-size muffin cups, or grease bottoms only with shortening or cooking spray.

2 In large bowl, stir ½ cup sugar, oil, egg and almond extract. Beat in sour cream and milk with spoon until blended. Stir in flour, baking powder, salt, baking soda and poppy seed until well blended. Divide batter evenly among muffin cups. Sprinkle with 1 tablespoon sugar and the almonds.

3 Bake 14 to 17 minutes or until toothpick inserted in center comes out clean. Remove muffins from pan to cooling rack. Serve warm if desired.

1 Muffin: Calories 180 (Calories from Fat 90); Total Fat 10g (Saturated Fat 2.5g; Trans Fat 0g); Cholesterol 25mg; Sodium 160mg; Total Carbohydrate 21g (Dietary Fiber 0g); Protein 3g **Exchanges:** 1 Starch, ½ Other Carbohydrate, 1½ Fat **Carbohydrate Choices:** 1½

bake smart The traditional bread basket lined with a clean paper or cloth napkin is still the ideal way to serve warm-from-the-oven muffins. The napkin holds in some warmth while the open weave of the basket lets steam escape, which could otherwise condense and make the muffins soggy.

cherry-streusel muffins

prep time: 20 minutes | start to finish: 45 minutes + 12 MUFFINS

topping

- 3 tablespoons packed brown sugar
- 3 tablespoons all-purpose flour
- 2 tablespoons finely chopped sliced almonds
- ¼ teaspoon ground cinnamon
- 2 tablespoons cold butter

muffins

- 1 jar (10 oz) maraschino cherries, drained, ¼ cup juice reserved
- 1⅓ cups all-purpose flour
- ⅔ cup granulated sugar
- 1½ teaspoons baking powder
- ½ teaspoon salt
- ⅓ cup vegetable oil
- 1 teaspoon almond extract
- ½ teaspoon vanilla
- 2 eggs
- 3 tablespoons sliced almonds

1 Heat oven to 400°F. Place paper baking cup in each of 12 regular-size muffin cups.

2 In medium bowl, mix all topping ingredients except butter. Cut in butter, using pastry blender or fork, until crumbly. Set aside.

3 Chop cherries; set aside. In large bowl, mix 1⅓ cups flour, the granulated sugar, baking powder and salt. In small bowl, beat oil, reserved ¼ cup cherry juice, the almond extract, vanilla and eggs with fork until blended. Stir cherry juice mixture into flour mixture just until flour is moistened. Fold in cherries and 3 tablespoons almonds. Divide batter evenly among muffin cups. Sprinkle each with about 1 tablespoon topping.

4 Bake 19 to 23 minutes or until toothpick inserted in center comes out clean. Immediately remove muffins from pan to cooling rack. Serve warm if desired.

1 Muffin: Calories 260 (Calories from Fat 90); Total Fat 10g (Saturated Fat 2.5g; Trans Fat 0g); Cholesterol 35mg; Sodium 190mg; Total Carbohydrate 37g (Dietary Fiber 1g); Protein 3g **Exchanges:** 1 Starch, 1½ Other Carbohydrate, 2 Fat **Carbohydrate Choices:** 2½

mocha muffins

prep time: **10 minutes** + start to finish: **30 minutes** + 12 MUFFINS

2 cups all-purpose flour

2 tablespoons unsweetened baking cocoa

2½ teaspoons baking powder

½ teaspoon salt

⅓ cup packed brown sugar

1 cup milk

⅓ cup vegetable oil

1 tablespoon instant coffee granules or crystals

1 egg

1 cup semisweet chocolate chunks or chips

1 Heat oven to 400°F. Grease bottoms only of 12 regular-size muffin cups with shortening or cooking spray, or place paper baking cup in each muffin cup.

2 In medium bowl, mix flour, cocoa, baking powder and salt. In large bowl, beat brown sugar, milk, oil, coffee granules and egg with fork or whisk. Stir in flour mixture just until flour is moistened. Fold in chocolate chunks. Divide batter evenly among muffin cups.

3 Bake 18 to 20 minutes or until toothpick inserted in center comes out clean. Immediately remove from pan to cooling rack.

1 Muffin: Calories 250 (Calories from Fat 100); Total Fat 11g (Saturated Fat 4g; Trans Fat 0g); Cholesterol 15mg; Sodium 220mg; Total Carbohydrate 33g (Dietary Fiber 2g); Protein 4g **Exchanges:** 1½ Starch, ½ Other Carbohydrate, 2 Fat **Carbohydrate Choices:** 2

bake smart Be sure to use unsweetened baking cocoa, not hot chocolate mix.

For a bit of extra sweetness, drizzle muffins with a mixture of a teaspoon or two of brewed coffee and a spoonful of chocolate ready-to-spread frosting.

double-chocolate muffins

prep time: 15 minutes + start to finish: 40 minutes + 12 MUFFINS

1 cup Fiber One original bran cereal

1⅓ cups buttermilk

¼ cup vegetable oil

1 egg

¾ cup packed brown sugar

½ cup whole wheat flour

½ cup all-purpose flour

½ cup unsweetened baking cocoa

1 teaspoon baking soda

1 teaspoon vanilla

¼ teaspoon salt

⅓ cup miniature semisweet chocolate chips

1 Heat oven to 375°F. Place paper baking cup in each of 12 regular-size muffin cups. Place cereal in resealable food-storage plastic bag; seal bag and crush with rolling pin or meat mallet (or crush in food processor).

2 In medium bowl, mix crushed cereal and buttermilk; let stand 5 minutes. Stir in oil and egg. Stir in all remaining ingredients except chocolate chips. Stir in chocolate chips. Divide batter evenly among muffin cups.

3 Bake 15 to 20 minutes or until toothpick inserted in center comes out clean. Immediately remove muffins from pan to cooling rack. Serve warm.

1 Muffin: Calories 210 (Calories from Fat 70); Total Fat 7g (Saturated Fat 2g; Trans Fat 0g); Cholesterol 20mg; Sodium 360mg; Total Carbohydrate 31g (Dietary Fiber 4g); Protein 4g **Exchanges:** 1 Starch, 1 Other Carbohydrate, 1½ Fat **Carbohydrate Choices:** 2

bake smart Not only are these fantastic muffins really yummy, they're also packed with fiber. Getting fiber from a variety of food sources every day is beneficial in a healthy diet.

french breakfast puffs

1½ cups all-purpose flour

1½ teaspoons baking powder

½ teaspoon salt

¼ teaspoon ground nutmeg

⅓ cup shortening

1 cup sugar

1 egg

½ cup milk

1 teaspoon ground cinnamon

½ cup butter, melted

1 Heat oven to 350°F. Grease 12 regular-size muffin cups with shortening, or spray with cooking spray.

2 In small bowl, mix flour, baking powder, salt and nutmeg. In large bowl, stir shortening, ½ cup of the sugar and the egg until mixed. Stir in flour mixture alternately with milk. Divide batter evenly among muffin cups.

3 Bake 20 to 25 minutes or until tops are light golden brown and bottoms are golden brown.

4 Meanwhile, in shallow dish, mix remaining ½ cup sugar and the cinnamon. Place melted butter in another shallow dish. Immediately roll hot puffs in melted butter, then in cinnamon-sugar. Serve warm.

1 Puff: Calories 260 (Calories from Fat 130); Total Fat 14g (Saturated Fat 7g; Trans Fat 1.5g); Cholesterol 40mg; Sodium 220mg; Total Carbohydrate 29g (Dietary Fiber 0g); Protein 2g **Exchanges:** 1 Starch, 1 Other Carbohydrate, 2½ Fat **Carbohydrate Choices:** 2

almond–tres leches muffins

prep time: **20 minutes** ✛ start to finish: **50 minutes** ✛ **12 MUFFINS**

½ cup butter, softened

⅔ cup sugar

½ teaspoon almond extract

2 eggs

2 cups all-purpose flour

2 teaspoons baking powder

⅓ cup (from 14-oz can) sweetened condensed milk (not evaporated)

⅓ cup whipping cream

⅓ cup milk

¾ cup sliced almonds

Additional sweetened condensed milk (¼ cup)

1 Heat oven to 400°F. Grease 12 regular-size muffin cups with shortening, or place paper baking cup in each muffin cup.

2 In large bowl, beat butter and sugar with electric mixer on medium speed until smooth. Beat in almond extract and eggs. With spoon, stir in flour, baking powder, ⅓ cup condensed milk, the whipping cream, milk and ½ cup of the almonds just until moistened. Divide batter evenly among muffin cups. Sprinkle remaining ¼ cup almonds evenly over batter.

3 Bake 15 to 20 minutes or until light golden brown. Remove muffins from pan to cooling rack. Cool 10 minutes. Drizzle 1 teaspoon additional condensed milk over top of each muffin. Serve warm.

1 Muffin: Calories 310 (Calories from Fat 140); Total Fat 15g (Saturated Fat 8g; Trans Fat 0g); Cholesterol 70mg; Sodium 170mg; Total Carbohydrate 37g (Dietary Fiber 1g); Protein 6g **Exchanges:** ½ Starch, 2 Other Carbohydrate, ½ High-Fat Meat, 2 Fat **Carbohydrate Choices:** 2½

bake smart *Tres leches* simply refers to the three milk sources in this recipe—here it is the sweetened condensed milk, whipping cream and milk.

raspberry–white chocolate muffins

prep time: **10 minutes** ✛ start to finish: **30 minutes** ✛ **12 MUFFINS**

2 cups Original Bisquick mix

½ cup white vanilla baking chips

⅓ cup sugar

⅔ cup milk

2 tablespoons vegetable oil

1 egg

1 cup fresh raspberries

1 Heat oven to 400°F. Grease bottoms only of 12 regular-size muffin cups with shortening or cooking spray, or place paper baking cup in each muffin cup.

2 In large bowl, stir all ingredients except raspberries just until moistened. Fold in raspberries. Divide batter evenly among muffin cups.

3 Bake 15 to 18 minutes or until golden brown. Remove from pan to cooling rack. Serve warm.

1 Muffin: Calories 190 (Calories from Fat 80); Total Fat 8g (Saturated Fat 3.5g; Trans Fat 0g); Cholesterol 20mg; Sodium 310mg; Total Carbohydrate 26g (Dietary Fiber 0g); Protein 3g **Exchanges:** 1 Starch, ½ Other Carbohydrate, 1½ Fat **Carbohydrate Choices:** 2

bake smart For a sweet finish, dip muffin tops into melted butter and then into coarse or granulated sugar. Or drizzle tops of muffins with melted white vanilla baking chips.

strawberry-buttermilk muffins

prep time: 15 minutes ✛ start to finish: 45 minutes ✛ 16 MUFFINS

muffins

2	cups all-purpose flour
¾	cup granulated sugar
1	teaspoon baking soda
¼	teaspoon salt
1	cup buttermilk
½	cup vegetable oil
1	teaspoon vanilla
1	egg
1	cup chopped fresh strawberries

topping

⅓	cup packed brown sugar
3	tablespoons butter, melted
¼	teaspoon ground ginger
½	cup all-purpose flour
⅓	cup sliced almonds, toasted*

1 Heat oven to 375°F. Place paper baking cup in each of 16 regular-size muffin cups; spray baking cups with cooking spray.

2 In large bowl, mix 2 cups flour, the granulated sugar, baking soda and salt. Stir in buttermilk, oil, vanilla and egg just until moistened. Stir in strawberries. Divide batter evenly among muffin cups.

3 In small bowl, mix brown sugar, melted butter and ginger. Stir in ½ cup flour and the almonds with fork until crumbly. Sprinkle topping evenly over batter.

4 Bake 18 to 20 minutes or until toothpick inserted in center comes out clean. Cool 10 minutes; remove from pans to cooling rack. Serve warm.

*To toast almonds, bake in ungreased shallow pan at 375°F for 6 to 10 minutes, stirring occasionally, until light brown.

1 Muffin: Calories 240 (Calories from Fat 100); Total Fat 11g (Saturated Fat 3g; Trans Fat 0g); Cholesterol 20mg; Sodium 150mg; Total Carbohydrate 31g (Dietary Fiber 1g); Protein 3g **Exchanges:** 1 Starch, 1 Other Carbohydrate, 2 Fat **Carbohydrate Choices:** 2

bake smart It's easy to substitute fresh blueberries for the chopped strawberries in this recipe. The muffins are delicious with either fruit choice!

orange-almond streusel muffins

prep time: 15 minutes ✣ **start to finish: 30 minutes** ✣ **12 MUFFINS**

topping

- 2 tablespoons packed brown sugar
- 2 tablespoons sliced almonds
- 1 tablespoon Original Bisquick mix
- 1 tablespoon cold butter

muffins

- ⅓ cup packed brown sugar
- 1 teaspoon grated orange peel
- ½ cup orange juice
- ¼ cup vegetable oil
- ½ teaspoon almond extract
- 1 egg
- 2 cups Original Bisquick mix
- ¼ cup sliced almonds

1 Heat oven to 400°F. Place paper baking cup in each of 12 regular-size muffin cups, or grease bottoms only with shortening.

2 In medium bowl, mix 2 tablespoons brown sugar, 2 tablespoons almonds and 1 tablespoon Bisquick mix. Cut in butter with fork until crumbly; set aside.

3 In large bowl, mix all muffin ingredients except Bisquick mix and almonds. Stir in 2 cups Bisquick mix just until moistened. Stir in ¼ cup almonds. Divide batter evenly among muffin cups. Sprinkle evenly with streusel topping.

4 Bake 13 to 15 minutes or until golden brown. Immediately remove from pan to cooling rack. Serve warm.

1 Muffin: Calories 200 (Calories from Fat 90); Total Fat 11g (Saturated Fat 2.5g; Trans Fat 0.5g); Cholesterol 20mg; Sodium 270mg; Total Carbohydrate 23g (Dietary Fiber 0g); Protein 3g **Exchanges:** 1 Starch, ½ Other Carbohydrate, 2 Fat **Carbohydrate Choices:** 1½

bake smart If you have slivered almonds on hand, use them in place of the sliced almonds.

Serve these muffins warm with honey butter or cream cheese. Add fresh fruit and hot tea for a light breakfast, brunch or snack.

gluten-free banana–chocolate chip muffins

prep time: 25 minutes ÷ start to finish: 50 minutes ÷ 16 MUFFINS

½ cup white rice flour

½ cup tapioca flour

½ cup potato starch

¼ cup sweet white sorghum flour

¼ cup garbanzo and fava flour

½ teaspoon xanthan gum

1 teaspoon gluten-free baking powder

1 teaspoon baking soda

½ teaspoon salt

2 eggs

½ cup sunflower or canola oil or ghee (measured melted)

¼ cup gluten-free almond, soy or regular milk

1 cup mashed ripe bananas (2 medium)

⅔ cup packed brown sugar

2 teaspoons gluten-free vanilla

½ cup miniature semisweet chocolate chips

1 Heat oven to 350°F. Spray 16 regular-size muffin cups with cooking spray (without flour).

2 In small bowl, mix flours, xanthan gum, baking powder, baking soda and salt with whisk; set aside. In medium bowl, beat eggs, oil, milk, bananas, brown sugar and vanilla with electric mixer on medium speed until well blended. Gradually add flour mixture, beating until well blended. Stir in chocolate chips. Divide batter evenly among muffin cups.

3 Bake 18 to 20 minutes or until toothpick inserted in center comes out clean. Cool 5 minutes; remove from pan to cooling rack. Serve warm.

1 Muffin: Calories 220 (Calories from Fat 80); Total Fat 9g (Saturated Fat 2g; Trans Fat 0g); Cholesterol 25mg; Sodium 200mg; Total Carbohydrate 30g (Dietary Fiber 2g); Protein 2g **Exchanges:** 1 Starch, 1 Other Carbohydrate, 1½ Fat **Carbohydrate Choices:** 2

Jean Duane, Alternative Cook { www.alternativecook.com }

bake smart Cooking gluten free? Always read labels to make sure that each recipe ingredient is gluten free. Products and ingredient sources can vary.

This recipe is a great way to use bananas that are getting a little too ripe. You may find that you buy bananas just to make these muffins!

gluten-free lemon-blueberry muffins

prep time: 15 minutes ✛ start to finish: 40 minutes ✛ 12 MUFFINS

2 cups Bisquick Gluten Free mix

⅓ cup sugar

¾ cup milk

⅓ cup butter, melted

3 eggs, beaten

1 tablespoon grated lemon peel

1 cup fresh blueberries

2 tablespoons sugar

1 Heat oven to 400°F. Spray bottoms only of 12 regular-size muffin cups with cooking spray (without flour), or place paper baking cup in each muffin cup.

2 In large bowl, stir Bisquick mix, ⅓ cup sugar, the milk, butter, eggs and lemon peel just until moistened. Fold in blueberries. Divide batter evenly among muffin cups. Sprinkle 2 tablespoons sugar evenly over muffins.

3 Bake 14 to 16 minutes or until set and lightly browned. Cool 5 minutes. Remove muffins from pan to cooling rack. Serve warm.

1 Muffin: Calories 180 (Calories from Fat 60); Total Fat 7g (Saturated Fat 3.5g; Trans Fat 0g); Cholesterol 65mg; Sodium 280mg; Total Carbohydrate 27g (Dietary Fiber 1g); Protein 3g **Exchanges:** ½ Starch, 1 Other Carbohydrate, 1½ Fat **Carbohydrate Choices:** 2

bake smart Cooking gluten free? Always read labels to make sure that each recipe ingredient is gluten free. Products and ingredient sources can vary.

You can use frozen blueberries instead of fresh—thaw them completely and pat away excess moisture with a paper towel.

beer and chile cornbread muffins

prep time: 15 minutes ✛ start to finish: 40 minutes ✛ 12 MUFFINS

2 eggs

1 cup Mexican or other beer

¼ cup butter, melted

¾ cup all-purpose flour

¾ cup yellow or blue cornmeal

½ cup sugar

2 teaspoons baking powder

½ teaspoon salt

½ cup vacuum-packed whole kernel corn (from 11-oz can)

1 medium (5 inch) poblano chile, seeded, chopped

1 serrano chile, seeded, finely chopped

½ cup shredded Monterey Jack and Cheddar cheese blend (2 oz)

1 Heat oven to 400°F. Place paper baking cup in each of 12 regular-size muffin cups, or grease bottoms only with shortening.

2 In medium bowl, beat eggs with fork. Stir in beer and melted butter. Stir in remaining ingredients all at once just until flour is moistened (batter will be lumpy). Divide batter evenly among muffin cups (cups will be full).

3 Bake 15 to 20 minutes or until golden brown and toothpick inserted in center comes out clean. Cool 3 minutes. Remove muffins from pan to cooling rack. Serve warm.

1 Muffin: Calories 180 (Calories from Fat 60); Total Fat 6g (Saturated Fat 3.5g; Trans Fat 0g); Cholesterol 50mg; Sodium 260mg; Total Carbohydrate 25g (Dietary Fiber 1g); Protein 4g **Exchanges:** 1½ Starch, 1 Fat **Carbohydrate Choices:** 1½

bake smart Poblano chiles are large and fairly mild in flavor. They add a delicious, fresh taste to these cornbread muffins.

basil-corn muffins

prep time: 15 minutes ✛ start to finish: 45 minutes ✛ 12 MUFFINS

1½ cups all-purpose flour

½ cup yellow cornmeal

½ cup sugar

3 teaspoons baking
powder

½ teaspoon salt

¾ cup fresh whole kernel
corn

2 tablespoons chopped
fresh basil leaves

¾ cup milk

½ cup butter, melted

1 egg, slightly beaten

1 Heat oven to 375°F. Place paper baking cup in each of 12 regular-size muffin cups.

2 In large bowl, mix flour, cornmeal, sugar, baking powder and salt with whisk. Stir in corn and basil. In medium bowl, mix milk, melted butter and egg. Stir into flour mixture just until moistened. Divide batter evenly among muffin cups.

3 Bake 20 to 22 minutes or until toothpick inserted in center comes out clean. Cool 5 minutes; remove from pan to cooling rack. Serve warm.

1 Muffin: Calories 210 (Calories from Fat 80); Total Fat 9g (Saturated Fat 5g; Trans Fat 0g); Cholesterol 35mg; Sodium 300mg; Total Carbohydrate 28g (Dietary Fiber 1g); Protein 3g **Exchanges:** 1 Starch, 1 Other Carbohydrate, 1½ Fat **Carbohydrate Choices:** 2

bake smart Peak-season fresh corn is ideal for this recipe. If it's unavailable, use frozen corn and thaw before adding it to the batter.

popovers

prep time: 10 minutes ✛ start to finish: 45 minutes ✛ 6 POPOVERS

2 eggs
1 cup all-purpose flour
1 cup milk
½ teaspoon salt

1 Heat oven to 450°F. Generously grease 6-cup popover pan with shortening. Heat popover pan in oven 5 minutes.

2 Meanwhile, in medium bowl, beat eggs slightly with fork or whisk. Beat in remaining ingredients just until smooth (do not overbeat or popovers may not puff as high). Divide batter evenly among popover cups.

3 Bake 20 minutes. Reduce oven temperature to 325°F. Bake 10 to 15 minutes longer or until deep golden brown. Immediately remove from pan. Serve hot.

1 Popover: Calories 120 (Calories from Fat 25); Total Fat 3g (Saturated Fat 1g; Trans Fat 0g); Cholesterol 75mg; Sodium 240mg; Total Carbohydrate 18g (Dietary Fiber 0g); Protein 6g **Exchanges:** 1 Starch, 1 Fat **Carbohydrate Choices:** 1

bake smart After baking the popovers, pierce each popover with the point of a sharp knife to let the steam out, and cool completely on a cooling rack. If you don't serve them right away, just reheat uncovered on an ungreased cookie sheet at 350°F for 5 minutes.

maple, bacon and cheddar muffins

prep time: 20 minutes ✛ start to finish: 40 minutes ✛ 12 MUFFINS

8 oz maple-smoked bacon, cut into 1-inch pieces

1 egg

¾ cup milk

2 tablespoons butter, melted

2 cups Original Bisquick mix

¾ cup shredded Cheddar cheese (3 oz)

¼ teaspoon chili powder

1 Heat oven to 400°F. Place paper baking cup in each of 12 regular-size muffin cups. Spray baking cups with cooking spray. In 10-inch skillet, cook bacon over medium-high heat, stirring frequently, until crisp. Remove bacon from skillet; drain on paper towels.

2 Meanwhile, in medium bowl, beat egg slightly. Stir in remaining ingredients and the bacon just until moistened. Divide batter evenly among muffin cups.

3 Bake 16 to 19 minutes or until golden brown. Immediately remove from pan to cooling rack. Serve warm.

1 Muffin: Calories 170 (Calories from Fat 90); Total Fat 10g (Saturated Fat 4.5g; Trans Fat 0.5g); Cholesterol 35mg; Sodium 470mg; Total Carbohydrate 13g (Dietary Fiber 0g); Protein 6g **Exchanges:** 1 Starch, ½ High-Fat Meat, 1 Fat **Carbohydrate Choices:** 1

bake smart Jazz up these breakfast muffins by substituting Cheddar-Jack with jalapeño peppers cheese blend for the plain Cheddar cheese. You can find this shredded cheese blend in the dairy section of your supermarket.

scones

prep time: 15 minutes ✛ start to finish: 35 minutes ✛ 8 SCONES

1¾ cups all-purpose flour

3 tablespoons granulated sugar

2½ teaspoons baking powder

½ teaspoon salt

⅓ cup cold butter, cut into 8 pieces

1 egg, beaten

½ teaspoon vanilla

4 to 6 tablespoons whipping cream

Additional whipping cream

Coarse sugar or additional granulated sugar

1 Heat oven to 400°F. In large bowl, mix flour, 3 tablespoons granulated sugar, baking powder and salt. Cut in butter, using pastry blender or fork, until mixture looks like fine crumbs. Stir in egg, vanilla and just enough of the 4 to 6 tablespoons whipping cream so dough leaves side of bowl.

2 Place dough on lightly floured surface; gently roll in flour to coat. Knead lightly 10 times. On ungreased cookie sheet, roll or pat dough into 8-inch round. Cut into 8 wedges with sharp knife that has been dipped in flour, but do not separate wedges. Brush with additional whipping cream; sprinkle with coarse sugar.

3 Bake 14 to 16 minutes or until light golden brown. Immediately remove scones from cookie sheet to cooling rack; carefully separate wedges. Serve warm.

1 Scone: Calories 240 (Calories from Fat 100); Total Fat 11g (Saturated Fat 6g; Trans Fat 0.5g); Cholesterol 55mg; Sodium 360mg; Total Carbohydrate 31g (Dietary Fiber 0g); Protein 4g **Exchanges:** 1 Starch, 1 Other Carbohydrate, 2 Fat **Carbohydrate Choices:** 2

cherry–chocolate chip scones: Stir in ½ cup each of dried cherries and miniature semisweet chocolate chips with the egg, vanilla and whipping cream.

currant scones: Stir in ½ cup dried currants or raisins with the egg, vanilla and whipping cream.

raspberry–white chocolate scones: Substitute almond extract for the vanilla; increase whipping cream to ½ cup. Stir in ¾ cup frozen unsweetened raspberries (do not thaw) and ⅔ cup white vanilla baking chips with the egg, almond extract and whipping cream. Omit kneading step; on ungreased cookie sheet, pat dough into 8-inch round. Continue as directed, except bake 18 to 23 minutes. Raspberries will color the dough slightly.

making scones

Roll or pat dough into 8-inch round on ungreased cookie sheet.

Cut into 8 wedges with sharp knife or pizza cutter dipped in flour; do not separate.

coffeehouse scones

prep time: 20 minutes ✛ start to finish: 40 minutes ✛ 10 SCONES

2 cups all-purpose flour

⅓ cup sugar

1 teaspoon baking powder

½ teaspoon baking soda

¼ teaspoon salt

½ cup cold butter

¾ cup miniature semisweet chocolate chips

¾ cup buttermilk

5 teaspoons instant espresso coffee powder or granules

1 teaspoon vanilla

1 egg yolk

1 tablespoon milk

1 tablespoon sugar

2 oz semisweet baking chocolate, chopped

1 Heat oven to 400°F. Line cookie sheet with cooking parchment paper.

2 In large bowl, mix flour, ⅓ cup sugar, the baking powder, baking soda and salt. Cut in butter, using pastry blender or fork, until mixture looks like fine crumbs. Stir in chocolate chips. In medium bowl, stir buttermilk, coffee powder, vanilla and egg yolk with whisk. Stir into flour mixture just until soft dough forms.

3 On floured surface, press or roll dough to ½-inch thickness. Cut with floured 3-inch round cutter. On cookie sheet, place rounds about 1 inch apart. Brush dough with milk; sprinkle with 1 tablespoon sugar.

4 Bake 15 to 17 minutes or until golden brown. Remove from cookie sheet to cooling rack.

5 In small microwavable bowl, microwave baking chocolate uncovered on High 30 to 45 seconds until softened and chocolate can be stirred smooth. Drizzle over scones.

1 Scone: Calories 330 (Calories from Fat 150); Total Fat 17g (Saturated Fat 10g; Trans Fat 0g); Cholesterol 45mg; Sodium 270mg; Total Carbohydrate 38g (Dietary Fiber 2g); Protein 5g **Exchanges:** 2 Starch, ½ Other Carbohydrate, 3 Fat **Carbohydrate Choices:** 2½

glazed orange-ginger scones

prep time: 20 minutes ✛ **start to finish: 40 minutes** ✛ **8 SCONES**

2 cups all-purpose flour

⅓ cup granulated sugar

2 tablespoons chopped crystallized ginger

1 tablespoon baking powder

1 tablespoon grated orange peel

½ teaspoon salt

½ cup cold butter, cut into small pieces

¾ cup whipping cream

2 tablespoons fresh orange juice

2 tablespoons whipping cream

½ cup powdered sugar

3 to 4 teaspoons milk or whipping cream

1 Heat oven to 425°F. Line cookie sheet with cooking parchment paper. In large bowl, mix flour, granulated sugar, ginger, baking powder, orange peel and salt until blended. Cut in butter, using pastry blender or fork, until mixture looks like fine crumbs. Stir in ¾ cup whipping cream and the orange juice until soft dough forms.

2 On lightly floured surface, pat dough into 7-inch round. Cut into 8 wedges. On cookie sheet, place wedges about 2 inches apart. Brush dough with 2 tablespoons whipping cream.

3 Bake 15 to 18 minutes or until golden brown. In small bowl, mix powdered sugar and enough milk until thin enough to drizzle. Drizzle over scones. Serve warm.

1 Scone: Calories 390 (Calories from Fat 190); Total Fat 21g (Saturated Fat 13g; Trans Fat 1g); Cholesterol 65mg; Sodium 440mg; Total Carbohydrate 44g (Dietary Fiber 1g); Protein 4g **Exchanges:** 1½ Starch, 1½ Other Carbohydrate, 4 Fat **Carbohydrate Choices:** 3

apricot and white chocolate scones

prep time: 20 minutes ✛ start to finish: 40 minutes ✛ 8 SCONES

1¾ cups all-purpose flour

¼ cup sugar

2 teaspoons baking powder

¼ teaspoon salt

⅓ cup cold butter

⅓ cup finely chopped dried apricots

⅔ cup white vanilla baking chips

1 egg

About ⅓ cup half-and-half

1 Heat oven to 400°F. Lightly grease cookie sheet with shortening or cooking spray. In large bowl, mix flour, sugar, baking powder and salt. Cut in butter, using pastry blender or fork, until mixture looks like fine crumbs. Reserve 2 tablespoons apricots for topping. Stir remaining apricots and ⅓ cup of the baking chips into crumb mixture. Stir in egg and just enough half-and-half so dough leaves side of bowl and forms a ball.

2 On lightly floured surface, knead dough lightly 10 times. On cookie sheet, roll or pat dough into 8-inch round. Cut into 8 wedges, but do not separate.

3 Bake 14 to 16 minutes or until golden brown. Immediately remove from cookie sheet to cooling rack; carefully separate wedges.

4 In small resealable freezer plastic bag, place remaining ⅓ cup baking chips; seal bag. Microwave on High about 1 minute or until softened. Gently squeeze bag until chips are smooth; cut off tiny corner of bag. Squeeze bag to drizzle melted chips over scones. Sprinkle with reserved 2 tablespoons apricots. Drizzle remaining melted chips over apricots and scones. Serve warm or cool.

1 Scone: Calories 330 (Calories from Fat 130); Total Fat 15g (Saturated Fat 10g; Trans Fat 0g); Cholesterol 50mg; Sodium 300mg; Total Carbohydrate 43g (Dietary Fiber 1g); Protein 5g **Exchanges:** 1½ Starch, 1½ Other Carbohydrate, 3 Fat **Carbohydrate Choices:** 3

bake smart It's easy to use kitchen scissors sprayed with cooking spray to finely chop the dried apricots.

maple-nut scones

prep time: 20 minutes ✛ start to finish: 40 minutes ✛ 8 SCONES

topping

- 3 tablespoons all-purpose flour
- 2 tablespoons granulated sugar
- 2 tablespoons finely chopped nuts, toasted✳
- 2 tablespoons cold butter

scones

- 2 cups all-purpose flour
- 2 tablespoons packed brown sugar
- 2 teaspoons baking powder
- ¼ teaspoon salt
- ½ cup cold butter
- ½ cup coarsely chopped nuts, toasted✳
- ⅓ cup real maple syrup or maple-flavored syrup
- 1 egg
  About 2 tablespoons milk
  Additional milk

1 Heat oven to 400°F (375°F for dark or nonstick cookie sheet). In small bowl, mix 3 tablespoons flour, the granulated sugar and 2 tablespoons nuts. Cut in 2 tablespoons butter, using pastry blender or fork, until crumbly; set aside.

2 In large bowl, mix 2 cups flour, the brown sugar, baking powder and salt. Cut in ½ cup butter, using pastry blender or fork, until mixture looks like fine crumbs. Stir in ½ cup nuts. Stir in maple syrup, egg and just enough of the 2 tablespoons milk so dough leaves side of bowl and starts to form a ball.

3 Place dough on lightly floured surface; gently roll in flour to coat. Knead lightly 10 times. On ungreased cookie sheet, roll or pat dough into 8-inch round. Brush with additional milk. Sprinkle with topping. Cut into 8 wedges, but do not separate.

4 Bake 15 to 18 minutes or until golden brown. Immediately remove from cookie sheet; carefully separate wedges. Serve warm.

✳To toast nuts, bake in ungreased shallow pan at 400°F for 4 to 6 minutes, stirring occasionally, until light brown.

1 Scone: Calories 390 (Calories from Fat 200); Total Fat 22g (Saturated Fat 8g; Trans Fat 1g); Cholesterol 65mg; Sodium 300mg; Total Carbohydrate 43g (Dietary Fiber 2g); Protein 5g **Exchanges:** 2 Starch, 1 Other Carbohydrate, 4 Fat **Carbohydrate Choices:** 3

bake smart Serve these tender scones warm with a dollop of honey butter or a drizzle of maple syrup.

easy cranberry-orange scones

prep time: **20 minutes** ✛ start to finish: **1 hour** ✛ **8 SCONES**

1 cup whole wheat flour
1 cup all-purpose flour
¼ cup granulated sugar
2 teaspoons grated orange peel
1½ teaspoons cream of tartar
¾ teaspoon baking soda
¼ teaspoon salt
⅓ cup cold butter
⅓ cup milk
¼ cup orange juice
½ cup sweetened dried cranberries
⅓ cup powdered sugar
2 to 3 teaspoons milk

1 Heat oven to 350°F. In large bowl, mix flours, granulated sugar, orange peel, cream of tartar, baking soda and salt. Cut in butter, using pastry blender or fork, until mixture looks like fine crumbs. Stir in ⅓ cup milk, the orange juice and cranberries just until dry ingredients are moistened.

2 On ungreased cookie sheet, pat dough into 8-inch round. Cut into 8 wedges, but do not separate.

3 Bake 20 to 25 minutes or until golden brown. Cool 5 minutes; remove from cookie sheet to cooling rack. Cool 10 minutes; carefully separate wedges.

4 In small bowl, mix powdered sugar and 2 to 3 teaspoons milk until thin enough to drizzle. Drizzle over scones. Serve warm or cool.

1 Scone: Calories 260 (Calories from Fat 80); Total Fat 8g (Saturated Fat 5g; Trans Fat 0g); Cholesterol 20mg; Sodium 250mg, Total Carbohydrate 42g (Dietary Fiber 3g); Protein 4g **Exchanges:** 1 Starch, 2 Other Carbohydrate, 1½ Fat **Carbohydrate Choices:** 3

bake smart Use dried blueberries instead of the cranberries if you'd like. You can also substitute grated lemon peel for the orange peel.

dried cherry–lemon scones

prep time: 15 minutes ✛ start to finish: 30 minutes ✛ 10 SCONES

2 cups all-purpose flour

¼ cup sugar

2 teaspoons grated lemon peel

1½ teaspoons cream of tartar

¾ teaspoon baking soda

¼ teaspoon salt

½ cup cold butter

⅓ to ½ cup buttermilk

½ cup dried cherries

Milk

Additional sugar, if desired

1 Heat oven to 425°F. In medium bowl, mix flour, ¼ cup sugar, the lemon peel, cream of tartar, baking soda and salt. Cut in butter, using pastry blender or fork, until mixture looks like fine crumbs. Stir in enough buttermilk so dough leaves side of bowl and forms a ball. Stir in cherries.

2 Onto ungreased cookie sheet, drop dough by about ⅓ cupfuls about 1 inch apart. Brush with milk. Sprinkle with additional sugar.

3 Bake 10 to 15 minutes or until light brown. Immediately remove from cookie sheet to cooling rack. Serve warm or cool.

1 Scone: Calories 220 (Calories from Fat 90); Total Fat 10g (Saturated Fat 5g; Trans Fat 0.5g); Cholesterol 25mg; Sodium 230mg; Total Carbohydrate 30g (Dietary Fiber 1g); Protein 3g **Exchanges:** 1½ Starch, ½ Other Carbohydrate, 1½ Fat **Carbohydrate Choices:** 2

bake smart Despite its name, buttermilk is not full of butter. In fact, it's similar to 2% or skim milk in fat content. Traditionally, buttermilk is a fermented beverage made from the liquid that remained after butter was churned from fresh cream. Today, buttermilk is made by exposing milk to good bacteria (just like making yogurt), causing it to become acidic. The acid tenderizes cakes and breads and enhances flavor, just like a squirt of lemon brightens a soup.

rosemary-lemon cream scones

prep time: 25 minutes + start to finish: 50 minutes + 8 SCONES

scones

- 2½ cups Original Bisquick mix
- ⅓ cup granulated sugar
- 2 tablespoons cold butter
- 1 egg, beaten
- 1 container (6 oz) lemon burst low-fat yogurt
- ¼ cup whipping cream
- 1 tablespoon grated lemon peel
- 1 tablespoon finely chopped fresh rosemary leaves
- 1 tablespoon heavy whipping cream
- 1 tablespoon granulated sugar

lemon drizzle

- ½ cup powdered sugar
- 1 tablespoon lemon juice

1 Heat oven to 400°F. Generously spray cookie sheet with cooking spray. In large bowl, mix Bisquick mix and ⅓ cup granulated sugar. Cut in butter, using pastry blender or fork, until mixture looks like coarse crumbs.

2 In small bowl, mix egg, yogurt and ¼ cup whipping cream. Stir into crumb mixture just until combined. Stir in lemon peel and rosemary. Place dough on cookie sheet.

3 With greased hands, pat dough into 8-inch round. Brush dough with 1 tablespoon whipping cream; sprinkle with 1 tablespoon granulated sugar. With sharp knife dipped in additional Bisquick mix, cut into 8 wedges, but do not separate.

4 Bake 15 to 20 minutes or until light golden brown. Immediately remove from cookie sheet to cooling rack; carefully separate wedges. Cool 5 minutes. Meanwhile, in small bowl, mix powdered sugar and lemon juice. Drizzle over scones. Serve warm.

1 Scone: Calories 310 (Calories from Fat 100); Total Fat 11g (Saturated Fat 5g; Trans Fat 1.5g); Cholesterol 45mg; Sodium 500mg; Total Carbohydrate 47g (Dietary Fiber 1g); Protein 4g **Exchanges:** 1½ Starch, 1½ Other Carbohydrate, 2 Fat **Carbohydrate Choices:** 3

double-orange scones with orange butter

prep time: 15 minutes + start to finish: 35 minutes + 8 SCONES

scones

- 2 cups all-purpose flour
- 4 tablespoons sugar
- 2½ teaspoons baking powder
- 2 teaspoons grated orange peel
- ⅓ cup cold butter
- ½ cup mandarin orange segments (from 11 oz-can), chopped, drained
- ¼ cup milk
- 1 egg, slightly beaten

orange butter

- ½ cup butter, softened
- 2 tablespoons orange marmalade

1 Heat oven to 400°F. Lightly spray cookie sheet with cooking spray.

2 In large bowl, mix flour, 3 tablespoons of the sugar, the baking powder and orange peel. Cut in ⅓ cup butter, using pastry blender or fork, until mixture looks like coarse crumbs. Add orange segments, milk and egg; stir with fork just until mixture leaves side of bowl and soft dough forms.

3 Place dough on floured surface. Knead lightly 10 times. On cookie sheet, roll or pat dough into 7-inch round. Sprinkle with remaining 1 tablespoon sugar. Cut into 8 wedges; separate slightly.

4 Bake 15 to 20 minutes or until golden brown. Meanwhile, in small bowl, beat ½ cup butter until light and fluffy; stir in marmalade. Serve with warm scones.

1 Scone: Calories 350 (Calories from Fat 180); Total Fat 20g (Saturated Fat 12g; Trans Fat 1g); Cholesterol 80mg; Sodium 300mg; Total Carbohydrate 37g (Dietary Fiber 1g); Protein 4g **Exchanges:** 1½ Starch, 1 Other Carbohydrate, 4 Fat **Carbohydrate Choices:** 2½

bake smart When grating orange peel, be sure to grate only the orange part of the skin. The white part, or pith, is very bitter.

pecan–banana bread scones

prep time: 20 minutes ✛ start to finish: 50 minutes ✛ 8 SCONES

2½ cups all-purpose flour

⅓ cup packed brown sugar

2 teaspoons baking powder

1 teaspoon ground cinnamon

½ teaspoon salt

½ cup cold butter

¾ cup chopped pecans, toasted*

½ cup sour cream

1 cup mashed bananas (2 medium)

½ cup canned dulce de leche (caramelized sweetened condensed milk)

1 Heat oven to 400°F. Line cookie sheet with cooking parchment paper.

2 In large bowl, mix flour, brown sugar, baking powder, cinnamon and salt. Cut in butter, using pastry blender or fork, until mixture looks like coarse crumbs. Stir in ½ cup of the pecans. Stir in sour cream and bananas until soft dough forms.

3 On lightly floured surface, knead dough lightly 5 times. On cookie sheet, press dough with floured hands to 8-inch round. Cut into 8 wedges, but do not separate.

4 Bake 25 to 30 minutes or until golden brown. Remove from cookie sheet to cooling rack; carefully separate wedges.

5 In small microwavable bowl, microwave dulce de leche on High 30 seconds or until pourable. Drizzle over scones. Sprinkle with remaining ¼ cup pecans. Serve warm.

✱To toast pecans, bake in ungreased shallow pan at 400°F for 4 to 6 minutes, stirring occasionally, until light brown.

1 Scone: Calories 470 (Calories from Fat 210); Total Fat 24g (Saturated Fat 11g; Trans Fat 0.5g); Cholesterol 45mg; Sodium 410mg; Total Carbohydrate 58g (Dietary Fiber 3g); Protein 7g **Exchanges:** 2 Starch, 2 Other Carbohydrate, 4½ Fat **Carbohydrate Choices:** 4

bake smart Stirring mashed bananas into the batter gives these scones a texture similiar to banana-nut bread. They require a slightly longer baking time than most scones.

lemon-blueberry scones

prep time. 15 minutes + start to finish: 50 minutes + 8 SCONES

2 cups all-purpose flour

3 teaspoons baking powder

¼ cup sugar

⅓ cup cold butter, cut into small pieces

2 teaspoons grated lemon peel

½ cup dried blueberries

1 cup whipping cream

½ teaspoon vanilla

1 Heat oven to 425°F. Line cookie sheet with cooking parchment paper. In food processor bowl with metal blade, place flour, baking powder and 3 tablespoons of the sugar. Cover; process with on-and-off pulses 6 times or until blended. Add butter, scattering evenly over dry ingredients, and lemon peel. Cover; process with on-and-off pulses 12 times or until consistency of coarse crumbs.

2 Transfer crumb mixture to large bowl. Add blueberries, tossing with fork until blended. Add whipping cream and vanilla, tossing with fork just until dough begins to form, about 30 seconds (do not overmix).

3 On cookie sheet, press dough into 8-inch round. Cut into 8 wedges; separate wedges slightly. Sprinkle remaining 1 tablespoon sugar evenly over wedges.

4 Bake 14 to 16 minutes or until golden brown. Remove from cookie sheet to cooling rack; cool 10 minutes. Serve warm or cool.

1 Scone: Calories 320 (Calories from Fat 170); Total Fat 19g (Saturated Fat 12g; Trans Fat 0.5g); Cholesterol 60mg; Sodium 260mg; Total Carbohydrate 33g (Dietary Fiber 1g); Protein 4g **Exchanges:** 1½ Starch, ½ Other Carbohydrate, 3½ Fat **Carbohydrate Choices:** 2

chocolate scones

prep time: **15 minutes** ✛ start to finish: **40 minutes** ✛ **10 SCONES**

2 cups Original Bisquick mix

¼ cup sugar

3 tablespoons unsweetened dark baking cocoa

⅓ cup cold butter

1½ cups milk chocolate chips

⅓ cup whipping cream

2 teaspoons vanilla

1 egg

2 tablespoons whipping cream

1 Heat oven to 425°F. Line cookie sheet with cooking parchment paper. In large bowl, stir Bisquick mix, sugar and cocoa. Cut in butter, using pastry blender or fork, until mixture looks like coarse crumbs. Stir in 1 cup of the chocolate chips.

2 In small bowl, mix ⅓ cup whipping cream, the vanilla and egg. Add to crumb mixture, stirring with fork until soft dough forms. On cookie sheet, pat dough into 8-inch round. Cut into 10 wedges, but do not separate.

3 Bake 15 minutes or until set. Remove from cookie sheet to cooling rack; carefully separate wedges. Cool 10 minutes.

4 In small microwavable bowl, microwave 2 tablespoons whipping cream and remaining ½ cup chocolate chips uncovered on High 30 to 60 seconds or until chips can be stirred smooth. Drizzle over scones.

1 Scone: Calories 360 (Calories from Fat 190); Total Fat 21g (Saturated Fat 12g; Trans Fat 1.5g); Cholesterol 55mg; Sodium 330mg; Total Carbohydrate 37g (Dietary Fiber 2g); Protein 5g **Exchanges:** 1½ Starch, 1 Other Carbohydrate, 4 Fat **Carbohydrate Choices:** 2½

pear-nut scones

prep time: 15 minutes + start to finish: 35 minutes + 8 SCONES

1¾ cups all-purpose flour

⅓ cup packed brown sugar

2 teaspoons baking powder

¼ teaspoon salt

⅓ cup cold butter

1 egg

½ cup half-and-half

1 cup chopped peeled pear (1 medium)

⅓ cup chopped pecans

1 Heat oven to 400°F. In large bowl, mix flour, brown sugar, baking powder and salt. Cut in butter, using pastry blender or fork, until mixture looks like fine crumbs. Stir in egg and half-and-half until soft dough forms. Stir in pear and pecans.

2 Onto ungreased cookie sheet, drop dough by slightly rounded ⅓ cupfuls.

3 Bake 16 to 18 minutes or until golden brown. Immediately remove from cookie sheet to cooling rack. Serve warm.

1 Scone: Calories 280 (Calories from Fat 120); Total Fat 14g (Saturated Fat 6g; Trans Fat 0g); Cholesterol 50mg; Sodium 270mg; Total Carbohydrate 35g (Dietary Fiber 2g); Protein 4g **Exchanges:** 1½ Starch, 1 Other Carbohydrate, 2½ Fat **Carbohydrate Choices:** 2

bake smart If you prefer apple scones, just use chopped peeled apple in place of the pear and use any type of nuts you wish.

Drizzle warm scones with caramel topping. They'll be "pear-fectly" scrumptious!

gluten-free strawberries-and-cream scones

prep time: 20 minutes ✛ start to finish: 50 minutes ✛ 10 SCONES

1 cup white rice flour
½ cup tapioca flour
¼ cup millet flour
¼ cup potato starch
2 teaspoons xanthan gum
3 tablespoons sugar
1 tablespoon gluten-free baking powder
½ teaspoon salt
6 tablespoons cold unsalted butter, cut into ¼-inch pieces
½ cup chopped fresh strawberries
1¼ cups whipping cream

1 Heat oven to 375°F. Line cookie sheet with cooking parchment paper.

2 In large bowl, mix flours, potato starch, xanthan gum, 2 tablespoons of the sugar, the baking powder and salt with whisk. Cut in butter, using pastry blender or fork, until mixture looks like coarse crumbs. Add strawberries; stir gently to coat with crumb mixture. Stir in 1 cup plus 2 tablespoons whipping cream, mixing just until combined.

3 Onto cookie sheet, drop dough by ¼ cupfuls about 2 inches apart. Brush with remaining 2 tablespoons whipping cream; sprinkle with remaining 1 tablespoon sugar.

4 Bake 25 to 30 minutes or until golden and puffed. Remove from cookie sheet to cooling rack. Serve warm.

1 Scone: Calories 280 (Calories from Fat 150); Total Fat 17g (Saturated Fat 10g; Trans Fat 0.5g); Cholesterol 50mg; Sodium 280mg; Total Carbohydrate 29g (Dietary Fiber 1g); Protein 2g **Exchanges:** 1 Starch, 1 Other Carbohydrate, 3 Fat **Carbohydrate Choices:** 2

Silvana Nardone, Silvana's Kitchen { www.silvanaskitchen.com }

bake smart If you can't find millet flour at your local supermarket, increase the white rice flour to 1¼ cups.

Cooking gluten free? Always read labels to make sure that each recipe ingredient is gluten free. Products and ingredient sources can vary.

gluten-free cinnamon scones

prep time: 10 minutes ÷ start to finish: 30 minutes ÷ 8 SCONES

scones

- 1 cup potato starch
- ⅔ cup tapioca flour
- ⅔ cup white rice flour
- 6 tablespoons sugar
- 4 teaspoons gluten-free baking powder
- 1 teaspoon baking soda
- 1 teaspoon ground cinnamon
- ½ teaspoon salt
- 2 eggs
- ⅔ cup melted ghee or coconut oil
- ¼ cup gluten-free almond, rice, soy or regular milk
- 1 teaspoon xanthan gum
- 1 teaspoon guar gum

topping

- 2 tablespoons sugar
- 1 teaspoon cinnamon

1 Heat oven to 400°F. Line cookie sheet with cooking parchment paper; spray with cooking spray (without flour). In medium bowl, mix flours, 6 tablespoons sugar, the baking powder, baking soda, 1 teaspoon cinnamon and the salt.

2 In small bowl, beat eggs, melted ghee, milk and both gums with electric mixer until well blended. Add egg mixture to dry ingredients; beat with electric mixer on low speed until blended.

3 Coat work surface and hands with oil. Place dough on work surface; pat dough into round, about 1 inch thick. Cut into 8 wedges; place about 1 inch apart on cookie sheet. In small bowl, mix all topping ingredients; sprinkle over dough.

4 Bake 14 to 18 minutes or until set. Remove from cookie sheet to cooling rack. Serve warm.

1 Scone: Calories 400 (Calories from Fat 180); Total Fat 20g (Saturated Fat 16g; Trans Fat 0g); Cholesterol 55mg; Sodium 570mg; Total Carbohydrate 54g (Dietary Fiber 1g); Protein 2g **Exchanges:** 1½ Starch, 1 Fruit, 1 Other Carbohydrate, 3½ Fat **Carbohydrate Choices:** 3½

chocolate scones: Omit the cinnamon-sugar topping and stir ¼ cup miniature chocolate chips into the batter.

Jean Duane, Alternative Cook { www.alternativecook.com }

bake smart Cooking gluten free? Always read labels to make sure that each recipe ingredient is gluten free. Products and ingredient sources can vary.

parmesan-chive scones

prep time: **10 minutes** ✛ start to finish: **25 minutes** ✛ **6 SCONES**

2½ cups Bisquick Heart Smart® mix

1 cup shredded Parmesan cheese (4 oz)

¼ cup chopped fresh chives

1 egg

1 cup fat-free plain yogurt (from 2-lb container)

1 Heat oven to 425°F. Lightly grease cookie sheet with shortening or cooking spray.

2 In large bowl, stir Bisquick mix, cheese and chives. In small bowl, beat egg and yogurt; add to dry ingredients, stirring just until moistened.

3 On lightly floured surface, knead dough lightly with floured hands 4 or 5 times. On cookie sheet, pat dough into 9-inch round. Using knife sprayed with cooking spray, cut dough into 6 wedges, but do not separate.

4 Bake 12 minutes or until lightly golden. Serve warm.

1 Scone: Calories 290 (Calories from Fat 80); Total Fat 9g (Saturated Fat 3.5g; Trans Fat 0g); Cholesterol 45mg; Sodium 770mg; Total Carbohydrate 38g (Dietary Fiber 0g); Protein 13g **Exchanges:** 2 Starch, ½ Other Carbohydrate, 1 High-Fat Meat **Carbohydrate Choices:** 2½

cheddar-chiles cornbread scones

prep time: 20 minutes + start to finish: 45 minutes + 8 SCONES

1¼ cups white whole wheat flour

1 cup cornmeal

1 tablespoon sugar

2 teaspoons baking powder

½ teaspoon salt

½ cup cold butter, cut into 8 pieces

¼ cup milk

1 egg, beaten

¾ cup shredded Cheddar cheese (3 oz)

1 can (4.5 oz) chopped green chiles, undrained

⅔ cup crumbled crisply cooked bacon, if desired

Honey, if desired

1 Heat oven to 425°F. Grease cookie sheet with shortening or cooking spray. In large bowl, mix flour, cornmeal, sugar, baking powder and salt. Cut in butter, using pastry blender or fork, until mixture looks like coarse crumbs. Stir in milk, egg, cheese, chiles and bacon.

2 Place dough on lightly floured surface. Knead lightly 10 times. On cookie sheet, roll or pat dough into 8-inch round. Cut into 8 wedges, but do not separate.

3 Bake 18 to 23 minutes or until golden brown. Immediately remove from cookie sheet to cooling rack; carefully separate wedges. Serve warm with honey.

1 Scone: Calories 310 (Calories from Fat 150); Total Fat 17g (Saturated Fat 10g; Trans Fat 0.5g); Cholesterol 65mg; Sodium 510mg; Total Carbohydrate 33g (Dietary Fiber 2g); Protein 7g **Exchanges:** 1 Starch, 1 Other Carbohydrate, ½ High-Fat Meat, 2½ Fat **Carbohydrate Choices:** 2

bake smart White whole wheat flour can be used in any recipe. It's the best of both worlds—100% whole grain but with a lighter taste and color. Start substituting 25% or 50% of the all-purpose flour with white whole wheat flour, gradually increasing the proportion as desired.

onion–poppy seed scones

prep time: 15 minutes ✛ start to finish: 40 minutes ✛ 12 SCONES

3 tablespoons vegetable oil

¼ cup chopped onion

1¾ cups white whole wheat flour

½ cup old-fashioned oats

2 tablespoons sugar

1 tablespoon poppy seed

3 teaspoons baking powder

1 teaspoon ground mustard

½ teaspoon salt

½ cup buttermilk

¼ cup fat-free egg product

1 tablespoon fat-free egg product

1 Heat oven to 400°F. Spray cookie sheet with cooking spray or line with cooking parchment paper.

2 In 8-inch skillet, heat 1 tablespoon of the oil over medium-high heat. Add onion to oil; cook 3 to 4 minutes, stirring frequently, until tender and just beginning to brown; remove from heat.

3 In large bowl, stir flour, oats, sugar, poppy seed, baking powder, mustard and salt; set aside. In small bowl, stir together buttermilk, ¼ cup egg product, the cooked onions and remaining 2 tablespoons oil. Add flour mixture to onion mixture all at once; stir just until moistened.

4 On lightly floured surface, knead dough 10 times. On cookie sheet, lightly roll or pat dough into 8-inch round about ¾ inch thick. With sharp knife dipped in additional flour, cut round into 12 wedges. Carefully pull wedges out about ½ inch to create small amount of space between each scone. Brush scones with 1 tablespoon egg product. Bake 15 to 18 minutes or until golden brown. Immediately remove from cookie sheet to cooling rack; cool 5 minutes. Serve warm.

1 Scone: Calories 130 (Calories from Fat 40); Total Fat 4.5g (Saturated Fat 0g; Trans Fat 0g); Cholesterol 0mg; Sodium 240mg; Total Carbohydrate 20g (Dietary Fiber 1g); Protein 3g **Exchanges:** 1 Starch, ½ Other Carbohydrate, ½ Fat **Carbohydrate Choices:** 1

bake smart To keep scones tender, handle the dough as little as possible. After kneading a few times, the dough should hold its shape, but it may still look a bit rough.

glazed fruit-filled drop biscuits

prep time: **15 minutes** ✛ start to finish: **30 minutes** ✛ **12 BISCUITS**

biscuits

- 2 cups Original Bisquick mix
- ¼ cup butter, softened
- 2 tablespoons granulated sugar
- ⅔ cup milk or half-and-half
- ¼ cup preserves (any flavor)

vanilla glaze

- ⅔ cup powdered sugar
- 2 teaspoons water
- ¼ teaspoon vanilla

1 Heat oven to 450°F. Lightly grease cookie sheet with shortening or cooking spray.

2 In medium bowl, stir Bisquick mix, butter and granulated sugar until crumbly. Stir in milk until dough forms; beat 15 strokes. Onto cookie sheet, drop dough by rounded tablespoonfuls about 2 inches apart. Make shallow well in center of each with back of spoon dipped in water; fill each with 1 teaspoon preserves.

3 Bake 10 to 15 minutes or until golden brown. Immediately remove from cookie sheet to cooling rack.

4 In small bowl, beat all glaze ingredients with spoon until smooth, stirring in additional water if necessary. Drizzle glaze over biscuits. Serve warm.

1 Biscuit: Calories 170 (Calories from Fat 60); Total Fat 6g (Saturated Fat 3g; Trans Fat 1g); Cholesterol 10mg; Sodium 250mg; Total Carbohydrate 27g (Dietary Fiber 0g); Protein 2g **Exchanges:** ½ Starch, 1½ Other Carbohydrate, 1 Fat **Carbohydrate Choices:** 2

double-drizzled raspberry rolls

prep time: **15 minutes** + start to finish: **35 minutes** + **8 ROLLS**

3 cups Original Bisquick mix

⅔ cup milk or water

2 tablespoons sour cream

2 tablespoons granulated sugar

1 teaspoon grated orange peel

1 cup seedless red raspberry jam

1 cup powdered sugar

3 tablespoons whipping cream

1 Heat oven to 425°F. Line cookie sheet with cooking parchment paper. In large bowl, stir Bisquick mix, milk, sour cream, granulated sugar and orange peel until soft dough forms.

2 On surface sprinkled with additional Bisquick mix, knead dough 5 times. Roll dough into 16×12-inch rectangle, about ¼ inch thick. Spread ⅔ cup of the jam over dough to within 1 inch of edges. Starting with 12-inch side, roll up tightly. Pinch edges to seal. With sharp knife, cut dough into 8 slices. On cookie sheet, place slices cut side down.

3 Bake 15 to 16 minutes or until golden brown.

4 In small bowl, mix powdered sugar and whipping cream until smooth. In small microwavable bowl, microwave remaining ⅓ cup jam uncovered on High 10 to 20 seconds or until melted. Spoon melted jam on top of rolls. Drizzle glaze over jam. Serve warm.

1 Roll: Calories 400 (Calories from Fat 70); Total Fat 8g (Saturated Fat 3g; Trans Fat 2g); Cholesterol 10mg; Sodium 490mg; Total Carbohydrate 76g (Dietary Fiber 1g); Protein 4g **Exchanges:** 1½ Starch, 3½ Other Carbohydrate, 1½ Fat **Carbohydrate Choices:** 5

banana–chocolate chip biscuits

prep time: 10 minutes ✛ start to finish: 35 minutes ✛ 24 BISCUITS

2½ cups all-purpose flour

1 tablespoon granulated sugar

1 teaspoon baking powder

½ teaspoon baking soda

½ teaspoon salt

⅓ cup cold butter

1 cup miniature semisweet chocolate chips

½ cup chopped ripe banana (1 medium)

1 cup buttermilk

2 teaspoons turbinado sugar (raw sugar)

1 Heat oven to 400°F. Line 17×12-inch half-sheet pan with cooking parchment paper.

2 In large bowl, mix flour, granulated sugar, baking powder, baking soda and salt with whisk. Cut in butter, using pastry blender or fork, until mixture looks like fine crumbs. Stir in chocolate chips and banana. Stir in buttermilk until dough leaves side of bowl.

3 Onto pan, drop dough by 2 tablespoonfuls about 1 inch apart. Sprinkle with turbinado sugar.

4 Bake 12 minutes or until golden brown. Cool 5 minutes; remove from pan to cooling rack. Serve warm.

1 Biscuit: Calories 120 (Calories from Fat 45); Total Fat 5g (Saturated Fat 3g; Trans Fat 0g); Cholesterol 10mg; Sodium 130mg; Total Carbohydrate 17g (Dietary Fiber 1g); Protein 2g **Exchanges:** ½ Starch, ½ Other Carbohydrate, 1 Fat **Carbohydrate Choices:** 1

bake smart Serve these chocolate-studded biscuits with honey or your favorite preserves.

glazed raisin-cinnamon biscuits

prep time: 15 minutes ✛ start to finish: 25 minutes ✛ 12 BISCUITS

biscuits

2½ cups Original Bisquick mix

½ cup raisins

⅔ cup milk

2 tablespoons granulated sugar

1 teaspoon ground cinnamon

vanilla glaze

⅔ cup powdered sugar

1 tablespoon water

¼ teaspoon vanilla

1 Heat oven to 450°F. In medium bowl, stir all biscuit ingredients just until soft dough forms.

2 Place dough on surface generously sprinkled with additional Bisquick mix; gently roll dough in Bisquick mix to coat. Shape dough into a ball; knead 10 times. Roll to ½-inch thickness; cut with 2½-inch round cutter dipped in Bisquick mix. On ungreased cookie sheet, place rounds about 2 inches apart.

3 Bake 8 to 10 minutes or until golden brown.

4 In small bowl, mix all glaze ingredients with spoon until smooth. Drizzle glaze over biscuits. Serve warm.

1 Biscuit: Calories 170 (Calories from Fat 35); Total Fat 4g (Saturated Fat 1g; Trans Fat 0.5g); Cholesterol 0mg; Sodium 310mg; Total Carbohydrate 31g (Dietary Fiber 0g); Protein 3g **Exchanges:** 1 Starch, 1 Other Carbohydrate, ½ Fat **Carbohydrate Choices:** 2

bake smart To make drop biscuits, instead of kneading and rolling the dough, drop it by 12 to 15 rounded spoonfuls onto an ungreased cookie sheet. Bake 10 to 12 minutes or until golden brown.

Sweetened dried cranberries can be used in place of the raisins for a slightly tart flavor.

If you don't have a round biscuit cutter, a glass that's 2½ inches in diameter is a good substitute.

cream cheese drop danish

prep time: 15 minutes ✛ start to finish: 25 minutes ✛ 12 SWEET ROLLS

cream cheese filling

- 1 package (3 oz) cream cheese, softened
- 1 tablespoon granulated sugar
- 1 tablespoon milk

sweet dough

- 2 cups Original Bisquick mix
- 2 tablespoons granulated sugar
- ¼ cup butter, softened
- ⅔ cup milk

vanilla glaze

- ¾ cup powdered sugar
- 1 tablespoon warm water
- ¼ teaspoon vanilla

1 Heat oven to 450°F. Lightly grease cookie sheet with shortening or cooking spray. In small bowl, mix all filling ingredients until smooth; set aside.

2 In medium bowl, stir Bisquick mix, 2 tablespoons granulated sugar and the butter until mixture looks like coarse crumbs. Stir in ⅔ cup milk until dough forms; beat with spoon 15 strokes.

3 Onto cookie sheet, drop dough by rounded tablespoonfuls about 2 inches apart. Make shallow well in center of each with back of spoon; fill each with about 1 teaspoon filling.

4 Bake 8 to 10 minutes or until golden brown. Meanwhile, in small bowl, mix all glaze ingredients until smooth and thin enough to drizzle. Drizzle glaze over warm rolls. Store covered in refrigerator.

1 Sweet Roll: Calories 190 (Calories from Fat 80); Total Fat 9g (Saturated Fat 5g; Trans Fat 1g); Cholesterol 20mg; Sodium 300mg; Total Carbohydrate 24g (Dietary Fiber 0g); Protein 3g **Exchanges:** ½ Starch, 1 Other Carbohydrate, 2 Fat **Carbohydrate Choices:** 1½

bake smart Make two batches of these—one batch with the cream cheese filling and the second batch filled with your favorite flavor of preserves or jam.

easy cream biscuits

prep time: 15 minutes ✛ **start to finish:** 30 minutes ✛ 12 BISCUITS

1¾ cups all-purpose flour

2½ teaspoons baking powder

½ teaspoon salt

1 to 1¼ cups whipping cream

1 Heat oven to 450°F. In large bowl, mix flour, baking powder and salt. Stir in 1 cup whipping cream. Add remaining whipping cream, 1 tablespoon at a time, until dough leaves side of bowl and forms a ball. (If dough is too dry, mix in 1 to 2 teaspoons more whipping cream.)

2 Place dough on lightly floured surface; gently roll in flour to coat. Knead lightly 10 times, sprinkling with flour if dough is too sticky. Roll or pat to ½-inch thickness. Cut with floured 2- to 2¼-inch biscuit cutter. On ungreased cookie sheet, place biscuits about 1 inch apart.

3 Bake 10 to 12 minutes or until golden brown. Immediately remove from cookie sheet to cooling rack. Serve warm.

1 Biscuit: Calories 140 (Calories from Fat 70); Total Fat 8g (Saturated Fat 5g; Trans Fat 0g); Cholesterol 30mg; Sodium 210mg; Total Carbohydrate 15g (Dietary Fiber 0g); Protein 2g **Exchanges:** 1 Other Carbohydrate, 1½ Fat **Carbohydrate Choices:** 1

cinnamon-raisin cream biscuits: Stir in 2 tablespoons sugar, 1 teaspoon ground cinnamon and ⅓ cup raisins or dried currants with the flour.

chocolate chip cream biscuits: Stir in 1 tablespoon sugar and ¼ cup miniature semisweet chocolate chips with the flour.

cranberry cream biscuits: Stir in 2 tablespoons sugar, ¼ teaspoon ground nutmeg and ½ cup sweetened dried cranberries with the flour.

herbed cream biscuits: Stir in ½ teaspoon dried Italian seasoning with the flour.

sweet potato–bacon biscuits

prep time: 20 minutes ✛ start to finish: 35 minutes ✛ 8 BISCUITS

1½ cups all-purpose flour

3 teaspoons baking powder

¼ teaspoon salt

8 slices bacon, crisply cooked, crumbled

½ teaspoon chopped fresh thyme leaves

¼ cup butter, frozen

⅔ cup mashed canned sweet potatoes (from 15-oz can)

2 tablespoons buttermilk

2 tablespoons butter, melted

1 Heat oven to 450°F. In large bowl, mix flour, baking powder and salt; stir in bacon and thyme. Shred frozen butter, using large holes of grater; add to flour mixture and toss to coat. Stir in sweet potatoes and buttermilk just until soft dough forms.

2 Place dough on lightly floured surface; gently roll in flour to coat. Knead lightly 4 or 5 times. Press or roll dough to ¾-inch thickness. Cut with floured 2½-inch biscuit cutter. On ungreased cookie sheet, place biscuits about 1 inch apart.

3 Bake 12 to 15 minutes or until light golden brown. Brush with melted butter. Serve warm.

1 Biscuit: Calories 180 (Calories from Fat 60); Total Fat 7g (Saturated Fat 3g; Trans Fat 0g); Cholesterol 15mg; Sodium 480mg; Total Carbohydrate 24g (Dietary Fiber 1g); Protein 6g **Exchanges:** 1½ Starch, 1½ Fat **Carbohydrate Choices:** 1½

bake smart Coarsely shredding frozen butter is a nifty way to disperse small butter pieces into biscuit dough, making biscuits that are tender and flaky.

bacon biscuits with orange butter

prep time: 20 minutes ✛ start to finish: 30 minutes ✛ 8 SERVINGS (1 BISCUIT AND 1 TABLESPOON BUTTER)

8	slices bacon, cut into ½-inch pieces
1¼	cups Original Bisquick mix
½	cup yellow cornmeal
¼	cup sugar
½	cup milk
¼	cup butter, softened
3	tablespoons orange marmalade
1	tablespoon honey

1 Heat oven to 425°F. In 10-inch nonstick skillet, cook bacon over medium-high heat, stirring frequently, until crisp. Drain on paper towels.

2 In medium bowl, stir Bisquick mix, cornmeal, sugar and bacon. Stir in milk until soft dough forms. Onto ungreased cookie sheet, drop dough by 8 spoonfuls.

3 Bake 7 to 9 minutes or until golden brown.

4 In small bowl, beat butter, marmalade and honey with whisk until blended. Serve warm biscuits with orange butter.

1 Biscuit: Calories 260 (Calories from Fat 110); Total Fat 12g (Saturated Fat 6g; Trans Fat 1g); Cholesterol 25mg; Sodium 450mg; Total Carbohydrate 34g (Dietary Fiber 1g); Protein 5g **Exchanges:** 1 Starch, 1 Other Carbohydrate, ½ Medium-Fat Meat, 2 Fat **Carbohydrate Choices:** 2

bake smart Try serving these biscuits with other flavored butters. Simply substitute your favorite flavor of jam, jelly or preserves for the orange marmalade.

Save time by purchasing cooked real bacon pieces in a jar or package rather than cooking sliced bacon.

cheese 'n onion drop biscuits

prep time: **15 minutes** ✛ start to finish: **30 minutes** ✛ **12 BISCUITS**

1 cup whole wheat flour

1 cup all-purpose flour

4 teaspoons baking powder

1 tablespoon sugar

¾ teaspoon salt

⅓ cup cold butter

1½ cups shredded Cheddar cheese (6 oz)

½ cup chopped green onions (8 medium)

1 cup milk

1 Heat oven to 450°F. In large bowl, mix flours, baking powder, sugar and salt. Cut in butter, using pastry blender or fork, until mixture is crumbly. Stir in cheese, onions and milk just until moistened.

2 Onto ungreased cookie sheet, drop dough by 12 spoonfuls about 2 inches apart.

3 Bake 12 to 15 minutes or until golden brown. Immediately remove from cookie sheet to cooling rack. Serve warm.

1 Biscuit: Calories 190 (Calories from Fat 90); Total Fat 10g (Saturated Fat 7g; Trans Fat 0g); Cholesterol 30mg; Sodium 440mg; Total Carbohydrate 18g (Dietary Fiber 1g); Protein 6g **Exchanges:** 1 Starch, ½ High-Fat Meat, 1 Fat **Carbohydrate Choices:** 1

bake smart For a spicy flavor twist, add ½ teaspoon chili powder to the flour mixture.

parmesan-herb biscuits

prep time: **15 minutes** ✛ start to finish: **25 minutes** ✛ 12 BISCUITS

2 cups all-purpose flour

¼ cup chopped fresh parsley or 4 teaspoons parsley flakes

3 tablespoons grated Parmesan cheese

1 tablespoon sugar

3 teaspoons baking powder

½ teaspoon salt

1½ teaspoons chopped fresh or ½ teaspoon dried basil leaves

1 to 1¼ cups whipping cream

1 tablespoon butter, melted

1 Heat oven to 425°F. In large bowl, mix flour, parsley, 2 tablespoons of the cheese, the sugar, baking powder, salt and basil. Add ¾ cup of the whipping cream; stir with fork just until dry ingredients are moistened. (Stir in additional whipping cream, 1 tablespoon at a time, if necessary, to form a soft dough.)

2 Place dough on lightly floured surface; gently roll in flour to coat. Knead lightly about 10 times or until dough forms a smooth ball. Press or roll dough to ½-inch-thick square. Cut dough into 12 rectangles. On ungreased large cookie sheet, place rectangles about 1 inch apart.

3 Brush dough with melted butter; sprinkle with remaining 1 tablespoon cheese.

4 Bake 8 to 10 minutes or until light golden brown. Serve warm.

1 Biscuit: Calories 150 (Calories from Fat 70); Total Fat 8g (Saturated Fat 5g; Trans Fat 0g); Cholesterol 25mg; Sodium 260mg; Total Carbohydrate 18g (Dietary Fiber 0g); Protein 3g **Exchanges:** 1 Starch, 1½ Fat **Carbohydrate Choices:** 1

bake smart Serve warm biscuits with shaped butter cutouts made easily with mini cookie cutters.

hearty three-grain biscuits

prep time: 10 minutes + start to finish: 25 minutes + 10 BISCUITS

¾ cup whole wheat flour

½ cup all-purpose flour

½ cup whole-grain cornmeal

3 teaspoons baking powder

¼ teaspoon salt

¼ cup shortening

½ cup old-fashioned or quick-cooking oats

About ¾ cup milk

1 Heat oven to 450°F. In large bowl, mix flours, cornmeal, baking powder and salt. Cut in shortening, using pastry blender or fork, until mixture looks like fine crumbs. Stir in oats. Stir in just enough milk so dough leaves side of bowl and forms a ball.

2 On lightly floured surface, knead dough lightly 10 times. Roll or pat to ½-inch thickness. Cut with floured 2½-inch round cutter. On ungreased cookie sheet, place biscuits about 1 inch apart for crusty sides; touching for soft sides. Brush with milk and sprinkle with additional oats if desired.

3 Bake 10 to 12 minutes or until golden brown. Immediately remove from cookie sheet. Serve warm.

1 Biscuit: Calories 150 (Calories from Fat 50); Total Fat 6g (Saturated Fat 1.5g; Trans Fat 1g); Cholesterol 0mg; Sodium 210mg; Total Carbohydrate 21g (Dietary Fiber 2g); Protein 4g **Exchanges:** 1 Starch, ½ Other Carbohydrate, 1 Fat **Carbohydrate Choices:** 1½

bake smart These tasty biscuits contain three grains: cornmeal, whole wheat and oats. Combining grains adds flavor, texture, variety and fun.

cheesy bacon pull-apart biscuits

prep time: 25 minutes ✛ start to finish: 50 minutes ✛ 8 BISCUITS

8 slices bacon

4½ cups Original Bisquick mix

1⅓ cups milk

6 medium green onions, chopped (6 tablespoons)

¼ teaspoon garlic powder

¼ teaspoon ground red pepper (cayenne)

1½ cups shredded sharp Cheddar cheese (6 oz)

¾ cup shredded mozzarella cheese (3 oz)

1 Heat oven to 400°F. In 9-inch cast-iron skillet, cook bacon until crisp; drain on paper towels. Crumble bacon; set aside. Reserve 2 tablespoons bacon drippings in skillet, coating bottom and side completely. Discard any remaining drippings.

2 In large bowl, stir Bisquick mix, milk, ¼ cup of the onions, the garlic powder and red pepper until soft dough forms. On surface sprinkled with additional Bisquick mix, pat dough to 1-inch thickness. Cut with 2½-inch round cutter. Arrange rounds in skillet; sprinkle ¾ cup of the Cheddar cheese evenly between rounds.

3 Bake 15 to 17 minutes or until lightly browned. Sprinkle mozzarella cheese and remaining ¾ cup Cheddar cheese on tops of biscuits. Bake 2 to 4 minutes longer or until cheese is melted. Sprinkle with bacon and remaining 2 tablespoons onions. Serve warm.

1 Biscuit: Calories 450 (Calories from Fat 190); Total Fat 21g (Saturated Fat 9g; Trans Fat 3g); Cholesterol 40mg; Sodium 1100mg; Total Carbohydrate 47g (Dietary Fiber 2g); Protein 17g **Exchanges:** 2½ Starch, ½ Other Carbohydrate, 1½ Medium-Fat Meat, 2½ Fat **Carbohydrate Choices:** 3

gluten-free cheese-garlic biscuits

prep time: 5 minutes ✛ start to finish: 15 minutes ✛ 10 BISCUITS

biscuits

- 2 cups Bisquick Gluten Free mix
- ¼ teaspoon garlic powder
- ¼ cup cold butter
- ⅔ cup milk
- ½ cup shredded Cheddar cheese (2 oz)
- 3 eggs

garlic-butter topping

- ¼ cup butter, melted
- ¼ teaspoon garlic powder

1 Heat oven to 425°F. In medium bowl, mix Bisquick mix and ¼ teaspoon garlic powder. Cut in ¼ cup butter, using pastry blender or fork, until mixture looks like coarse crumbs. Stir in milk, cheese and eggs until soft dough forms.

2 Onto ungreased cookie sheet, drop dough by rounded tablespoonfuls about 3 inches apart.

3 Bake 8 to 10 minutes or until light golden brown. In small bowl, mix ¼ cup melted butter and ¼ teaspoon garlic powder; brush over warm biscuits before removing from cookie sheet. Serve warm.

1 Biscuit: Calories 230 (Calories from Fat 120); Total Fat 13g (Saturated Fat 8g; Trans Fat 0g); Cholesterol 95mg; Sodium 400mg; Total Carbohydrate 22g (Dietary Fiber 0g); Protein 5g **Exchanges:** 1½ Starch, 2½ Fat **Carbohydrate Choices:** 1½

bake smart Cooking gluten free? Always read labels to make sure that each recipe ingredient is gluten free. Products and ingredient sources can vary.

Serve these quick biscuits with fresh fruit for a delicious light breakfast.

Five-Grain Buttermilk-Cranberry Bread
(page 105)

quick bread loaves

banana bread

prep time: 15 minutes + start to finish: 3 hours 25 minutes + 2 LOAVES (12 SLICES EACH)

1¼ cups sugar

½ cup butter, softened

2 eggs

1½ cups mashed very ripe bananas (3 medium)

½ cup buttermilk

1 teaspoon vanilla

2½ cups all-purpose flour

1 teaspoon baking soda

1 teaspoon salt

1 cup chopped nuts, if desired

1 Heat oven to 350°F. Grease bottoms only of 2 (8×4-inch) loaf pans or 1 (9×5-inch) loaf pan.

2 In large bowl, stir sugar and butter until well mixed. Stir in eggs until well mixed. Stir in bananas, buttermilk and vanilla; beat with spoon until smooth. Stir in flour, baking soda and salt just until moistened. Stir in nuts. Divide batter evenly between 8-inch pans or pour into 9-inch pan.

3 Bake 8-inch loaves about 1 hour, 9-inch loaf about 1 hour 15 minutes, or until toothpick inserted in center comes out clean. Cool in pans on cooling rack 10 minutes.

4 Loosen sides of loaves from pans; remove from pans and place top side up on cooling rack. Cool completely, about 2 hours, before slicing. Wrap tightly and store at room temperature up to 4 days, or refrigerate.

1 Slice: Calories 150 (Calories from Fat 40); Total Fat 4.5g (Saturated Fat 2.5g; Trans Fat 0g); Cholesterol 30mg; Sodium 190mg; Total Carbohydrate 24g (Dietary Fiber 0g); Protein 2g **Exchanges:** ½ Starch, 1 Other Carbohydrate, 1 Fat **Carbohydrate Choices:** 1½

blueberry-banana bread: Omit nuts. Stir 1 cup fresh or frozen (thawed) and drained blueberries into batter.

bake smart Although the true origin of banana bread is not known, this enduring favorite has been around at least since the 1930s. This version is our favorite in the Betty Crocker Kitchens.

sour cream–cranberry bread

prep time. 20 minutes ✛ start to finish: 3 hours 30 minutes ✛ 1 LOAF (12 SLICES)

bread

- 2⅓ cups Bisquick Heart Smart mix
- ¾ cup granulated sugar
- 2 tablespoons grated orange peel
- ½ cup reduced-fat sour cream
- ¼ cup vegetable oil
- ¼ cup fat-free (skim) milk
- 5 egg whites or ¾ cup fat-free egg product
- ¾ cup fresh or frozen cranberries, chopped

glaze

- ½ cup powdered sugar
- 2 to 3 teaspoons orange juice

1 Heat oven to 375°F. Generously grease bottom only of 9×5-inch loaf pan with shortening or cooking spray.

2 In medium bowl, stir all bread ingredients except cranberries with fork or whisk until moistened. Stir in cranberries. Pour into pan.

3 Bake 50 to 55 minutes or until toothpick inserted in center comes out clean and top crust is deep golden brown. Cool 15 minutes. Loosen sides of loaf from pan; remove from pan and place top side up on cooling rack. Cool completely before slicing, about 2 hours. Wrap tightly and store at room temperature up to 4 days, or refrigerate.

4 In small bowl, stir all glaze ingredients until smooth and thin enough to drizzle. Drizzle glaze over bread just before serving.

1 Slice: Calories 220 (Calories from Fat 70); Total Fat 7g (Saturated Fat 1.5g; Trans Fat 0g); Cholesterol 0mg; Sodium 230mg; Total Carbohydrate 35g (Dietary Fiber 0g); Protein 3g **Exchanges:** 1 Starch, 1½ Other Carbohydrate, 1½ Fat **Carbohydrate Choices:** 2

bake smart Plan on using two oranges to get the 2 tablespoons grated orange peel called for here. Be sure to grate only the orange part of the skin. The white part, or pith, is very bitter.

rhubarb crumble loaf

prep time: **15 minutes** ✛ start to finish: **3 hours 10 minutes** ✛ 1 LOAF (12 SLICES)

bread

2½	cups all-purpose flour
1	teaspoon baking soda
½	teaspoon salt
1¼	cups packed brown sugar
½	cup vegetable oil
1	cup buttermilk
2	teaspoons vanilla
1	egg
½	cup chopped fresh or frozen (thawed) rhubarb

topping

½	cup coarsely chopped pecans
⅓	cup packed brown sugar
⅓	cup butter, softened
2	tablespoons chopped crystallized ginger
½	cup all-purpose flour

1 Heat oven to 375°F. Spray 9×5-inch loaf pan with cooking spray.

2 In medium bowl, mix 2½ cups flour, the baking soda and salt. In large bowl, mix 1¼ cups brown sugar, the oil, buttermilk, vanilla and egg until blended. Stir in rhubarb. Stir in flour mixture just until blended. Spread batter in pan.

3 In small bowl, mix pecans, ⅓ cup brown sugar, the butter and ginger. Stir in ½ cup flour with fork until mixture is crumbly. Sprinkle topping over batter.

4 Bake 20 minutes. Cover with foil; bake 55 minutes to 70 minutes or until toothpick inserted in center comes out clean. Cool 15 minutes. Loosen sides of loaf from pan; remove from pan to cooling rack. Cool completely, about 1 hour. Wrap tightly and store at room temperature up to 4 days, or refrigerate.

1 Slice: Calories 410 (Calories from Fat 170); Total Fat 19g (Saturated Fat 5g; Trans Fat 0g); Cholesterol 30mg; Sodium 280mg; Total Carbohydrate 56g (Dietary Fiber 1g); Protein 5g **Exchanges:** 1½ Starch, 2 Other Carbohydrate, 3½ Fat **Carbohydrate Choices:** 4

bake smart This moist loaf freezes well and is also a great choice for gift giving. Wrap in plastic wrap and tie with a pretty ribbon for someone special.

chai-spiced bread

prep time: **15 minutes** ✛ start to finish: **3 hours 55 minutes** ✛ **1 LOAF (16 SLICES)**

bread

- ¾ cup granulated sugar
- ½ cup butter, softened
- ½ cup cold brewed tea or water
- ⅓ cup milk
- 2 teaspoons vanilla
- 2 eggs
- 2 cups all-purpose flour
- 2 teaspoons baking powder
- ¾ teaspoon ground cardamom
- ½ teaspoon salt
- ¼ teaspoon ground cinnamon
- ⅛ teaspoon ground cloves

glaze

- 1 cup powdered sugar
- ¼ teaspoon vanilla
- 3 to 5 teaspoons milk
  Additional ground cinnamon

1 Heat oven to 400°F. Grease bottom only of 8×4- or 9×5-inch loaf pan with shortening or cooking spray.

2 In large bowl, beat granulated sugar and butter with electric mixer on medium speed until fluffy. On low speed, beat in tea, ⅓ cup milk, 2 teaspoons vanilla and the eggs until well combined (mixture will appear curdled). Stir in remaining bread ingredients just until moistened. Spread in pan.

3 Bake 50 to 60 minutes or until toothpick inserted in center comes out clean (do not underbake). Cool 10 minutes. Run knife or metal spatula around sides of pan to loosen loaf. Remove from pan to cooling rack; cool 30 minutes.

4 In small bowl, stir powdered sugar, ¼ teaspoon vanilla and 3 teaspoons of the milk; add additional milk, 1 teaspoon at a time, until spreadable. Spread glaze over bread. Sprinkle with additional cinnamon. Cool completely, about 2 hours, before slicing. Wrap tightly and store at room temperature up to 4 days, or refrigerate.

1 Slice: Calories 190 (Calories from Fat 60); Total Fat 7g (Saturated Fat 4g; Trans Fat 0g); Cholesterol 40mg; Sodium 190mg; Total Carbohydrate 30g (Dietary Fiber 0g); Protein 3g **Exchanges:** 1 Starch, 1 Other Carbohydrate, 1 Fat **Carbohydrate Choices:** 2

bake smart *Chai* is the Hindi word for tea made with milk and spices such as cardamom, cinnamon, cloves, ginger, nutmeg and pepper.

Serve this bread with fresh fruit and tea as a snack or dessert.

chocolate-pistachio bread

prep time: 15 minutes + start to finish: 4 hours 35 minutes + 1 LOAF (24 SLICES)

⅔ cup granulated sugar

½ cup butter, melted

¾ cup milk

1 egg

1½ cups all-purpose flour

1 cup chopped pistachio nuts

½ cup semisweet chocolate chips

⅓ cup unsweetened baking cocoa

2 teaspoons baking powder

¼ teaspoon salt

Decorator sugar crystals, if desired

1 Heat oven to 350°F. Generously grease bottom only of 9×5-inch glass or shiny metal loaf pan with shortening (do not use dark-colored bakeware or bread will burn around edges).

2 In large bowl, mix granulated sugar, butter, milk and egg until well blended. Stir in all remaining ingredients except sugar crystals. Pour into pan. Sprinkle with sugar crystals.

3 Bake 60 to 70 minutes or until toothpick inserted in center comes out clean. Cool in pan on cooling rack 10 minutes.

4 Run knife or metal spatula around sides of pan to loosen loaf. Remove from pan to cooling rack. Cool completely, about 3 hours, before slicing. Wrap tightly and store at room temperature up to 4 days, or refrigerate.

1 Slice: Calories 150 (Calories from Fat 70); Total Fat 8g (Saturated Fat 3g; Trans Fat 0g); Cholesterol 20mg; Sodium 120mg; Total Carbohydrate 16g (Dietary Fiber 1g); Protein 3g **Exchanges:** ½ Starch, ½ Other Carbohydrate, 1½ Fat **Carbohydrate Choices:** 1

double chocolate–walnut bread: Substitute chocolate milk for the regular milk and walnuts for the pistachio nuts.

bake smart The baked and cooled loaf may be wrapped tightly and frozen up to 3 months.

chocolate-cherry bread

prep time: **15 minutes** ✛ start to finish: **2 hours 40 minutes** ✛ 1 LOAF (12 SLICES)

2 cups all-purpose flour

1½ teaspoons baking powder

½ teaspoon baking soda

¼ teaspoon salt

¾ cup sugar

½ cup butter, softened

2 eggs

1 teaspoon almond extract

1 teaspoon vanilla

1 container (8 oz) sour cream

½ cup chopped dried cherries

½ cup bittersweet or dark chocolate chips

1 Heat oven to 350°F. Grease 9x5-inch loaf pan with shortening; lightly flour. In medium bowl, mix flour, baking powder, baking soda and salt; set aside.

2 In large bowl, beat sugar and butter with electric mixer on medium speed until light and fluffy, about 2 minutes. Beat in eggs until well mixed. Beat in almond extract and vanilla. On low speed, alternately add flour mixture with sour cream, beating just until blended after each addition. Stir in cherries and chocolate chips. Spread batter in pan.

3 Bake 1 hour 10 minutes to 1 hour 15 minutes or until toothpick inserted in center comes out clean. Cool 10 minutes; remove from pan to cooling rack. Cool completely, about 1 hour. Wrap tightly and store at room temperature up to 4 days, or refrigerate.

1 Slice: Calories 310 (Calories from Fat 130); Total Fat 15g (Saturated Fat 9g; Trans Fat 0g); Cholesterol 60mg, Sodium 260mg; Total Carbohydrate 39g (Dietary Fiber 1g); Protein 4g **Exchanges:** 1½ Starch, 1 Other Carbohydrate, 3 Fat **Carbohydrate Choices:** 2½

ginger-topped pumpkin bread

prep time: 15 minutes ✛ start to finish: 2 hours 35 minutes ✛ 2 LOAVES (24 SLICES EACH)

bread

- 1 can (15 oz) pumpkin (not pumpkin pie mix)
- 1⅔ cups granulated sugar
- ⅔ cup unsweetened applesauce
- ½ cup milk
- 2 teaspoons vanilla
- 1 cup fat-free egg product or 2 eggs plus 4 egg whites
- 3 cups all-purpose flour
- 2 teaspoons baking soda
- 1 teaspoon salt
- 1 teaspoon ground cinnamon
- ½ teaspoon baking powder
- ½ teaspoon ground cloves

glaze and topping

- ⅔ cup powdered sugar
- 2 to 3 teaspoons warm water
- ¼ teaspoon vanilla
- 3 tablespoons finely chopped crystallized ginger

1 Heat oven to 350°F. Grease bottoms only of 2 (8×4- or 9×5-inch) loaf pans with shortening or cooking spray.

2 In large bowl, mix pumpkin, granulated sugar, applesauce, milk, vanilla and egg product. Stir in remaining bread ingredients. Pour into pans.

3 Bake 1 hour to 1 hour 10 minutes or until toothpick inserted in center comes out clean. Cool 10 minutes. Run knife or metal spatula around sides of pans to loosen loaves. Remove from pans to cooling rack. Cool completely, about 1 hour.

4 In small bowl, mix powdered sugar, water and ¼ teaspoon vanilla until thin enough to drizzle. Drizzle over loaves. Sprinkle with ginger. Wrap tightly and store at room temperature up to 4 days, or refrigerate up to 10 days.

1 Slice: Calories 70 (Calories from Fat 0); Total Fat 0g (Saturated Fat 0g; Trans Fat 0g); Cholesterol 0mg; Sodium 120mg; Total Carbohydrate 16g (Dietary Fiber 0g); Protein 1g **Exchanges:** ½ Starch, ½ Other Carbohydrate **Carbohydrate Choices:** 1

bake smart You'll find crystallized ginger in glass jars or plastic bags with the other baking ingredients at the grocery store.

Applesauce is the ingredient that adds moistness and depth to this updated favorite; ginger adds a new look and taste.

zucchini bread

prep time: **15 minutes** ✛ start to finish: **3 hours 25 minutes** ✛ **2 LOAVES (12 SLICES EACH)**

3 cups shredded zucchini (2 to 3 medium)

1⅔ cups sugar

⅔ cup vegetable oil

2 teaspoons vanilla

4 eggs

3 cups all-purpose or whole wheat flour

2 teaspoons baking soda

1 teaspoon salt

1 teaspoon ground cinnamon

½ teaspoon baking powder

½ teaspoon ground cloves

½ cup chopped nuts

½ cup raisins, if desired

1 Heat oven to 350°F. Grease bottoms only of 2 (8×4-inch) loaf pans or 1 (9×5-inch) loaf pan with shortening or cooking spray.

2 In large bowl, stir zucchini, sugar, oil, vanilla and eggs until well mixed. Stir in all remaining ingredients except nuts and raisins. Stir in nuts and raisins. Divide batter evenly between 8-inch pans or pour into 9-inch pan.

3 Bake 8-inch loaves 50 to 60 minutes, 9-inch loaf 1 hour 10 minutes to 1 hour 20 minutes, or until toothpick inserted in center comes out clean. Cool in pans on cooling rack 10 minutes.

4 Loosen sides of loaves from pans; remove from pans and place top side up on cooling rack. Cool completely, about 2 hours, before slicing. Wrap tightly and store at room temperature up to 4 days, or refrigerate up to 10 days.

1 Slice: Calories 200 (Calories from Fat 80); Total Fat 9g (Saturated Fat 1.5g; Trans Fat 0g); Cholesterol 35mg; Sodium 230mg; Total Carbohydrate 27g (Dietary Fiber 1g); Protein 3g **Exchanges:** 1 Starch, 1 Other Carbohydrate, 1½ Fat **Carbohydrate Choices:** 2

cranberry bread: Omit zucchini, cinnamon, cloves and raisins. Stir in ½ cup milk and 2 teaspoons grated orange peel with the oil. Stir 3 cups fresh or frozen (thawed and drained) cranberries into batter. Bake 1 hour to 1 hour 10 minutes.

orange zucchini bread: Stir in 2 teaspoons grated orange peel with the flour mixture.

pumpkin bread: Substitute 1 can (15 oz) pumpkin (not pumpkin pie mix) for the zucchini.

bake smart You don't need to peel the zucchini if it is very fresh and green. Older, larger zucchini may require peeling before shredding. The peel adds little green flecks to the bread.

whole wheat banana bread with caramel glaze

prep time: 30 minutes ⁙ start to finish: 3 hours 55 minutes ⁙ 1 LOAF (12 SLICES)

bread

2 cups white whole wheat flour

1 teaspoon baking soda

½ teaspoon baking powder

½ teaspoon salt

½ cup butter, softened

½ cup granulated sugar

½ cup packed brown sugar

2 eggs

1⅓ cups mashed very ripe bananas (3 medium)

½ cup chopped pecans, toasted*

glaze

½ cup packed brown sugar

3 tablespoons whipping cream

2 tablespoons butter, cut up

1 tablespoon light corn syrup

½ cup chopped pecans, toasted*

1 Heat oven to 325°F. Spray bottom only of 9×5-inch loaf pan with cooking spray. In medium bowl, stir flour, baking soda, baking powder and salt with whisk.

2 In large bowl, beat ½ cup butter, granulated sugar and ½ cup brown sugar with electric mixer on medium speed 3 minutes or until light and fluffy. Beat in eggs one at a time, beating well after each addition. On low speed, beat in bananas. Beat in flour mixture just until moistened. Stir in ½ cup pecans. Spoon into pan.

3 Bake 1 hour 10 minutes to 1 hour 20 minutes or until toothpick inserted in center comes out clean. Cool in pan on cooling rack 10 minutes.

4 Loosen sides of loaf from pan; remove from pan and place top side up on cooling rack. Cool completely, about 2 hours.

5 Meanwhile, in 1-quart saucepan, combine all glaze ingredients except pecans. Bring to a boil over medium heat, stirring frequently, until sugar has melted. Boil, without stirring, 45 to 60 seconds or until thickened. Pour into small bowl; refrigerate 30 to 40 minutes or until cool enough to spread, stirring occasionally. Spread caramel over top of cooled bread; sprinkle ½ cup chopped pecans over caramel. Let stand until set.

*To toast pecans, bake in ungreased shallow pan at 325°F for 7 to 11 minutes, stirring occasionally, until light brown.

1 Slice: Calories 390 (Calories from Fat 170); Total Fat 19g (Saturated Fat 8g; Trans Fat 0g); Cholesterol 65mg; Sodium 340mg; Total Carbohydrate 50g (Dietary Fiber 3g); Protein 5g **Exchanges:** 1½ Starch, 2 Other Carbohydrate, 3½ Fat **Carbohydrate Choices:** 3

bake smart For the best banana flavor, use the ripest bananas with dark skin. Save ripe bananas for future use in bread by freezing them whole in resealable freezer plastic bags. They become mushy and are perfect for banana bread or smoothies.

When stirring the caramel, make sure all of the sugar is dissolved before it boils and thickens, or crystallization can occur. If there is sugar that has not dissolved on the side of the pan, use a pastry brush dipped in water to wash the sugar crystals down into the caramel before boiling.

poppy seed–lemon bread

prep time: **15 minutes** ✢ start to finish: **3 hours 25 minutes** ✢ **1 LOAF (16 SLICES)**

2 cups all-purpose flour

1 cup sugar

¼ cup grated lemon peel

1 cup milk

¾ cup vegetable oil

2 tablespoons poppy seed

2 teaspoons baking powder

½ teaspoon salt

2 eggs, slightly beaten

1 Heat oven to 350°F. Generously grease bottom only of 9×5-inch loaf pan with shortening; lightly flour. (Do not use cooking spray.)

2 In large bowl, stir together all ingredients until moistened. Pour into pan.

3 Bake 55 to 65 minutes or until toothpick inserted in center comes out clean. Cool 5 minutes. Loosen sides of loaf from pan; remove from pan and place top side up on cooling rack. Cool completely, about 2 hours. Wrap tightly and store at room temperature up to 4 days, or refrigerate.

1 Slice: Calories 220 (Calories from Fat 110); Total Fat 12g (Saturated Fat 2g; Trans Fat 0g); Cholesterol 25mg; Sodium 150mg; Total Carbohydrate 26g (Dietary Fiber 1g); Protein 3g **Exchanges:** 1 Starch, ½ Other Carbohydrate, 2½ Fat **Carbohydrate Choices:** 2

bake smart You'll want to purchase poppy seed in small amounts as this nutty-flavored spice can spoil easily. Store poppy seed tightly covered in the refrigerator for 3 to 6 months.

ginger-carrot-nut bread

prep time: 15 minutes | start to finish: 3 hours 25 minutes + 1 LOAF (16 SLICES)

2   eggs
¾   cup packed brown sugar
⅓   cup vegetable oil
½   cup milk
1   teaspoon vanilla
2   cups all-purpose flour
2   teaspoons baking powder
1   teaspoon ground ginger
½   teaspoon salt
1   cup shredded carrots (2 medium)
½   cup chopped nuts

1 Move oven rack to low position so that tops of pans will be in center of oven. Heat oven to 350°F. Grease bottom only of 8×4-inch loaf pan with shortening; lightly flour (or spray bottom of pan with baking spray with flour).

2 In large bowl, beat eggs and brown sugar with electric mixer on medium speed until creamy. Beat in oil, milk and vanilla. On low speed, beat in flour, baking powder, ginger and salt until smooth. Stir in carrots and nuts. Spread in pan.

3 Bake 50 to 60 minutes or until toothpick inserted in center comes out clean. Cool in pans on cooling rack 10 minutes.

4 Loosen sides of loaves from pan; remove from pan and place top side up on cooling rack. Cool completely, about 2 hours, before slicing. Wrap tightly and store at room temperature up to 4 days, or refrigerate.

1 Slice: Calories 180 (Calories from Fat 70); Total Fat 8g (Saturated Fat 1.5g; Trans Fat 0g); Cholesterol 25mg; Sodium 170mg; Total Carbohydrate 24g (Dietary Fiber 1g); Protein 3g **Exchanges:** 1 Starch, ½ Other Carbohydrate, 1½ Fat **Carbohydrate Choices:** 1½

bake smart Serve slices of this fragrant loaf with whipped cream cheese.

The reason only the bottom of the pan is greased is to help the loaf rise correctly and keep the loaf from sinking around the edges.

cinnamon bubble loaf

prep time: 15 minutes ✛ start to finish: 55 minutes ✛ 1 LOAF (12 SLICES)

loaf

- 2 tablespoons granulated sugar
- 1½ teaspoons ground cinnamon
- 3½ cups Original Bisquick mix
- ⅓ cup granulated sugar
- 3 tablespoons butter, softened
- ½ cup milk
- 1 teaspoon vanilla
- 1 egg
- 2 tablespoons butter, melted

glaze, if desired

- ½ cup powdered sugar
- 2 to 3 teaspoons water

1 Heat oven to 375°F. Grease bottom and sides of 9×5-inch loaf pan with shortening or cooking spray. In small bowl, mix 2 tablespoons granulated sugar and the cinnamon; set aside.

2 In medium bowl, stir Bisquick mix, ⅓ cup granulated sugar, 3 tablespoons softened butter, the milk, vanilla and egg until soft dough forms.

3 Shape dough into 1-inch balls; roll in cinnamon-sugar. Place dough randomly in pan. Sprinkle with any remaining cinnamon-sugar. Drizzle 2 tablespoons melted butter over dough balls.

4 Bake 25 to 30 minutes or until golden brown. Cool in pan on cooling rack 10 minutes. Meanwhile, in small bowl, mix all glaze ingredients until smooth and thin enough to drizzle.

5 Loosen sides of loaves from pan; remove loaf from pan to cooling rack. Drizzle glaze over loaf. Serve warm.

1 Slice: Calories 250 (Calories from Fat 90); Total Fat 10g (Saturated Fat 4.5g; Trans Fat 1.5g); Cholesterol 30mg; Sodium 470mg; Total Carbohydrate 36g (Dietary Fiber 1g); Protein 3g **Exchanges:** 1½ Starch, 1 Other Carbohydrate, 2 Fat **Carbohydrate Choices:** 2½

apple-fig bread with honey glaze

prep time: 20 minutes ✚ start to finish: 3 hours 30 minutes ✚ 1 LOAF (12 SLICES)

bread

- 1½ cups all-purpose flour
- 1½ teaspoons ground cinnamon
- 1 teaspoon baking powder
- ½ teaspoon salt
- ½ teaspoon ground nutmeg
- ¼ teaspoon ground allspice
- ⅔ cup granulated sugar
- ½ cup vegetable oil
- 1 egg
- 1 egg yolk
- 1½ teaspoons vanilla
- ½ cup milk
- 1 cup chopped peeled apples
- ½ cup dried figs, chopped

glaze

- ⅓ to ½ cup powdered sugar
- 2 tablespoons honey
- 1 tablespoon butter, softened
- Dash ground allspice

1 Heat oven to 350°F. Spray bottom only of 8×4-inch loaf pan with cooking spray. In medium bowl, stir flour, cinnamon, baking powder, salt, nutmeg and ¼ teaspoon allspice with whisk.

2 In large bowl, beat granulated sugar and oil with electric mixer on medium speed 1 minute or until blended. Beat in egg and egg yolk, one at a time, beating well after each addition. Beat in vanilla.

3 Beat flour mixture into sugar mixture alternately with milk on low speed, beating after each addition until smooth. Stir in apples and figs. Pour into pan.

4 Bake 55 to 65 minutes or until toothpick inserted in center comes out clean. Cool in pan on cooling rack 10 minutes.

5 Loosen sides of loaf from pan; remove from pan and place top side up on cooling rack. Cool completely, about 2 hours.

6 In small bowl, beat ⅓ cup powdered sugar, the honey, butter and dash of allspice until smooth, slowly adding additional powdered sugar for desired glaze consistency. Spread glaze over top of loaf. Let stand until set. (Glaze will remain slightly tacky to the touch.) Wrap tightly and store in refrigerator.

1 Slice: Calories 260 (Calories from Fat 100); Total Fat 11g (Saturated Fat 1.5g; Trans Fat 0g); Cholesterol 40mg; Sodium 160mg; Total Carbohydrate 36g (Dietary Fiber 1g); Protein 3g **Exchanges:** 1 Starch, 1½ Other Carbohydrate, 2 Fat **Carbohydrate Choices:** 2½

bake smart Use sweet-tart apples such as Braeburn, Gala or Honeycrisp for this recipe.

Raisins or chopped dates can be substituted for the figs.

five-grain buttermilk-cranberry bread

prep time: 15 minutes ✛ start to finish: 1 hour 25 minutes ✛ 1 LOAF (12 SLICES)

1 cup 5-grain rolled whole-grain cereal or old-fashioned oats

3 cups white whole wheat flour

⅓ cup packed brown sugar

1 teaspoon baking soda

1 teaspoon cream of tartar

¾ teaspoon salt

¼ cup cold butter, cut into small pieces

½ cup sweetened dried cranberries, cherries or raisins

1 egg

1½ cups buttermilk

1 Heat oven to 375°F. Grease cookie sheet with shortening or cooking spray. Reserve 1 tablespoon of the cereal.

2 In large bowl, mix remaining cereal, the flour, brown sugar, baking soda, cream of tartar and salt. Cut in butter, using pastry blender or fork, until mixture looks like coarse crumbs. Stir in dried cranberries.

3 In small bowl, beat egg and buttermilk with whisk until well blended. Reserve 1 tablespoon buttermilk mixture. Stir remaining buttermilk mixture into dry ingredients, stirring just until mixture is moistened; dough will be soft. On floured surface, knead dough 5 or 6 times.

4 On large cookie sheet, shape dough into 7-inch round. Using sharp knife, cut large X shape ¼ inch deep into top of dough. Brush top of dough with reserved buttermilk mixture; sprinkle with reserved cereal.

5 Bake 35 to 40 minutes or until top is golden brown. Remove from pan to cooling rack. Cool 30 minutes. Using serrated knife, cut into 12 slices or wedges to serve.

1 Slice: Calories 230 (Calories from Fat 60); Total Fat 6g (Saturated Fat 3g; Trans Fat 0g); Cholesterol 30mg; Sodium 320mg; Total Carbohydrate 38g (Dietary Fiber 4g); Protein 6g **Exchanges:** 2 Starch, ½ Other Carbohydrate, 1 Fat **Carbohydrate Choices:** 2½

bake smart If you don't have white whole wheat flour, you could use all-purpose flour instead for a loaf that is just as delicious.

oatmeal-streusel bread

prep time: 25 minutes ✛ start to finish: 3 hours 55 minutes ✛ 1 LOAF (12 SLICES)

streusel

- ¼ cup packed brown sugar
- ¼ cup chopped walnuts, toasted*
- 2 teaspoons ground cinnamon

bread

- 1 cup all-purpose flour
- ½ cup whole wheat flour
- ½ cup old-fashioned oats
- 2 tablespoons ground flaxseed or flaxseed meal
- 1 teaspoon baking powder
- ½ teaspoon salt
- ¼ teaspoon baking soda
- ¾ cup packed brown sugar
- ⅔ cup vegetable oil
- 2 eggs
- ¼ cup sour cream
- 2 teaspoons vanilla
- ½ cup milk

icing

- ¾ to 1 cup powdered sugar
- 1 tablespoon milk
- 2 teaspoons light corn syrup

1 Heat oven to 350°F. Spray bottom only of 9×5-inch loaf pan with cooking spray. In small bowl, stir together all streusel ingredients; set aside.

2 In medium bowl, stir flours, oats, flaxseed, baking powder, salt and baking soda with whisk until blended.

3 In large bowl, beat ¾ cup brown sugar and the oil with electric mixer on medium speed 1 minute or until blended. Beat in eggs one at a time, beating well after each addition. Beat in sour cream and vanilla.

4 Beat flour mixture into sugar mixture alternately with ½ cup milk on low speed, beating after each addition until smooth. Spoon one-third of batter in pan (about 1 cup); sprinkle with half of the streusel (about ⅓ cup). Top with half of remaining batter (about 1 cup), spreading gently. Sprinkle with remaining streusel mixture. Top with remaining batter. Gently run knife through batter to swirl.

5 Bake 50 to 55 minutes or until toothpick inserted in center comes out clean. Cool on cooling rack 10 minutes.

6 Loosen sides of loaf from pan; remove from pan and place top side up on cooling rack. Cool completely, about 2 hours.

7 In small bowl, beat all icing ingredients, adding enough of the powdered sugar for desired drizzling consistency. Drizzle icing over bread. Let stand until set. Wrap tightly and store at room temperature up to 4 days, or refrigerate.

*To toast walnuts, bake in ungreased shallow pan at 350°F for 7 to 11 minutes, stirring occasionally, until light brown.

1 Slice: Calories 320 (Calories from Fat 150); Total Fat 16g (Saturated Fat 2g; Trans Fat 0g); Cholesterol 40mg; Sodium 190mg; Total Carbohydrate 40g (Dietary Fiber 1g); Protein 4g **Exchanges:** 1½ Starch, 1 Other Carbohydrate, 3 Fat **Carbohydrate Choices:** 2½

bake smart Although this bread doesn't need to be refrigerated, doing so makes slicing it a bit easier.

For a flavor change, add 2 teaspoons grated orange peel in place of the vanilla. Then, use orange juice in place of the milk in the icing.

brown bread with raisins

prep time: 15 minutes | start to finish: 1 hour 45 minutes + 1 LOAF (32 SLICES)

1 cup all-purpose flour
1 cup whole wheat flour
1 cup whole-grain cornmeal
1 cup raisins
2 cups buttermilk
¾ cup molasses
2 teaspoons baking soda
1 teaspoon salt

1 Heat oven to 325°F. Grease 2-quart casserole dish with shortening or cooking spray.

2 In large bowl, beat all ingredients with electric mixer on low speed 30 seconds, scraping bowl constantly. Beat on medium speed 30 seconds, scraping bowl constantly. Pour into casserole.

3 Bake uncovered about 1 hour or until toothpick inserted in center comes out clean. Immediately loosen sides of bread with metal spatula and remove bread from casserole. Cool 30 minutes on cooling rack before slicing. Serve warm.

1 Slice: Calories 90 (Calories from Fat 0); Total Fat 0.5g (Saturated Fat 0g; Trans Fat 0g); Cholesterol 0mg; Sodium 170mg; Total Carbohydrate 19g (Dietary Fiber 0g); Protein 2g **Exchanges:** 1 Starch **Carbohydrate Choices:** 1

bake smart Created in colonial times and also called Boston brown bread, this authentic dark bread is made with cornmeal and molasses. Originally, it called for rye meal, which was available at the time. If you really like the flavor of rye, substitute ½ cup rye flour for ½ cup of the whole wheat flour.

blueberries 'n orange bread

prep time: **15 minutes** ✛ start to finish: **2 hours 10 minutes** ✛ 1 LOAF (18 SLICES)

bread

- 3 cups Original Bisquick mix
- ½ cup granulated sugar
- 1 tablespoon grated orange peel
- ½ cup milk
- 3 tablespoons vegetable oil
- 2 eggs
- 1 cup fresh or frozen (rinsed and drained) blueberries

glaze

- ½ cup powdered sugar
- 3 to 4 teaspoons orange juice

  Additional grated orange peel, if desired

1 Heat oven to 350°F. Grease bottom only of 9×5-inch loaf pan with shortening or cooking spray. In large bowl, stir all bread ingredients except blueberries until blended. Fold in blueberries. Pour into pan.

2 Bake 50 to 60 minutes or until toothpick inserted in center comes out clean. Cool 10 minutes. Loosen loaf from sides of pan; remove from pan to cooling rack. Cool completely, about 45 minutes.

3 In small bowl, mix powdered sugar and orange juice until smooth and thin enough to drizzle. Drizzle glaze over bread; sprinkle with additional orange peel.

1 Slice: Calories 150 (Calories from Fat 50); Total Fat 6g (Saturated Fat 1.5g; Trans Fat 1g); Cholesterol 25mg; Sodium 250mg; Total Carbohydrate 24g (Dietary Fiber 0g); Protein 2g **Exchanges:** 1 Starch, ½ Other Carbohydrate, 1 Fat **Carbohydrate Choices:** 1½

bake smart Try other fruit combinations, such as lemon-raspberry or orange-cranberry. Substitute lemon peel and juice for the orange peel and juice, and fresh or frozen raspberries or cranberries for the blueberries.

gluten-free glazed lemon-pecan bread

prep time: **15 minutes** ✛ start to finish: **1 hour 10 minutes** ✛ 1 LOAF (12 SLICES)

bread

- ½ cup white rice flour
- ½ cup tapioca flour
- ½ cup potato starch
- ¼ cup sweet white sorghum flour
- ¼ cup garbanzo and fava flour
- 1 teaspoon xanthan gum
- 1 teaspoon gluten-free baking powder
- 1 teaspoon baking soda
- ½ teaspoon salt
- 2 eggs
- ½ cup sunflower or canola oil or melted ghee
- ¼ cup almond milk, soymilk or regular milk
- ½ teaspoon cider vinegar
- 1 tablespoon grated lemon peel
- ¼ cup fresh lemon juice
- ⅔ cup granulated sugar
- ½ cup chopped pecans

glaze

- 2 tablespoons fresh lemon juice
- 1 cup gluten-free powdered sugar

1 Heat oven to 350°F. Spray 9×5-inch loaf pan with cooking spray (without flour).

2 In small bowl, mix flours, xanthan gum, baking powder, baking soda and salt with whisk; set aside. In medium bowl, beat eggs, oil, milk, vinegar, lemon peel, ¼ cup lemon juice and the granulated sugar with electric mixer on medium speed until well blended. Gradually add flour mixture, beating until well blended. Stir in pecans. Pour into pan.

3 Bake 20 minutes. Cover loaf with cooking parchment paper; bake 25 minutes longer or until golden brown. Cool 10 minutes. Loosen loaf from pan; remove from pan to cooling rack.

4 In small bowl, stir all glaze ingredients until smooth. With fork, poke holes in top of loaf; drizzle glaze over loaf. Serve warm.

1 Slice: Calories 300 (Calories from Fat 120); Total Fat 14g (Saturated Fat 1.5g; Trans Fat 0g); Cholesterol 35mg; Sodium 260mg; Total Carbohydrate 41g (Dietary Fiber 2g); Protein 3g **Exchanges:** 1 Starch, 1½ Other Carbohydrate, 2½ Fat **Carbohydrate Choices:** 3

Jean Duane, Alternative Cook { www.alternativecook.com }

bake smart Cooking gluten free? Always read labels to make sure that each recipe ingredient is gluten free. Products and ingredient sources can vary.

A zester makes grating lemons a breeze. Just go as deep as the outer skin, avoiding the pith (the bitter white part of the skin).

When you're ready to juice the lemon, roll it on the countertop before cutting it open. This releases the juice.

gluten-free best-ever banana bread

prep time: **15 minutes** ✛ start to finish: **2 hours 20 minutes** ✛ 1 LOAF (16 SLICES)

½ cup tapioca flour

½ cup white rice flour

½ cup potato starch

¼ cup garbanzo and fava flour

¼ cup sweet white sorghum flour

1 teaspoon xanthan gum

½ teaspoon guar gum

1 teaspoon gluten-free baking powder

1 teaspoon baking soda

1 teaspoon salt

1 teaspoon ground cinnamon

¾ cup packed brown sugar

1 cup mashed very ripe bananas (2 medium)

½ cup ghee (measured melted)

¼ cup almond milk, soymilk or regular milk

1 teaspoon gluten-free vanilla

2 eggs

1 Heat oven to 350°F. Generously spray bottom and sides of 9×5-inch loaf pan with cooking spray (without flour).

2 In small bowl, mix flours, xanthan gum, guar gum, baking powder, baking soda, salt and cinnamon; set aside. In medium bowl, beat remaining ingredients with whisk until blended. Add flour mixture; stir until thoroughly mixed. Pour into pan.

3 Bake 30 minutes. Cover with foil; bake 25 to 30 minutes longer or until toothpick inserted in center comes out almost clean. Cool 5 minutes. Loosen loaf from pan; remove from pan to cooling rack. Cool completely, about 1 hour. Store tightly wrapped in refrigerator.

1 Slice: Calories 200 (Calories from Fat 80); Total Fat 9g (Saturated Fat 5g; Trans Fat 0g); Cholesterol 40mg; Sodium 270mg; Total Carbohydrate 29g (Dietary Fiber 1g); Protein 2g **Exchanges:** 1 Starch, ½ Fruit, ½ Other Carbohydrate, 1½ Fat **Carbohydrate Choices:** 2

apple bread: Substitute applesauce for the mashed bananas.

pumpkin bread: Substitute canned pumpkin (not pumpkin pie mix) for the mashed bananas, and add ¼ teaspoon ground cloves and ¼ teaspoon ground nutmeg.

Jean Duane, Alternative Cook { www.alternativecook.com }

bake smart Cooking gluten free? Always read labels to make sure that each recipe ingredient is gluten free. Products and ingredient sources can vary.

blueberry-basil loaf

prep time: **20 minutes** + start to finish: **2 hours 40 minutes** + 1 LOAF (12 SLICES)

bread

1¼   cups fresh blueberries

1   tablespoon all-purpose flour

2¼   cups all-purpose flour

1   cup granulated sugar

2   teaspoons baking powder

1   teaspoon grated lemon peel

½   teaspoon salt

1   cup buttermilk

6   tablespoons butter, melted

1   teaspoon vanilla

2   eggs

¼   cup coarsely chopped fresh basil leaves

topping

½   cup packed brown sugar

¼   cup butter, melted

⅔   cup all-purpose flour

1 Heat oven to 375°F. Spray 9×5-inch loaf pan with cooking spray. In small bowl, toss blueberries with 1 tablespoon flour; set aside.

2 In large bowl, mix 2¼ cups flour, the granulated sugar, baking powder, lemon peel and salt. In medium bowl, beat buttermilk, 6 tablespoons melted butter, the vanilla and eggs with whisk until well blended. Stir into flour mixture. Gently fold in blueberries and basil. Spread in pan.

3 In medium bowl, mix brown sugar and ¼ cup butter until blended. Using fork, stir in ⅔ cup flour until mixture is crumbly. Sprinkle topping over batter.

4 Bake 1 hour 5 minutes to 1 hour 10 minutes or until toothpick inserted in center comes out clean. (If loaf becomes too brown, cover with foil during last 30 minutes of baking.) Cool 10 minutes. Loosen loaf from pan; remove from pan to cooling rack. Cool completely, about 1 hour.

1 Slice: Calories 340 (Calories from Fat 100); Total Fat 11g (Saturated Fat 7g; Trans Fat 0g); Cholesterol 60mg; Sodium 300mg; Total Carbohydrate 53g (Dietary Fiber 1g); Protein 5g **Exchanges:** 1½ Starch, 2 Other Carbohydrate, 2 Fat **Carbohydrate Choices:** 3½

bake smart Freeze blueberries before adding them to the batter to prevent them from sinking to the bottom of the loaf.

savory sweet potato pan bread

prep time: **15 minutes** ✛ start to finish: **40 minutes** ✛ 1 LOAF (8 WEDGES)

1½ cups uncooked shredded dark-orange sweet potato (about ½ potato)

½ cup sugar

¼ cup vegetable oil

2 eggs

¾ cup all-purpose flour

¾ cup whole wheat flour

2 teaspoons dried minced onion

1 teaspoon dried rosemary leaves, crumbled

1 teaspoon baking soda

½ teaspoon salt

¼ teaspoon baking powder

2 teaspoons sesame seed

1 Heat oven to 350°F. Grease bottom only of 9-inch round pan with shortening or cooking spray.

2 In large bowl, mix sweet potato, sugar, oil and eggs. Stir in all remaining ingredients except sesame seed. Spread in pan. Sprinkle sesame seed over batter.

3 Bake 20 to 25 minutes or until golden brown. Serve warm.

1 Wedge: Calories 240 (Calories from Fat 80); Total Fat 9g (Saturated Fat 1g; Trans Fat 0g); Cholesterol 55mg; Sodium 340mg; Total Carbohydrate 34g (Dietary Fiber 3g); Protein 5g **Exchanges:** 1 Starch, 1½ Other Carbohydrate, 1½ Fat **Carbohydrate Choices:** 2

bake smart Sweet potatoes add sweetness, extra flavor and color to this delicious savory bread. It's an excellent choice to serve with dinner, or eat as a snack. Keep leftovers tightly covered.

best-ever oatmeal-flax bread

prep time: 10 minutes + start to finish: 3 hours 10 minutes + 1 LOAF (16 SLICES)

1½ cups whole wheat flour

1 cup all-purpose flour

⅔ cup packed dark brown sugar

½ cup old-fashioned oats

⅓ cup ground flaxseed or flaxseed meal

1 teaspoon baking soda

1 teaspoon salt

1⅔ cups buttermilk

1 tablespoon old-fashioned oats

1 Heat oven to 350°F. Spray 8×4-inch loaf pan with cooking spray.

2 In large bowl, mix flours, brown sugar, ½ cup oats, the flaxseed, baking soda and salt. Stir in buttermilk just until mixed. Pour into pan. Sprinkle with 1 tablespoon oats.

3 Bake 45 to 55 minutes or until toothpick inserted in center comes out clean. Cool 5 minutes. Loosen loaf from pan; remove from pan to cooling rack. Cool completely, about 2 hours, before slicing.

1 Slice: Calories 140 (Calories from Fat 15); Total Fat 2g (Saturated Fat 0g; Trans Fat 0g); Cholesterol 0mg; Sodium 250mg; Total Carbohydrate 27g (Dietary Fiber 3g); Protein 4g **Exchanges:** 1 Starch, 1 Other Carbohydrate **Carbohydrate Choices:** 2

bake smart The flaxseed in this recipe replaces eggs and much of the oil used in other quick breads.

irish yogurt bread

prep time: 10 minutes ✛ start to finish: 30 minutes ✛ 8 WEDGES

1¾ cups all-purpose flour

½ cup dried currants or raisins

1½ teaspoons baking powder

¼ teaspoon baking soda

¼ teaspoon salt

1 container (6 oz) lemon burst, orange creme or French vanilla yogurt

2 tablespoons vegetable oil

1 Heat oven to 375°F. Lightly grease bottom and side of 9-inch round pan with shortening.

2 In medium bowl, mix flour, currants, baking powder, baking soda and salt. In small bowl, mix yogurt and oil; stir into flour mixture just until moistened. Spread in pan.

3 Bake 20 minutes or until toothpick inserted in center comes out clean. Cool 5 to 10 minutes before serving. Serve warm or cool.

1 Wedge: Calories 180 (Calories from Fat 35); Total Fat 4g (Saturated Fat 0.5g; Trans Fat 0g); Cholesterol 0mg; Sodium 220mg; Total Carbohydrate 31g (Dietary Fiber 1g); Protein 4g **Exchanges:** 1½ Starch, ½ Other Carbohydrate, ½ Fat **Carbohydrate Choices:** 2

bake smart For a quick, fruity topping for these tasty wedges, mix equal parts of plain or flavored yogurt and your favorite preserves and drizzle over the top.

cornbread

prep time: **10 minutes** + start to finish: **35 minutes** +

1 cup milk
¼ cup butter, melted
1 egg
1¼ cups yellow, white or blue cornmeal
1 cup all-purpose flour
½ cup sugar
1 tablespoon baking powder
½ teaspoon salt

1 Heat oven to 400°F. Grease bottom and side of 9-inch round pan or 8-inch square pan with shortening or cooking spray.

2 In large bowl, beat milk, butter and egg with whisk. Stir in remaining ingredients all at once just until flour is moistened (batter will be lumpy). Pour into pan.

3 Bake 20 to 25 minutes or until golden brown and toothpick inserted in center comes out clean. Serve warm.

1 Wedge: Calories 170 (Calories from Fat 45); Total Fat 5g (Saturated Fat 2.5g; Trans Fat 0g); Cholesterol 30mg; Sodium 260mg; Total Carbohydrate 29g (Dietary Fiber 0g); Protein 4g **Exchanges:** 1 Starch, 1 Other Carbohydrate, 1 Fat **Carbohydrate Choices:** 2

bacon cornbread: Make recipe as directed. Stir 4 slices cooked, crumbled bacon into batter before pouring into pan.

corn muffins: Grease bottoms only of 12 regular-size muffin cups with shortening or cooking spray, or line with paper baking cups. Fill cups about three-quarters full. Bake as directed in step 3.

gluten-free cornbread

prep time. 15 minutes + start to finish: 55 minutes + 9 SERVINGS

¾ cup cornmeal

½ cup tapioca flour

¼ cup white rice flour

¼ cup sweet white sorghum flour

¼ cup potato starch

2 teaspoons gluten-free baking powder

1 teaspoon baking soda

1 teaspoon salt

½ teaspoon xanthan gum

½ teaspoon guar gum

1¼ cups almond milk, soymilk or regular milk

1 teaspoon cider vinegar

⅓ cup sugar

2 eggs

¼ cup ghee (measured melted)

1 Heat oven to 400°F. Spray bottom and sides of 8-inch square (2-quart) glass baking dish with cooking spray (without flour).

2 In medium bowl, mix cornmeal, all flours, the baking powder, baking soda, salt, xanthan gum and guar gum; set aside.

3 In medium bowl, beat milk, vinegar, sugar and eggs with electric mixer on medium speed until frothy. Gradually add ghee, beating constantly until thoroughly mixed. Add cornmeal mixture; beat on low speed about 1 minute or until well blended. Pour into baking dish.

4 Bake 20 to 25 minutes or until top springs back when touched lightly in center and cornbread pulls away from sides of baking dish. Cool 15 minutes. Serve warm.

1 Serving: Calories 240 (Calories from Fat 80); Total Fat 9g (Saturated Fat 5g; Trans Fat 0g); Cholesterol 60mg; Sodium 540mg; Total Carbohydrate 37g (Dietary Fiber 1g); Protein 4g **Exchanges:** 1½ Starch, 1 Other Carbohydrate, 1½ Fat **Carbohydrate Choices:** 2½

Jean Duane, Alternative Cook { www.alternativecook.com }

bake smart Vinegar is added to balance the pH and to boost the leavening.

Ghee is clarified butter and is measured when melted. Just microwave it on High a minute or two to melt it. If you'd prefer, substitute sunflower or corn oil for the ghee in this recipe.

pecan-topped cornbread with honey butter

prep time: 20 minutes ✛ start to finish: 1 hour 5 minutes ✛ 12 WEDGES

cornbread

- 1 cup cornmeal
- 1 cup all-purpose flour
- ⅓ cup sugar
- ¼ cup butter, melted
- 2 teaspoons baking powder
- ¼ teaspoon salt
- 3 eggs
- 1 can (14.75 oz) cream-style corn
- ¼ cup chopped pecans

honey butter

- ½ cup butter, softened (do not use margarine)
- ¼ cup honey
  Dash salt

1 Heat oven to 375°F. Spray 9- or 8-inch round pan with baking spray with flour.

2 In medium bowl, stir all cornbread ingredients except pecans until well blended. Pour into pan. Sprinkle pecans evenly over batter.

3 Bake 35 to 45 minutes or until toothpick inserted in center comes out clean.

4 In small bowl, beat ½ cup butter with spoon until creamy. Slowly beat in honey and salt until well blended. Serve with warm cornbread.

1 Wedge: Calories 300 (Calories from Fat 140); Total Fat 15g (Saturated Fat 8g; Trans Fat 0g); Cholesterol 85mg; Sodium 320mg; Total Carbohydrate 35g (Dietary Fiber 1g); Protein 5g **Exchanges:** 1 Starch, 1½ Other Carbohydrate, 3 Fat **Carbohydrate Choices:** 2

bake smart Keep your cornmeal fresh by storing it in the refrigerator or freezer.

zesty cheddar bread

prep time: **10 minutes** ÷ start to finish: **1 hour 20 minutes** ÷ **1 LOAF (12 SLICES)**

1 cup buttermilk

⅓ cup butter, melted

1 tablespoon sugar

2 tablespoons finely chopped chipotle chiles in adobo sauce (from 7-oz can)

2 eggs

2 cups all-purpose flour

1 cup shredded Cheddar cheese (4 oz)

2 teaspoons baking powder

1 teaspoon baking soda

½ teaspoon salt

1 Heat oven to 400°F. Grease bottom only of 8×4- or 9×5-inch loaf pan with shortening or cooking spray.

2 In large bowl, stir buttermilk, butter, sugar, chiles and eggs until well mixed. Stir in remaining ingredients just until moistened. Spread in pan.

3 Bake 8-inch pan 45 to 55 minutes, 9-inch pan 40 to 50 minutes, or until toothpick inserted in center comes out clean (do not underbake). Cool in pan on cooling rack 15 minutes. Loosen sides of loaf from pan; remove from pan and place top side up on cooling rack. Serve warm, if desired.

1 Slice: Calories 180 (Calories from Fat 90); Total Fat 10g (Saturated Fat 6g; Trans Fat 0g); Cholesterol 60mg; Sodium 430mg; Total Carbohydrate 18g (Dietary Fiber 0g); Protein 6g **Exchanges:** 1 Starch, ½ High-Fat Meat, 1 Fat **Carbohydrate Choices:** 1

bake smart Double-check the expiration date on your baking powder and baking soda before using in recipes. If you're not sure the baking powder is still good, combine 1 teaspoon with ⅓ cup hot water—if it bubbles, it's fine to use.

Lemon Filled Doughnuts
(page 132)

doughnuts and coffee cakes

aztec chocolate doughnuts

prep time: 1 hour 10 minutes ✛ start to finish: 2 hours 50 minutes ✛ 16 DOUGHNUTS

doughnuts

- 3 eggs
- ¾ cup granulated sugar
- ½ cup buttermilk
- 3 tablespoons butter, melted
- 1 teaspoon vanilla
- ¾ cup unsweetened baking cocoa
- 1¾ cups all-purpose flour
- 1½ teaspoons baking powder
- ¾ teaspoon ground cinnamon
- ½ teaspoon baking soda
- ½ teaspoon salt
  Vegetable oil

glaze

- ¼ cup butter
- 3 tablespoons milk
- 1 tablespoon light corn syrup
- ⅛ teaspoon ground cinnamon
- ¾ cup dark chocolate chips
- 1 to 1½ cups powdered sugar
- 1½ teaspoons vanilla

1 In medium bowl, beat eggs, granulated sugar, buttermilk, 3 tablespoons butter and 1 teaspoon vanilla with whisk until blended. Stir in cocoa. Stir in all remaining doughnut ingredients except oil just until moistened. Grease another medium bowl with shortening. Place dough in bowl, turning dough to grease all sides. Cover bowl with plastic wrap; refrigerate 1 hour.

2 Place dough on generously floured surface. Roll dough in flour to coat. With floured rolling pin, roll dough to ⅜-inch thickness. Cut with floured 3-inch cookie cutter.

3 Line 2 cookie sheets with cooking parchment paper. Place dough rounds on cookie sheets about 1 inch apart. Cut out centers using floured 1-inch cookie cutter. Reroll scraps to cut additional doughnuts. Cover cookie sheets loosely with towels; let stand at room temperature while heating oil.

4 In 4-quart Dutch oven or heavy 3-quart saucepan, heat 2 inches oil to 375°F. Place cooling rack on cookie sheet. Fry doughnuts in oil, 3 or 4 at a time, about 2 minutes, turning over every 30 seconds, until deep brown and puffed (do not undercook or centers will be raw). Remove from oil with slotted spoon to cooling rack. Cool completely, about 20 minutes.

5 In 1½-quart microwavable bowl, microwave ¼ cup butter, the milk, corn syrup and ⅛ teaspoon cinnamon on High 45 seconds or until mixture can be stirred smooth. Stir in chocolate chips. Microwave an additional 30 seconds; carefully stir until chocolate melts and mixture is smooth (stirring too quickly can cause air bubbles in glaze). Stir in 1 cup powdered sugar and the vanilla until smooth. Stir in additional powdered sugar, 1 tablespoon at a time, until consistency of thick syrup. Dip top of each doughnut into glaze; let excess drip off. Place doughnuts on cooling rack, allowing excess glaze to drip onto cookie sheet. Let stand until glaze is set, about 30 minutes.

1 Doughnut: Calories 290 (Calories from Fat 130); Total Fat 14g (Saturated Fat 6g; Trans Fat 0g); Cholesterol 55mg; Sodium 220mg; Total Carbohydrate 36g (Dietary Fiber 2g); Protein 4g **Exchanges:** 1½ Starch, 1 Other Carbohydrate, 2½ Fat **Carbohydrate Choices:** 2½

bake smart For the best results, maintain the temperature of the oil. Heat the oil back to 375°F before cooking each new batch of doughnuts. Also, turning the doughnuts frequently helps ensure that they cook thoroughly.

applesauce doughnuts

prep time: 40 minutes ✛ start to finish: 1 hour 40 minutes ✛ 18 DOUGHNUTS

3⅓ cups all-purpose flour

1 cup applesauce

¾ cup sugar

2 tablespoons shortening

3 teaspoons baking powder

1 teaspoon ground cinnamon

½ teaspoon salt

2 eggs

Vegetable oil

Cinnamon-sugar mixture, if desired

1 Beat 1⅓ cups of the flour and all remaining ingredients except oil and cinnamon-sugar in large bowl with electric mixer on low speed, scraping bowl constantly, until blended. Beat on medium speed 2 minutes, scraping bowl occasionally. Stir in remaining 2 cups flour. Cover and refrigerate about 1 hour or until dough stiffens.

2 In deep fryer or 3-quart saucepan, heat 2 to 3 inches oil to 375°F. Divide dough in half. Place half of dough on well-floured cloth-covered surface; gently roll in flour to coat. Gently roll dough to ⅜-inch thickness. Cut with floured doughnut cutter. Repeat with remaining dough.

3 Fry doughnuts in oil, 2 or 3 at a time, sliding in with a wide spatula and turning as they rise to surface. Fry 1 to 1½ minutes on each side or until golden brown. Remove from oil with slotted spoon; drain on paper towels. Sprinkle hot doughnuts with cinnamon-sugar.

1 Doughnut: Calories 230 (Calories from Fat 100); Total Fat 11g (Saturated Fat 2g; Trans Fat 0g); Cholesterol 20mg; Sodium 150mg; Total Carbohydrate 29g (Dietary Fiber 1g); Protein 3g **Exchanges:** 1 Starch, 1 Other Carbohydrate, 2 Fat **Carbohydrate Choices:** 2

bake smart The key to perfect doughnuts is maintaining the oil temperature at 375°F. Use a deep-frying thermometer for best results.

Do you like your doughnuts completely coated? Place the cinnamon-sugar in a plastic or paper bag, and shake one or two doughnuts at a time in the mixture until coated.

lemon-filled doughnuts

prep time: 1 hour 30 minutes ÷ start to finish: 4 hours ÷ 32 DOUGHNUTS

doughnuts

1 cup warm milk
(105°F to 115°F)

2 packages fast-acting
dry yeast (4½ teaspoons)

4½ to 5 cups all-purpose
flour

½ cup granulated sugar

1 teaspoon salt

3 eggs

⅓ cup butter, softened

Vegetable oil

filling

2 jars (10 oz each)
lemon curd

topping

1½ teaspoons powdered
sugar

1 Pour warm milk into large bowl; stir in yeast until dissolved. Add 2 cups of the flour, the granulated sugar, salt, and eggs; mix with electric mixer on low speed 30 seconds, scraping bowl occasionally. On medium speed, beat 2 minutes, scraping bowl occasionally. Add butter, 1 tablespoon at a time, mixing well after each addition. Stir in enough remaining flour, ½ cup at a time, to form a soft dough.

2 Place dough on lightly floured surface. Knead dough 2 minutes or until dough is smooth and springy. Grease large bowl with butter. Place dough in bowl, turning dough to grease all sides. Cover bowl with plastic wrap; let rise in warm place about 1 hour 45 minutes or until doubled in size.

3 Sprinkle 2 cookie sheets with flour; set aside. Place dough on generously floured surface. Roll dough in flour to coat. With floured rolling pin, roll dough into 16×8-inch rectangle. Using sharp knife or pizza cutter, cut dough into 8 rows by 4 rows, forming 32 squares (pieces may be slightly uneven in shape, especially corners, since dough stretches when cut). On lightly floured surface, dust both sides of each piece with flour; place on cookie sheets about 2 inches apart. Loosely cover doughnuts with plastic wrap sprayed with cooking spray; let rise in warm place 30 to 40 minutes or until slightly risen.

4 In 4-quart Dutch oven or heavy 3-quart saucepan, heat 2 inches oil to 325°F over medium heat. Cover cooling rack with paper towels. Fry doughnuts in oil, 4 or 5 at a time, about 1 minute per side, until golden brown on both sides. Remove from oil with slotted spoon to cooling rack. Cool completely, about 30 minutes.

5 Fill decorating bag fitted with writing tip (¼-inch opening) with lemon curd. To fill each doughnut, while holding doughnut in hand, insert tip into side of doughnut. Slowly squeeze about 1 tablespoon lemon curd into center until you feel the doughnut plump up, moving tip from one side to the other to completely fill doughnut. Sprinkle filled doughnuts with powdered sugar.

1 Doughnut: Calories 200 (Calories from Fat 70); Total Fat 8g (Saturated Fat 2.5g; Trans Fat 0g); Cholesterol 40mg; Sodium 105mg; Total Carbohydrate 28g (Dietary Fiber 0g); Protein 3g **Exchanges:** 1 Starch, 1 Other Carbohydrate, 1½ Fat **Carbohydrate Choices:** 2

bake smart You can make the dough the night before. Instead of letting it rise in a warm place for the first rise, place the covered bowl in the refrigerator for up to 12 hours. Then continue as directed in the recipe.

Try to keep the oil temperature as constant as possible. Too cool, and the doughnuts will absorb more oil and take longer to cook. Too hot, and the doughnuts will get done on the outside too quickly, leaving the centers still doughy. It will take about 20 minutes to heat the oil to 325°F.

These doughnuts can be filled with a variety of fillings. Try lime curd or any flavor of jelly.

buttons and bows

prep time: 15 minutes + start to finish: 25 minutes + 8 ROLLS

2 cups Original Bisquick mix

2 tablespoons sugar

1 teaspoon ground nutmeg

⅛ teaspoon ground cinnamon

⅓ cup milk

1 egg

¼ cup butter, melted

½ cup sugar

1 Heat oven to 400°F. In medium bowl, stir Bisquick mix, 2 tablespoons sugar, the nutmeg, cinnamon, milk and egg until soft dough forms.

2 On surface sprinkled with additional Bisquick mix, roll dough into a ball; knead about 5 times. Press or roll dough to ½-inch thickness. Cut dough with doughnut cutter dipped in Bisquick mix. To make bow shapes, hold opposite sides of each ring of dough, then twist to make a figure 8. On ungreased cookie sheet, place bows and buttons (the dough from the center of each ring).

3 Bake 8 to 10 minutes or until light golden brown. Immediately dip each roll in melted butter, then in ½ cup sugar. Serve warm.

1 Roll: Calories 250 (Calories from Fat 90); Total Fat 10g (Saturated Fat 5g; Trans Fat 1.5g); Cholesterol 45mg; Sodium 420mg; Total Carbohydrate 36g (Dietary Fiber 0g); Protein 3g **Exchanges:** 1 Starch, 1½ Other Carbohydrate, 2 Fat **Carbohydrate Choices:** 2½

gluten-free doughnut holes

prep time: **45 minutes** ✛ start to finish: **45 minutes** ✛ 24 DOUGHNUT HOLES

Vegetable oil

¼ cup granulated sugar

½ teaspoon ground cinnamon

1¼ cups Bisquick Gluten Free mix

¼ cup packed brown sugar

¼ teaspoon ground nutmeg

2 tablespoons butter, melted

⅓ cup buttermilk

1 egg, beaten

1 In deep fryer or 2-quart heavy saucepan, heat 2 to 3 inches oil to 375°F. In shallow bowl, mix granulated sugar and cinnamon; set aside.

2 In medium bowl, mix remaining ingredients until smooth. Shape dough into 1¼-inch balls. Fry balls in oil, 5 or 6 at a time, 1 to 2 minutes or until golden brown on all sides. Remove from oil with slotted spoon; drain on paper towels. Immediately roll in cinnamon-sugar.

1 Doughnut Hole: Calories 60 (Calories from Fat 20); Total Fat 2g (Saturated Fat 1g; Trans Fat 0g); Cholesterol 10mg; Sodium 85mg; Total Carbohydrate 10g (Dietary Fiber 0g); Protein 0g **Exchanges:** ½ Starch, ½ Fat **Carbohydrate Choices:** ½

bake smart If you don't have buttermilk on hand, mix 1 teaspoon white vinegar in ⅓ cup milk. Let stand 5 minutes.

cake doughnuts

prep time: 15 minutes + start to finish: 45 minutes + 24 DOUGHNUTS

Vegetable oil

3⅓ cups all-purpose flour

1 cup granulated sugar

¾ cup milk

3 teaspoons baking powder

½ teaspoon salt

½ teaspoon ground cinnamon

¼ teaspoon ground nutmeg

2 tablespoons shortening

2 eggs

Rainbow Doughnut Icing (page 140), if desired

1 In deep fryer or 3-quart saucepan, heat 3 to 4 inches oil to 375°F.

2 In large bowl, beat 1½ cups of the flour and all remaining ingredients except Rainbow Doughnut Icing with electric mixer on low speed 30 seconds, scraping bowl constantly. Beat on medium speed 2 minutes, scraping bowl occasionally. Stir in remaining flour.

3 On generously floured surface, roll dough lightly to coat. Gently roll to ⅜-inch thickness. Cut dough with floured 2½-inch doughnut cutter.

4 Fry doughnuts in oil, 2 or 3 at a time, turning as they rise to the surface. Fry 2 to 3 minutes or until golden brown on both sides. Remove from oil with slotted spoon; drain on paper towels. Cool slightly and frost with doughnut icing.

1 Doughnut: Calories 190 (Calories from Fat 45); Total Fat 5g (Saturated Fat 1g; Trans Fat 0g); Cholesterol 20mg; Sodium 120mg; Total Carbohydrate 35g (Dietary Fiber 0g); Protein 3g **Exchanges:** 1 Starch, 1 Other Carbohydrate, 1 Fat **Carbohydrate Choices:** 2

bake smart These old-fashioned doughnuts are perfect for dipping into your favorite hot beverage. If you'd like to make buttermilk doughnuts, you can substitute buttermilk for the milk, decrease the baking powder to 2 teaspoons and add 1 teaspoon baking soda.

The doughnuts are also great plain or just sprinkled with granulated or powdered sugar instead of the icing.

rainbow doughnut icing

prep time: 30 minutes ✛ start to finish: 30 minutes ✛ 2½ CUPS ICING (FOR 12 DOUGHNUTS)

4½ cups powdered sugar

6 tablespoons milk

4 tablespoons light corn syrup

Red, orange, yellow, green, blue and purple gel icing color (not liquid food color)

12 Cake Doughnuts (page 139) or purchased plain cake doughnuts

1 In large bowl, mix powdered sugar, milk and corn syrup until smooth. Divide icing evenly among 6 small bowls. Add a different color gel to each bowl; stir to blend. Place each color icing in small resealable food-storage plastic bag. Cut off tiny corner of each bag.

2 Place cooling rack on large cookie sheet; place doughnuts on rack. To make a rainbow on each doughnut, pipe one stripe of red, orange, yellow, green, blue and purple icing over top and slightly over edge of doughnut so that colors just touch. Pipe 1 or 2 doughnuts at a time so icing can blend together slightly before setting. Icing will spread slightly and drip down side. Let stand at least 30 minutes or until icing is set. Store in tightly covered container.

1 Serving: Calories 400 (Calories from Fat 100); Total Fat 11g (Saturated Fat 2.5g; Trans Fat 2g); Cholesterol 20mg; Sodium 120mg; Total Carbohydrate 74g (Dietary Fiber 0g); Protein 3g **Exchanges:** 1 Starch, 4 Other Carbohydrate, 2 Fat **Carbohydrate Choices:** 5

bake smart The icing may seem thick at first, but don't be tempted to thin it. It will flow just enough to drip slightly down the side of each doughnut. If it's too thin, it won't set up and will run off the doughnut.

Try coloring the icing red, white and blue for a patriotic theme or the colors of your favorite sports team. Experiment with different patterns: Spoon one color over the top, then add drops of another color. Watch the pattern it makes as the icing spreads. Kids will love to experiment with this.

Sparkle it up—immediately after icing the doughnuts, sprinkle with colored sugar or edible glitter.

sugared doughnuts

prep time: 30 minutes + start to finish: 3 hours 15 minutes + 20 DOUGHNUTS

⅔ cup milk

¼ cup water

¼ cup butter, softened

1 egg

3 cups bread flour

¼ cup sugar

1 teaspoon salt

2½ teaspoons bread machine or fast-acting dry yeast

Vegetable oil

Additional sugar, if desired

1 Measure carefully, placing all ingredients except vegetable oil and additional sugar in bread machine pan in the order recommended by the manufacturer.

2 Select Dough/Manual cycle. Do not use delay cycle.

3 Remove dough from pan, using lightly floured hands. Cover and let rest 10 minutes on lightly floured board.

4 Roll dough to ⅜-inch thickness on lightly floured board. Cut with floured doughnut cutter. Cover and let rise on board 35 to 45 minutes or until slightly raised.

5 In deep fryer or heavy Dutch oven, heat 2 to 3 inches oil to 375°F. Fry doughnuts in oil, 2 or 3 at a time, turning as they rise to the surface. Fry 2 to 3 minutes or until golden brown on both sides. Remove from oil with slotted spoon to cooling rack. Roll warm doughnuts in sugar.

1 Doughnut: Calories 190 (Calories from Fat 110); Total Fat 12g (Saturated Fat 3g; Trans Fat 0g); Cholesterol 15mg; Sodium 150mg; Total Carbohydrate 18g (Dietary Fiber 0g); Protein 3g **Exchanges:** 1 Starch, 2½ Fat **Carbohydrate Choices:** 1

bake smart If you don't have a doughnut cutter, you still can make great doughnuts. Roll the dough out into a rectangle until it is ⅜ inch thick. Cut the dough into 20 squares. With your fingers, form a hole about an inch wide in the center of each square. The hole will help the doughnut fry evenly, so the center will not be undercooked and doughy. Try covering these square doughnuts with powdered sugar and a touch of cinnamon after they are cooked. Yum!

double-streusel coffee cake

prep time: 15 minutes ✛ start to finish: 1 hour 10 minutes ✛ 6 SERVINGS

streusel

- ⅔ cup Original Bisquick mix
- ⅔ cup packed brown sugar
- 1 teaspoon ground cinnamon
- 3 tablespoons cold butter

coffee cake

- 2 cups Original Bisquick mix
- ½ cup milk or water
- 2 tablespoons granulated sugar
- 1½ teaspoons vanilla
- 1 egg

1 Heat oven to 375°F. Spray 9-inch round pan with cooking spray.

2 In small bowl, mix ⅔ cup Bisquick mix, the brown sugar and cinnamon. Cut in butter, using pastry blender or fork, until crumbly; set aside.

3 In medium bowl, stir all coffee cake ingredients until blended. Spread about 1 cup of the batter in pan. Sprinkle with about ¾ cup of the streusel. Drop and carefully spread remaining batter over streusel. Sprinkle remaining streusel over top.

4 Bake 20 to 24 minutes or until golden brown. Cool 30 minutes before serving.

1 Serving: Calories 410 (Calories from Fat 120); Total Fat 14g (Saturated Fat 6g; Trans Fat 2.5g); Cholesterol 50mg; Sodium 720mg; Total Carbohydrate 64g (Dietary Fiber 1g); Protein 5g **Exchanges:** 2 Starch, 2 Other Carbohydrate, 2½ Fat **Carbohydrate Choices:** 4

bake smart A drizzle of almond glaze adds a nice finishing touch. Stir ¾ cup powdered sugar, 1 tablespoon milk and ½ teaspoon almond extract until thin enough to drizzle. Drizzle glaze over warm coffee cake.

Cold butter is needed to create a "just right" streusel texture and a crust that's easy to handle.

cranberry-almond coffee cake

prep time: **15 minutes** ✛ start to finish: **1 hour 10 minutes** ✛ 8 SERVINGS

coffee cake

6 tablespoons butter, softened

¾ cup packed brown sugar

2 eggs

1 teaspoon almond extract

2 cups Original Bisquick mix

¾ cup milk

1 cup fresh or frozen (do not thaw) cranberries

streusel

⅓ cup old-fashioned oats

⅓ cup sliced almonds, toasted✳

¼ cup packed brown sugar

2 tablespoons butter, softened

1 Heat oven to 350°F. Spray 9-inch springform pan with cooking spray. In large bowl, beat 6 tablespoons butter and ¾ cup brown sugar with electric mixer on medium speed until creamy. Add eggs, one at a time, beating well after each addition. Stir in almond extract. On low speed, beat in Bisquick mix alternately with milk until smooth. Stir in cranberries. Spread batter in pan.

2 In small bowl, mix all streusel ingredients with fork until crumbly. Sprinkle over batter.

3 Bake 38 to 42 minutes or until toothpick inserted in center comes out clean. Cool 10 minutes. Remove side of pan before serving. Serve warm.

✳To toast almonds, bake in ungreased shallow at 350°F for 6 to 10 minutes, stirring occasionally, until light brown.

1 Serving: Calories 400 (Calories from Fat 170); Total Fat 19g (Saturated Fat 9g; Trans Fat 1.5g); Cholesterol 80mg; Sodium 440mg; Total Carbohydrate 52g (Dietary Fiber 2g); Protein 6g **Exchanges:** 2 Starch, 1½ Other Carbohydrate, 3½ Fat **Carbohydrate Choices:** 3½

bake smart For the best results, do not thaw the frozen cranberries before stirring them into the batter.

danish apple-almond cake

prep time: **20 minutes** ✛ start to finish: **2 hours** ✛ 8 SERVINGS

½ cup butter, softened

½ cup granulated sugar

3 eggs

1 teaspoon almond extract

1½ cups Original Bisquick mix

3 medium baking apples, peeled, cut into eighths

1 teaspoon powdered sugar

¼ cup sliced almonds, toasted if desired※

1 Heat oven to 325°F. Spray bottom of 9-inch springform pan with cooking spray.

2 In large bowl, beat butter and granulated sugar with electric mixer on high speed 1 minute. Add eggs and almond extract; beat on medium speed about 10 seconds. Add Bisquick mix; beat on medium speed about 30 seconds or until combined.

3 Spread batter in bottom of pan. Press apple pieces, cut side down, into batter.

4 Bake 1 hour to 1 hour 10 minutes or until apples are tender and cake is golden brown. Cool 30 minutes. Remove side of pan. Sift or sprinkle powdered sugar over top of cake; sprinkle with almonds. Serve warm.

※To toast almonds, bake in ungreased shallow pan at 325°F for 7 to 11 minutes, stirring occasionally, until light brown.

1 Serving: Calories 320 (Calories from Fat 160); Total Fat 18g (Saturated Fat 9g; Trans Fat 1g); Cholesterol 110mg; Sodium 420mg; Total Carbohydrate 33g (Dietary Fiber 1g); Protein 5g **Exchanges:** 1½ Starch, ½ Other Carbohydrate, 3½ Fat **Carbohydrate Choices:** 2

bake smart Serve with coffee topped with an indulgent topping of whipped cream and a sprinkle of nutmeg.

cherry swirl coffee cake

prep time: 20 minutes ✛ **start to finish: 45 minutes** ✛ 18 SERVINGS

coffee cake

- 4 cups Original Bisquick mix
- ½ cup granulated sugar
- ¼ cup butter, melted
- ½ cup milk
- 1 teaspoon vanilla
- 1 teaspoon almond extract
- 3 eggs
- 1 can (21 oz) cherry pie filling

glaze

- 1 cup powdered sugar
- 1 to 2 tablespoons milk

1 Heat oven to 350°F. Grease bottom and sides of 1 (15×10×1-inch) pan or 2 (9-inch) square pans with shortening or cooking spray. In large bowl, stir all coffee cake ingredients except pie filling; beat vigorously with spoon 30 seconds.

2 Spread two-thirds of the batter (about 2½ cups) in 15×10×1-inch pan or one-third of the batter (about 1¼ cups) in each square pan. Spread pie filling over batter (filling may not cover batter completely). Drop remaining batter by tablespoonfuls onto pie filling.

3 Bake 20 to 25 minutes or until light brown. Meanwhile, in small bowl, stir all glaze ingredients until smooth and thin enough to drizzle. Drizzle glaze over warm coffee cake. Serve warm or cool.

1 Serving: Calories 240 (Calories from Fat 70); Total Fat 8g (Saturated Fat 3g; Trans Fat 1g); Cholesterol 45mg; Sodium 360mg; Total Carbohydrate 39g (Dietary Fiber 1g); Protein 4g **Exchanges:** 1 Starch, 1½ Other Carbohydrate, 1½ Fat **Carbohydrate Choices:** 2½

bake smart This recipe is easy to cut in half. Use one 9-inch square pan. Use 2 eggs, and substitute a 10-ounce jar of fruit preserves for the pie filling. Divide remaining ingredient amounts in half.

Use 1 can of your favorite flavor of pie filling instead of the cherry.

mixed fruit and yogurt coffee cake

prep time: 15 minutes ✛ start to finish: 1 hour 15 minutes ✛ 8 SERVINGS

- 1 package (7 oz) mixed dried fruit, coarsely chopped
- ½ cup orange juice
- 1½ cups Original Bisquick mix
- ½ cup sugar
- ⅓ cup plain fat-free yogurt
- 2 tablespoons butter, melted
- 1 teaspoon vanilla
- 1 egg

1 Heat oven to 350°F. Grease bottom and side of 9-inch round pan with shortening; lightly flour. In 1-quart saucepan, heat fruit and orange juice to boiling over medium heat. Reduce heat; simmer about 3 minutes, stirring occasionally, until thickened and fruit is soft. Set aside.

2 In medium bowl, stir remaining ingredients until mixed; pour into pan. Top with fruit mixture.

3 Bake 30 to 40 minutes or until golden brown and toothpick inserted in center comes out clean. Cool 20 minutes before serving.

1 Serving: Calories 260 (Calories from Fat 60); Total Fat 6g (Saturated Fat 3g; Trans Fat 1g); Cholesterol 35mg; Sodium 320mg; Total Carbohydrate 46g (Dietary Fiber 2g); Protein 4g **Exchanges:** 1 Starch, ½ Fruit, 1½ Other Carbohydrate, 1 Fat **Carbohydrate Choices:** 3

bake smart If necessary, cover the coffee cake with foil halfway through baking to keep the fruit from overbrowning.

cherry-pecan ring

prep time: 15 minutes ✛ start to finish: 50 minutes ✛ 10 SERVINGS

coffee cake

- ⅓ cup butter, melted
- ⅓ cup packed brown sugar
- 1 jar (6 oz) maraschino cherries (about 25 cherries), drained, stems removed
- ⅓ cup pecan halves
- 2 cups Original Bisquick mix
- 2 tablespoons granulated sugar
- ⅔ cup milk
- 2 tablespoons butter, softened
- 1 egg

glaze

- 1 cup powdered sugar
- 4 teaspoons water
- ½ teaspoon vanilla

1 Heat oven to 400°F. Spray 8- or 12-cup fluted tube cake pan with cooking spray. Pour ⅓ cup melted butter into pan; turn pan to coat with butter. Sprinkle brown sugar over butter. Arrange cherries and pecans on sugar mixture.

2 In medium bowl, stir Bisquick mix, granulated sugar, milk, 2 tablespoons softened butter and the egg until combined; beat vigorously 30 seconds. Spoon batter evenly over cherries and pecans.

3 Bake 20 to 25 minutes or until toothpick inserted in center comes out clean. Immediately place heatproof plate upside down on pan; carefully turn plate and pan over to remove coffee cake. Cool 10 minutes.

4 Meanwhile, in small bowl, mix all glaze ingredients until smooth and thin enough to drizzle, adding additional water, 1 teaspoon at a time, until desired consistency. Drizzle glaze over warm coffee cake.

1 Serving: Calories 320 (Calories from Fat 130); Total Fat 15g (Saturated Fat 7g; Trans Fat 1.5g); Cholesterol 45mg; Sodium 370mg; Total Carbohydrate 43g (Dietary Fiber 1g); Protein 3g **Exchanges:** 1 Starch, 2 Other Carbohydrate, 3 Fat **Carbohydrate Choices:** 3

bake smart For a Cherry-Almond Ring, use almonds instead of the pecans, and replace half of the vanilla in the glaze with almond flavoring.

strawberry cream brunch cake

prep time. 20 minutes + start to finish. 1 hour 35 minutes + 16 SERVINGS

filling

- 1 package (8 oz) cream cheese, softened
- ¼ cup sugar
- 2 tablespoons all-purpose flour
- 1 egg

cake

- 2¼ cups all-purpose flour
- ¾ cup sugar
- ¾ cup cold butter
- ½ teaspoon baking powder
- ½ teaspoon baking soda
- ¼ teaspoon salt
- ¾ cup sour cream
- 1 teaspoon almond extract
- 1 egg
- ½ cup strawberry or raspberry preserves
- ½ cup sliced almonds

1 Heat oven to 350°F. Grease bottom and side of 10-inch springform pan or 11×7-inch (2-quart) glass baking dish with shortening; lightly flour.

2 In small bowl, mix all filling ingredients until smooth; set aside.

3 In large bowl, mix 2¼ cups flour and ¾ cup sugar. Cut in butter, using pastry blender or fork, until mixture looks like coarse crumbs. Reserve 1 cup of the crumb mixture. Stir baking powder, baking soda, salt, sour cream, almond extract and egg into remaining crumb mixture. Spread batter over bottom and 2 inches up side (about ¼ inch thick) of pan.

4 Pour filling over batter. Carefully spoon preserves evenly over filling. Mix almonds and reserved crumb mixture; sprinkle over preserves.

5 Bake springform pan 50 to 60 minutes, 11×7-inch dish 35 to 45 minutes, or until filling is set and crust is deep golden brown. Cool 15 minutes; remove side of springform pan. Serve warm or cool. Store covered in refrigerator.

1 Serving: Calories 320 (Calories from Fat 160); Total Fat 18g (Saturated Fat 10g; Trans Fat 0.5g); Cholesterol 65mg; Sodium 230mg; Total Carbohydrate 35g (Dietary Fiber 1g); Protein 4g **Exchanges:** 1½ Starch, 1 Other Carbohydrate, 3½ Fat **Carbohydrate Choices:** 2

bake smart Cool cake completely, then wrap tightly and freeze for up to 1 month. To thaw, let stand at room temperature for several hours before serving.

lemon curd–filled butter cake

prep time: 25 minutes ✛ **start to finish: 2 hours 40 minutes** ✛ 12 SERVINGS

lemon curd

¼ cup granulated sugar

2 tablespoons cornstarch

¾ cup cold water

3 egg yolks

1 tablespoon grated lemon peel

3 tablespoons fresh lemon juice

cake

1 cup butter, softened

1 cup granulated sugar

5 whole eggs

1¾ cups all-purpose flour

2 teaspoons grated lemon peel

1½ teaspoons baking powder

1 teaspoon vanilla

⅓ cup slivered almonds, toasted※

Powdered sugar, if desired

1 Heat oven to 350°F. Grease bottom and side of 9-inch springform pan with shortening; lightly flour.

2 In 1-quart saucepan, mix ¼ cup granulated sugar and the cornstarch. Stir in water and egg yolks with whisk until well mixed and no lumps remain. Heat to boiling over medium heat, stirring constantly, until mixture begins to thicken. Cook and stir 1 minute; remove from heat. Stir in 1 tablespoon lemon peel and the lemon juice. Refrigerate uncovered 20 minutes, stirring once, until room temperature.

3 Meanwhile, in large bowl, beat butter and 1 cup granulated sugar with electric mixer on medium speed about 1 minute or until smooth. Beat in eggs, one at a time, just until blended, then continue beating on medium speed 2 minutes, scraping bowl once. On low speed, beat in flour, 2 teaspoons lemon peel, the baking powder and vanilla about 30 seconds or just until blended.

4 Spread half of batter (about 2 cups) in pan. Spoon lemon curd evenly onto batter, spreading to within ½ inch of edge. Drop remaining batter by tablespoonfuls around edge of lemon curd and pan; spread batter evenly and toward center to cover lemon curd. Sprinkle almonds over top.

5 Bake 45 to 55 minutes or until center is set, cake is firm to the touch and top is golden brown. Cool on cooling rack at least 1 hour (center will sink slightly). Run thin knife around side of cake; remove side of pan. Sprinkle with powdered sugar before serving. Store covered in refrigerator.

※To toast almonds, bake in ungreased shallow pan at 350°F for 6 to 10 minutes, stirring occasionally, until light brown.

1 Serving: Calories 360 (Calories from Fat 180); Total Fat 20g (Saturated Fat 9g; Trans Fat 1g); Cholesterol 180mg; Sodium 190mg; Total Carbohydrate 37g (Dietary Fiber 0g); Protein 6g **Exchanges:** 1 Starch, 1½ Other Carbohydrate, 4 Fat **Carbohydrate Choices:** 2½

bake smart Lemon curd can be made up to 1 day ahead; cover it with plastic wrap and refrigerate. When you're ready to make the cake, let the curd come to room temperature before spreading over the batter.

streusel-topped fruit brunch cake

prep time: 15 minutes ✛ start to finish: 1 hour ✛ 12 SERVINGS

cake

- 2 cups Wheat Chex® or Multi-Bran Chex® cereal
- 1½ cups orange juice
- ¼ cup vegetable oil
- 1 egg, slightly beaten
- 2 small bananas, thinly sliced
- 1 cup all-purpose flour
- ½ cup whole wheat flour
- ¾ cup granulated sugar
- ½ cup raisins, if desired
- 1 teaspoon baking soda
- 1 teaspoon ground cinnamon
- ½ teaspoon salt

topping

- ½ cup Wheat Chex or Multi-Bran Chex cereal
- ½ cup chopped nuts, if desired
- ⅓ cup packed brown sugar
- ¼ cup all-purpose flour
- 2 tablespoons butter, softened
- ½ teaspoon ground cinnamon

1 Heat oven to 350°F. Grease bottom and sides of 9-inch square pan with shortening or cooking spray. In large bowl, mix 2 cups cereal and the orange juice; let stand about 2 minutes or until cereal is soft.

2 Stir oil, egg and bananas into cereal mixture. Stir in remaining cake ingredients. Spread in pan.

3 Bake 35 to 40 minutes or until top springs back when touched lightly in center. Meanwhile, place ½ cup cereal in resealable food-storage plastic bag or between sheets of waxed paper; coarsely crush with rolling pin. In small bowl, mix crushed cereal and remaining topping ingredients until crumbly.

4 When cake is done, set oven control to broil. Sprinkle topping evenly over warm cake. Broil with top about 5 inches from heat 1 to 2 minutes or until bubbly (watch carefully to avoid burning).

1 Serving: Calories 280 (Calories from Fat 70); Total Fat 7g (Saturated Fat 1.5g; Trans Fat 0g); Cholesterol 25mg; Sodium 340mg; Total Carbohydrate 50g (Dietary Fiber 3g); Protein 4g **Exchanges:** 1½ Starch, 2 Other Carbohydrate, 1 Fat **Carbohydrate Choices:** 3

bake smart Fortified whole-grain cereals are a great source of vitamins and minerals, including iron.

sour cream coffee cake

prep time: 30 minutes ✢ start to finish: 2 hours ✢ 16 SERVINGS

filling

- ½ cup packed brown sugar
- ½ cup finely chopped nuts
- 1½ teaspoons ground cinnamon

coffee cake

- 3 cups all-purpose or whole wheat flour
- 1½ teaspoons baking powder
- 1½ teaspoons baking soda
- ¾ teaspoon salt
- 1½ cups granulated sugar
- ¾ cup butter, softened
- 1½ teaspoons vanilla
- 3 eggs
- 1½ cups sour cream

glaze

- ½ cup powdered sugar
- ¼ teaspoon vanilla
- 2 to 3 teaspoons milk

1 Heat oven to 350°F. Grease bottom and side of 10-inch angel food (tube) cake pan, 12-cup fluted tube cake pan or 2 (9×5-inch) loaf pans with shortening or cooking spray.

2 In small bowl, stir all filling ingredients until well mixed; set aside. In large bowl, stir flour, baking powder, baking soda and salt until well mixed; set aside.

3 In another large bowl, beat granulated sugar, butter, 1½ teaspoons vanilla and eggs with electric mixer on medium speed 2 minutes, scraping bowl occasionally. Beat about one-fourth of the flour mixture and sour cream at a time alternately into sugar mixture on low speed until blended.

4 For angel food or fluted tube cake pan, spread one-third of the batter (about 2 cups) in pan, then sprinkle with one-third of the filling; repeat twice. For loaf pans, spread one-fourth of the batter (about 1½ cups) in each pan, then sprinkle each with one-fourth of the filling; repeat once.

5 Bake angel food or fluted tube cake pan about 1 hour, loaf pans about 45 minutes, or until toothpick inserted near center comes out clean. Cool in pan on cooling rack 10 minutes.

6 Remove from pan to cooling rack. Cool 20 minutes. In small bowl, stir all glaze ingredients until smooth and thin enough to drizzle. Drizzle glaze over coffee cake. Serve warm if desired.

1 Serving: Calories 360 (Calories from Fat 150); Total Fat 16g (Saturated Fat 8g; Trans Fat 0.5g); Cholesterol 75mg; Sodium 360mg; Total Carbohydrate 49g (Dietary Fiber 1g); Protein 5g **Exchanges:** 2 Starch, 1 Other Carbohydrate, 3 Fat **Carbohydrate Choices:** 3

bake smart To remove the coffee cake from the pan, slide a narrow metal spatula between cake and tube along side of pan. For 2-piece pan, push up from bottom to release. Slide spatula between cake and base to release bottom of cake.

blackberry coffee cake

prep time: 25 minutes ✚ start to finish: 3 hours 10 minutes ✚ 16 SERVINGS

filling

1¼	cups frozen blackberries, thawed and well drained
½	cup finely chopped pecans
3	tablespoons granulated sugar
1½	teaspoons ground cinnamon

coffee cake

2¼	cups all-purpose flour
1	teaspoon baking powder
½	teaspoon baking soda
1¼	cups granulated sugar
1	cup butter, softened
1	teaspoon vanilla
2	eggs
1	container (8 oz) sour cream

glaze

1½	cups powdered sugar
3	to 4 teaspoons water

1 Heat oven to 350°F. Grease bottom and side of 10-inch angel food (tube) cake pan with shortening; lightly flour. In small bowl, stir all filling ingredients until mixed; set aside.

2 In medium bowl, mix flour, baking powder and baking soda; set aside. In large bowl, beat 1¼ cups granulated sugar, the butter, vanilla and eggs with electric mixer on medium speed 2 minutes, scraping bowl occasionally. On low speed, alternately add flour mixture with sour cream, beating just until blended after each addition.

3 Spread one-third of the batter in pan; sprinkle with half of the filling. Spoon another one-third of the batter by tablespoonfuls over filling; sprinkle with remaining filling. Spoon remaining batter over filling; spread evenly.

4 Bake 55 to 65 minutes or until toothpick inserted in center comes out clean. Cool in pan 10 minutes; remove from pan to cooling rack. Cool completely, about 1 hour 30 minutes.

5 In small bowl, mix all glaze ingredients until smooth and thin enough to drizzle. Drizzle glaze over coffee cake.

1 Serving: Calories 360 (Calories from Fat 160); Total Fat 18g (Saturated Fat 9g; Trans Fat 0.5g); Cholesterol 60mg; Sodium 190mg; Total Carbohydrate 46g (Dietary Fiber 1g); Protein 3g **Exchanges:** 1 Starch, 2 Other Carbohydrate, 3½ Fat **Carbohydrate Choices:** 3

bake smart Packed with sweet blackberries, this glorious coffee cake is a great make-ahead treat. Wrap it up tightly and tuck it away in your freezer for up to 2 months to serve when unexpected guests drop by. Drizzle with the glaze just before serving.

toffee–macadamia nut coffee cake

prep time: **10 minutes** ✛ start to finish: **2 hours 15 minutes** ✛ 8 SERVINGS

1⅔ cups all-purpose flour

¾ cup packed brown sugar

⅓ cup butter, softened

1 cup milk

2 teaspoons baking powder

½ teaspoon salt

1 egg

¼ cup toffee bits

¼ cup flaked coconut

¼ cup chopped macadamia nuts

1 Heat oven to 350°F. Grease bottom and sides of 9- or 8-inch square pan with shortening.

2 In large bowl, beat flour, brown sugar, butter, milk, baking powder, salt and egg with electric mixer on low speed 30 seconds. Beat on medium speed 2 minutes, scraping bowl occasionally. Stir in 2 tablespoons of the toffee bits. Pour batter into pan. Sprinkle remaining 2 tablespoons toffee bits, the coconut and nuts over batter.

3 Bake 32 to 35 minutes or until toothpick inserted in center comes out clean. Cool completely in pan on cooling rack, about 1 hour 30 minutes.

1 Serving: Calories 350 (Calories from Fat 140); Total Fat 15g (Saturated Fat 8g; Trans Fat 0g); Cholesterol 45mg; Sodium 370mg; Total Carbohydrate 48g (Dietary Fiber 1g); Protein 5g **Exchanges:** 1½ Starch, 1½ Other Carbohydrate, 3 Fat **Carbohydrate Choices:** 3

chocolate streusel coffee cake

prep time: 20 minutes ✛ start to finish: 1 hour 35 minutes ✛ 12 SERVINGS

coffee cake

- 1½ cups all-purpose flour
- ¾ cup granulated sugar
- 1 teaspoon ground cinnamon
- ¾ teaspoon baking powder
- ¼ teaspoon baking soda
- ½ teaspoon salt
- 3 tablespoons cold butter
- ⅔ cup buttermilk
- 1 egg
- 1 teaspoon vanilla

streusel

- ¼ cup all-purpose flour
- ¼ cup packed brown sugar
- 1 tablespoon unsweetened baking cocoa
- 1 tablespoon butter, softened
- ¼ cup miniature semisweet chocolate chips

1 Heat oven to 350°F. Grease bottom only of 8-inch square pan with shortening or cooking spray.

2 In large bowl, mix 1½ cups flour, the granulated sugar, cinnamon, baking powder, baking soda and salt. Cut in butter, using pastry blender or fork, until mixture is crumbly. Add buttermilk, egg and vanilla. Beat with electric mixer on medium speed 1 minute. Spread batter in pan.

3 In small bowl, mix all streusel ingredients except chocolate chips with whisk or fork. Sprinkle over batter. Sprinkle with chocolate chips.

4 Bake 35 to 45 minutes or until toothpick inserted in center comes out clean. Cool on cooling rack 30 minutes. Serve warm.

1 Serving: Calories 200 (Calories from Fat 45); Total Fat 5g (Saturated Fat 1.5g; Trans Fat 0g); Cholesterol 20mg; Sodium 210mg; Total Carbohydrate 34g (Dietary Fiber 1g); Protein 3g **Exchanges:** 1 Starch, 1 Other Carbohydrate, 1 Fat **Carbohydrate Choices:** 2

banana–chocolate chip coffee cake

prep time: **15 minutes** ✛ start to finish: **1 hour 15 minutes** ✛ 9 SERVINGS

coffee cake

2¼ cups Original Bisquick mix

1 cup mashed ripe bananas (2 medium)

½ cup miniature semisweet chocolate chips

¼ cup granulated sugar

⅓ cup milk

2 tablespoons butter, softened

½ teaspoon ground cinnamon

1 egg

glaze

1 cup powdered sugar

1 tablespoon milk

½ teaspoon vanilla

1 Heat oven to 375°F. Spray 8-inch square pan with cooking spray. In medium bowl, stir all coffee cake ingredients with whisk or spoon until blended. Spread in pan.

2 Bake 26 to 30 minutes or until golden brown and toothpick inserted in center comes out clean. Cool 30 minutes.

3 In small bowl, mix all glaze ingredients until smooth. If necessary, add additional milk, 1 teaspoon at a time, for desired consistency. Drizzle glaze over warm coffee cake. Serve warm.

1 Serving: Calories 310 (Calories from Fat 90); Total Fat 10g (Saturated Fat 5g; Trans Fat 1g); Cholesterol 30mg; Sodium 400mg; Total Carbohydrate 51g (Dietary Fiber 2g); Protein 4g **Exchanges:** 1 Starch, 2½ Other Carbohydrate, 2 Fat **Carbohydrate Choices:** 3½

bake smart For more chocolate flavor, omit the glaze and drizzle with 2 tablespoons melted white or semisweet chocolate instead.

banana-toffee mini cakes

prep time: 20 minutes + start to finish: 50 minutes + 12 MINI CAKES

coffee cakes

- 2 cups Original Bisquick mix
- ⅓ cup granulated sugar
- 1 cup mashed ripe bananas (2 medium)
- ⅔ cup milk
- 1 egg, slightly beaten
- ½ teaspoon ground allspice

topping

- ½ cup all-purpose flour
- ½ cup packed brown sugar
- ¼ cup cold butter
- 2 tablespoons peanut butter

glaze

- ½ cup white vanilla baking chips
- 2 tablespoons whipping cream

1 Heat oven to 400°F. Spray 12 regular-size muffin cups with cooking spray.

2 In medium bowl, stir all coffee cake ingredients with whisk or spoon until blended. Divide batter evenly among muffin cups.

3 In small bowl, mix flour and brown sugar. Cut in butter and peanut butter, using pastry blender or fork, until mixture looks like small peas. Sprinkle topping evenly over batter.

4 Bake 17 minutes or until toothpick inserted in center comes out clean. Cool 10 minutes. Gently run knife around edge of cups; remove to cooling rack.

5 In small microwavable bowl, microwave baking chips and whipping cream uncovered on High 30 to 60 seconds or until chips are melted; stir until smooth. Place sheet of waxed paper under cooling rack. Drizzle glaze back and forth over tops of cakes with tines of fork. Serve warm.

1 Mini Cake: Calories 300 (Calories from Fat 110); Total Fat 12g (Saturated Fat 7g; Trans Fat 1g); Cholesterol 30mg; Sodium 310mg; Total Carbohydrate 43g (Dietary Fiber 1g); Protein 4g **Exchanges:** 1½ Starch, 1½ Other Carbohydrate, 2 Fat **Carbohydrate Choices:** 3

carrot-walnut coffee cake

prep time: **15 minutes** ✛ start to finish: **1 hour 20 minutes** ✛ 9 SERVINGS

topping

- ½ cup Original Bisquick mix
- ⅓ cup packed brown sugar
- 2 tablespoons cold butter

coffee cake

- 2 cups Original Bisquick mix
- 2 tablespoons granulated sugar
- 1½ teaspoons pumpkin pie spice
- ½ cup chopped walnuts
- ½ cup shredded carrots
- ½ cup raisins
- ⅔ cup milk
- 2 tablespoons vegetable oil
- 1 egg

1 Heat oven to 375°F. In small bowl, mix ½ cup Bisquick mix and the brown sugar until well blended. Cut in butter, using pastry blender or fork, until mixture is crumbly; set aside.

2 In large bowl, stir 2 cups Bisquick mix, the granulated sugar, pumpkin pie spice, walnuts, carrots and raisins. Stir in milk, oil and egg with whisk or spoon until blended. Pour into ungreased 8-inch square pan. Sprinkle with topping.

3 Bake 30 to 35 minutes or until toothpick inserted in center comes out clean. Cool 30 minutes before serving. Serve warm, with honey, if desired.

1 Serving: Calories 320 (Calories from Fat 140); Total Fat 15g (Saturated Fat 4g; Trans Fat 1.5g); Cholesterol 30mg; Sodium 450mg; Total Carbohydrate 41g (Dietary Fiber 2g); Protein 5g **Exchanges:** 1½ Starch, 1 Other Carbohydrate, 3 Fat **Carbohydrate Choices:** 3

bake smart Try adding sweetened dried cranberries or cut-up dried apples in place of the raisins.

apples 'n brown sugar coffee cake

prep time: 15 minutes ✛ start to finish: 1 hour ✛ 8 SERVINGS

topping

⅔ cup Original Bisquick mix

⅔ cup packed brown sugar

1 teaspoon ground cinnamon

½ teaspoon ground nutmeg

¼ cup cold butter

coffee cake

2 cups Original Bisquick mix

3 tablespoons granulated sugar

⅔ cup milk or water

1 egg

2 medium cooking apples, peeled, thinly sliced (2 cups)

2 tablespoons chopped nuts

glaze

½ cup powdered sugar

2 to 3 teaspoons milk

1 Heat oven to 400°F. Spray 9-inch square pan with cooking spray. In small bowl, mix ⅔ cup Bisquick mix, the brown sugar, cinnamon and nutmeg. Cut in butter, using pastry blender or fork, until mixture looks like coarse crumbs; set aside.

2 In medium bowl, stir together 2 cups Bisquick mix, granulated sugar, ⅔ cup milk and the egg; beat vigorously 30 seconds. Spread half of the batter in pan. Arrange apple slices on batter; sprinkle with half of the streusel topping. Spread with remaining batter; sprinkle with remaining topping. Sprinkle with nuts.

3 Bake 25 minutes or until toothpick inserted in center comes out clean. Cool 20 minutes. In small bowl, stir glaze ingredients until thin enough to drizzle. Drizzle over warm coffee cake.

1 Serving: Calories 380 (Calories from Fat 120); Total Fat 13g (Saturated Fat 6g; Trans Fat 2g); Cholesterol 45mg; Sodium 550mg; Total Carbohydrate 62g (Dietary Fiber 2g); Protein 5g **Exchanges:** 1½ Starch, 2½ Other Carbohydrate, 2½ Fat **Carbohydrate Choices:** 4

bake smart This coffee cake is a great make-ahead treat to serve when unexpected guests drop by. Bake and cool the coffee cake, but don't glaze it. Wrap it tightly, and freeze for up to 2 months. Thaw and heat it in the microwave or oven, and glaze it just before serving.

easy apple coffee cake

prep time: 20 minutes ✛ start to finish: 3 hours 40 minutes ✛ 10 SERVINGS

⅔ cup water

3 tablespoons butter, softened

2 cups bread flour

3 tablespoons granulated sugar

1 teaspoon salt

1½ teaspoons bread machine or fast-acting dry yeast

1 cup canned apple pie filling

Powdered sugar, if desired

1 Measure carefully, placing all ingredients except pie filling and powdered sugar in bread machine pan in the order recommended by the manufacturer.

2 Select Dough/Manual cycle. Do not use delay cycle.

3 Remove dough from pan, using lightly floured hands. Cover and let rest 10 minutes on lightly floured surface.

4 Grease large cookie sheet. Roll dough into 13×8-inch rectangle on lightly floured surface. Place on cookie sheet. Spoon pie filling lengthwise down center third of rectangle. On each 13-inch side, using sharp knife, make cuts from filling to edge of dough at 1-inch intervals. Fold ends up over filling. Fold strips diagonally over filling, alternating sides and overlapping in center. Cover and let rise in warm place 30 to 45 minutes or until doubled in size. Dough is ready if indentation remains when touched.

5 Heat oven to 375°F. Bake 30 to 35 minutes or until golden brown. Remove from cookie sheet to cooling rack; cool. Sprinkle with powdered sugar.

1 Serving: Calories 180 (Calories from Fat 40); Total Fat 4.5g (Saturated Fat 2.5g; Trans Fat 0g); Cholesterol 10mg; Sodium 270mg; Total Carbohydrate 31g (Dietary Fiber 1g); Protein 3g **Exchanges:** 1 Starch, 1 Other Carbohydrate, 1 Fat **Carbohydrate Choices:** 2

bake smart Surprise your family with a different filling every time you make this cake. Try cherry, blueberry, peach or apricot pie filling. Canned poppy seed filling or lemon curd works, too!

Prevent a thin crust from forming on the surface by covering the dough while it rests. A handy way to cover the dough? Just turn the bread machine pan upside down over it.

gluten-free cinnamon streusel coffee cake

prep time: 10 minutes ✛ start to finish: 40 minutes ✛ 6 SERVINGS

topping

⅓ cup Bisquick Gluten Free mix

½ cup packed brown sugar

¾ teaspoon ground cinnamon

¼ cup cold butter

coffee cake

1¾ cups Bisquick Gluten Free mix

3 tablespoons granulated sugar

⅔ cup milk or water

1½ teaspoons gluten-free vanilla

3 eggs

1 Heat oven to 350°F. Spray 9-inch round or square pan with cooking spray (without flour). In small bowl, mix ⅓ cup Bisquick mix, the brown sugar and cinnamon. Cut in butter, using pastry blender or fork, until mixture is crumbly; set aside.

2 In medium bowl, stir all coffee cake ingredients until blended. Spread in pan; sprinkle with topping.

3 Bake 25 to 30 minutes or until golden brown. Store tightly covered.

1 Serving: Calories 380 (Calories from Fat 100); Total Fat 11g (Saturated Fat 6g; Trans Fat 0g); Cholesterol 130mg; Sodium 570mg; Total Carbohydrate 62g (Dietary Fiber 1g); Protein 6g **Exchanges:** 2 Starch, 2 Other Carbohydrate, 2 Fat **Carbohydrate Choices:** 4

bake smart Cooking gluten free? Always read labels to make sure that each recipe ingredient is gluten free. Products and ingredient sources can vary.

This coffee cake is perfect for brunch. Add a bowl of cut-up fresh fruit drizzled with poppy seed dressing and a plate of sliced cheeses to complete the menu.

cherry–white chocolate almond twist

prep time: 25 minutes ✛ start to finish: 3 hours 55 minutes ✛ 16 SERVINGS

bread dough

- ½ cup maraschino cherries
- ¾ cup plus 2 tablespoons water
- 1 teaspoon almond extract
- 2 tablespoons butter
- 3¼ cups bread flour
- 2 tablespoons sugar
- 1 teaspoon salt
- 2 teaspoons bread machine yeast or fast-acting dry yeast

filling

- ½ cup chopped white baking chips
- ⅓ cup chopped slivered almonds
- 2 tablespoons sugar
- 2 tablespoons butter, softened
- ¼ cup maraschino cherries, well drained

glaze

- ½ cup powdered sugar
- 2 to 4 teaspoons reserved maraschino cherry juice

1 Drain ½ cup cherries thoroughly; reserve 2 to 4 teaspoons cherry juice for glaze.

2 Measure carefully, placing ½ cup cherries and remaining bread dough ingredients in bread machine pan in the order recommended by the manufacturer.

3 Select Dough/Manual cycle. Do not use delay cycle.

4 Remove dough from pan, using lightly floured hands. Cover and let rest 10 minutes on lightly floured surface. In small bowl, mix baking chips, almonds and 2 tablespoons sugar.

5 Grease large cookie sheet with shortening. On floured surface, roll dough into 15×10-inch rectangle. Spread 2 tablespoons butter over dough. Sprinkle with almond mixture and ¼ cup cherries; press into dough. Starting with 15-inch side, roll up dough; press to seal seam. Place, seam side down, on cookie sheet.

6 Cut roll lengthwise in half. Place halves, filling side up and side by side, on cookie sheet; twist together gently and loosely. Pinch ends to seal. Cover and let rise in warm place about 45 minutes or until doubled in size.

7 Heat oven to 350°F. Bake 30 to 35 minutes or until golden brown. Remove from cookie sheet to cooling rack. Cool 20 minutes. In small bowl, stir powdered sugar and enough cherry juice for drizzling consistency. Drizzle over coffee cake.

1 Serving: Calories 220 (Calories from Fat 60); Total Fat 6g (Saturated Fat 3.5g; Trans Fat 0g); Cholesterol 10mg; Sodium 180mg; Total Carbohydrate 35g (Dietary Fiber 1g); Protein 4g **Exchanges:** 1½ Starch, 1 Other Carbohydrate, 1 Fat **Carbohydrate Choices:** 2

bake smart Be sure to use a sharp knife when cutting the roll lengthwise in half. This will help prevent the filling from pulling on the knife during cutting.

Maraschino cherries (pronounced either mar-uh-SKEE-noh or mar-uh-SHEE-noh) can be made from any variety of cherry, but the Royal Ann is most often used. The cherries are pitted and then marinated in a flavored sugar syrup. Almond flavoring is sometimes added to red cherries, and mint flavoring is sometimes added to green cherries. The cherries are then dyed with government-approved red or green dye, so they are safe to eat.

pear kuchen with ginger topping

prep time: 20 minutes ✛ start to finish: 3 hours 30 minutes ✛ 12 SERVINGS

bread dough

- ½ cup milk
- 2 tablespoons butter, softened
- 1 egg
- 2 cups bread flour
- 2 tablespoons sugar
- 1 teaspoon salt
- 1¾ teaspoons bread machine or fast-acting dry yeast

topping

- 3 cups sliced peeled pears
- 1 cup sugar
- 2 tablespoons butter, softened
- 1 tablespoon chopped crystallized ginger
- ½ cup whipping cream
- 1 egg yolk

1 Measure carefully, placing all bread dough ingredients in bread machine pan in the order recommended by the manufacturer.

2 Select Dough/Manual cycle. Do not use delay cycle.

3 Remove dough from pan, using lightly floured hands. Cover and let rest 10 minutes on lightly floured surface.

4 Grease 13×9-inch pan with shortening. Press dough evenly in bottom of pan. Arrange pears on dough. In small bowl, mix 1 cup sugar, 2 tablespoons butter and the ginger. Reserve 2 tablespoons of the topping; sprinkle remaining topping over pears. Cover and let rise in warm place 30 to 45 minutes or until doubled in size. Dough is ready if indentation remains when touched.

5 Heat oven to 375°F. Bake 20 minutes. Mix whipping cream and egg yolk; pour over hot kuchen. Bake 15 minutes longer or until golden brown. Sprinkle with reserved 2 tablespoons topping. Serve warm.

1 Serving: Calories 270 (Calories from Fat 80); Total Fat 9g (Saturated Fat 5g; Trans Fat 0g); Cholesterol 60mg; Sodium 240mg; Total Carbohydrate 44g (Dietary Fiber 2g); Protein 4g **Exchanges:** 1½ Starch, 1½ Other Carbohydrate, 1½ Fat **Carbohydrate Choices:** 3

bake smart Pears are flavorful and juicy when at their seasonal peak. If pears are not in season, you can make this kuchen with canned pears. You'll need 3 cups of well-drained, canned sliced pears.

When peaches are in season, make this custard-based kuchen with sliced peeled peaches. To peel the peaches easily, drop them into boiling water for just a minute, then remove them with a large slotted spoon. Immediately place them in iced water to stop the cooking. The peels will slip right off.

apricot–cream cheese ring

prep time: 25 minutes ✛ start to finish: 4 hours 10 minutes ✛ 10 SERVINGS

bread dough

- ⅓ cup water
- 2 tablespoons butter, softened
- 1 egg
- 2 cups bread flour
- 2 tablespoons sugar
- ½ teaspoon salt
- 1¾ teaspoons bread machine or fast-acting dry yeast

filling

- 1 package (3 oz) cream cheese, softened
- 1½ tablespoons bread flour
- ¼ cup apricot preserves
- 1 egg, beaten
- 2 tablespoons sliced almonds

1 Measure carefully, placing all bread dough ingredients in bread machine pan in the order recommended by the manufacturer.

2 Select Dough/Manual cycle. Do not use delay cycle.

3 Remove dough from pan, using lightly floured hands. Cover and let rest 10 minutes on lightly floured surface. In small bowl, mix cream cheese and 1½ tablespoons flour.

4 Grease 9-inch round pan with shortening. Roll dough into 15-inch round. Place in pan, letting side of dough hang over edge of pan. Spread cream cheese mixture over dough in pan; spoon apricot preserves onto cream cheese mixture. Make cuts along edge of dough at 1-inch intervals to about ½ inch above cream cheese mixture. Twist pairs of dough strips and fold over cream cheese mixture. Cover and let rise in warm place 40 to 50 minutes or until almost double.

5 Heat oven to 375°F. Brush beaten egg over dough. Sprinkle with almonds. Bake 30 to 35 minutes or until golden brown. Cool at least 30 minutes before cutting.

1 Serving: Calories 210 (Calories from Fat 70); Total Fat 7g (Saturated Fat 3.5g; Trans Fat 0g); Cholesterol 60mg; Sodium 180mg; Total Carbohydrate 30g (Dietary Fiber 1g); Protein 5g **Exchanges:** 1½ Starch, ½ Other Carbohydrate, 1½ Fat **Carbohydrate Choices:** 2

potica

prep time: 20 minutes ✛ start to finish: 4 hours 15 minutes ✛ 10 SERVINGS

bread dough

- ½ cup milk
- ¼ cup cold butter, cut into small pieces
- 1 egg
- 2 cups bread flour
- ¼ cup sugar
- ¼ teaspoon salt
- 1 teaspoon bread machine yeast or fast-acting dry yeast

filling

- 2 cups finely chopped or ground walnuts (about 7 oz)
- ⅓ cup honey
- ⅓ cup milk
- 3 tablespoons sugar
- 1 egg white, beaten

1 Measure carefully, placing all bread dough ingredients in bread machine pan in the order recommended by the manufacturer.

2 Select Dough/Manual cycle. Do not use delay cycle.

3 Remove dough from pan, using lightly floured hands. Cover and let rest 10 minutes on lightly floured surface. In small saucepan, combine all filling ingredients except egg white. Bring to a boil over medium heat, stirring frequently. Reduce heat; simmer uncovered 5 minutes, stirring occasionally. Spread in shallow dish; cover and refrigerate until chilled.

4 Grease large cookie sheet with shortening. Roll dough into 16×12-inch rectangle on lightly floured surface. Spread filling over dough to within ½ inch of edges. Starting with 16-inch side, roll up tightly; pinch seam to seal. Stretch and shape roll until even. Coil roll of dough to form a snail shape. Place on cookie sheet. Cover and let rise in warm place 30 to 60 minutes or until doubled in size. Dough is ready if indentation remains when touched.

5 Heat oven to 325°F. Brush egg white over dough. Bake 45 to 55 minutes or until golden brown. Remove from cookie sheet to cooling rack.

1 Serving: Calories 400 (Calories from Fat 190); Total Fat 21g (Saturated Fat 5g; Trans Fat 0g); Cholesterol 35mg; Sodium 115mg; Total Carbohydrate 42g (Dietary Fiber 2g); Protein 8g **Exchanges:** 3 Starch, 4 Fat **Carbohydrate Choices:** 3

bake smart Spread the filling to within ½ inch of the edges so it won't pop out when you roll up the dough or ooze out during baking.

crunchy wheat-and-honey twist

prep time: 20 minutes ✛ **start to finish: 4 hours 10 minutes** ✛ 16 SERVINGS

bread dough

- ¾ cup plus 2 tablespoons water
- 2 tablespoons honey
- 1 tablespoon butter, softened
- 1¼ cups whole wheat flour
- 1 cup bread flour
- ⅓ cup slivered almonds, toasted*
- 1 teaspoon salt
- 1 teaspoon bread machine or fast-acting dry yeast

topping

- Butter, melted
- 1 egg, slightly beaten
- 2 tablespoons sugar
- ¼ teaspoon ground cinnamon

1 Measure carefully, placing all bread dough ingredients in bread machine pan in the order recommended by the manufacturer.

2 Select Dough/Manual cycle. Do not use delay cycle.

3 Remove dough from pan, using lightly floured hands. Cover and let rest 10 minutes on lightly floured surface.

4 Grease large cookie sheet with shortening. Divide dough in half. Roll each half into 15-inch rope. Place ropes side by side on cookie sheet; twist together gently and loosely. Pinch ends to seal. Brush melted butter lightly over dough. Cover and let rise in warm place 45 to 60 minutes or until doubled in size. Dough is ready if indentation remains when touched.

5 Heat oven to 375°F. Brush egg over dough. Mix sugar and cinnamon; sprinkle over dough. Bake 25 to 30 minutes or until twist is golden brown and sounds hollow when tapped. Remove from cookie sheet to cooling rack; cool 20 minutes.

*To toast almonds, bake in ungreased shallow pan at 350°F for 6 to 10 minutes, stirring occasionally, until light brown.

1 Serving: Calories 120 (Calories from Fat 40); Total Fat 4.5g (Saturated Fat 1.5g; Trans Fat 0g); Cholesterol 20mg; Sodium 180mg; Total Carbohydrate 17g (Dietary Fiber 1g); Protein 3g **Exchanges:** 1 Starch, 1 Fat **Carbohydrate Choices:** 1

bake smart For added crunch, add some finely chopped almonds to the cinnamon-sugar mixture.

Bourbon-Orange Mini Loaves
(page 196)

mini breads

maple-glazed bacon drop doughnuts

prep time: 1 hour 20 minutes ✛ start to finish: 1 hour 20 minutes ✛ 24 DOUGHNUT BALLS

doughnuts

Vegetable oil

1 egg

½ cup milk

2 tablespoons butter, melted

1½ cups all-purpose flour

¼ cup packed brown sugar

2 teaspoons baking powder

½ teaspoon salt

½ teaspoon ground cinnamon

6 slices maple-flavored bacon, crisply cooked, crumbled

maple glaze

3 cups powdered sugar

⅓ cup water

⅓ cup maple-flavored syrup

1 In 3-quart heavy saucepan or 4-quart Dutch oven, heat 2 inches oil to 350°F.

2 Meanwhile, in large bowl, beat egg, milk and butter with fork. Stir in flour, brown sugar, baking powder, salt, cinnamon and bacon.

3 Carefully drop dough by heaping tablespoons, 6 balls at a time, into oil. Fry doughnut balls 30 seconds to 60 seconds on each side, or until golden brown; drain on paper towels until cooled, about 20 minutes.

4 In medium bowl, mix powdered sugar and water until smooth; stir in maple-flavored syrup. Add additional water, 1 teaspoon at a time, until thick glazing consistency. Dip cooled doughnut balls into glaze; let excess drip off. (If glaze disappears while drying, glaze may be too thin. Try dipping balls again, or thicken up glaze by adding a small amount of powdered sugar.) Place glazed doughnut balls on cooling rack; let stand until glaze is set, about 10 minutes.

1 Doughnut Ball: Calories 180 (Calories from Fat 60); Total Fat 7g (Saturated Fat 1.5g; Trans Fat 0g); Cholesterol 15mg; Sodium 150mg; Total Carbohydrate 27g (Dietary Fiber 0g); Protein 2g **Exchanges:** ½ Starch, 1½ Other Carbohydrate, 1½ Fat **Carbohydrate Choices:** 2

bake smart Instead of heaping tablespoons of dough, use a #60 or #70 ice-cream scoop (1¼ inches in diameter) to spoon the dough into the oil.

Cook bacon quickly in the microwave. Place slices on microwavable plate lined with paper towels; cover with paper towel. Microwave on High 3 to 5 minutes or until crisp.

snickerdoodle mini doughnuts

prep time: 45 minutes + start to finish: 1 hour 45 minutes + 26 MINI DOUGHNUTS

doughnuts

⅓ cup sugar

¼ cup butter, melted

2 eggs

⅓ cup milk

3 tablespoons sour cream

1 teaspoon vanilla

2 cups all-purpose flour

1½ teaspoons ground cinnamon

1 teaspoon cream of tartar

1 teaspoon baking powder

topping

¾ cup sugar

3 tablespoons ground cinnamon

6 tablespoons butter, melted

1 In medium bowl, mix ⅓ cup sugar, ¼ cup butter and the eggs until smooth. Stir in milk, sour cream and vanilla with whisk. Stir in flour, 1½ teaspoons cinnamon, the cream of tartar and baking powder just until moistened.

2 Grease medium bowl with shortening, turning dough to grease all sides. Place dough in bowl. Cover bowl with plastic wrap; refrigerate 1 hour.

3 Heat oven to 450°F. Line 2 cookie sheets with cooking parchment paper. Place dough on generously floured surface. Roll dough in flour to coat. With floured rolling pin, roll dough to ½-inch thickness. Cut dough with floured 1¾-inch round cookie cutter. Place dough rounds on cookie sheets about 1 inch apart. Cut out centers using floured ¾-inch round cookie cutter. Re-roll scraps to cut additional doughnuts.

4 Bake 8 to 10 minutes or until edges just turn light golden brown. Immediately remove from cookie sheet to cooling rack. Cool 3 minutes.

5 In small bowl, stir ¾ cup sugar and 3 tablespoons cinnamon. Place melted butter in another small bowl. Quickly dip both sides of each warm doughnut into butter; let excess drip off. Using spoon, roll each doughnut in cinnamon-sugar mixture to coat. Return doughnuts to cooling rack. Serve warm.

1 Mini Doughnut: Calories 120 (Calories from Fat 50); Total Fat 5g (Saturated Fat 3g; Trans Fat 0g); Cholesterol 30mg; Sodium 60mg; Total Carbohydrate 17g (Dietary Fiber 1g); Protein 1g **Exchanges:** ½ Starch, ½ Other Carbohydrate, 1 Fat **Carbohydrate Choices:** 1

bake smart Refrigerating the dough makes it easier to roll, but extra flour is still needed to keep the dough from sticking to the counter and rolling pin. Shake off any excess flour before placing the dough rounds on the cookie sheet.

Cream of tartar helps add the signature "snickerdoodle" texture and flavor to these doughnuts, distinguishing them from the regular cinnamon-sugar variety.

orange mini muffins

prep time: 15 minutes + start to finish: 35 minutes + 36 MINI MUFFINS

¾ cup milk

⅓ cup vegetable oil

¼ cup frozen (thawed) orange juice concentrate

2 teaspoons grated orange peel

1 egg, slightly beaten

2¼ cups all-purpose flour

¾ cup sugar

3 teaspoons baking powder

¼ teaspoon salt

1¼ teaspoons grated orange peel

1 Heat oven to 400°F. Grease bottoms only of 36 mini muffin cups. In large bowl, beat milk, oil, juice concentrate, 2 teaspoons orange peel and the egg with whisk until blended. Stir in flour, ½ cup of the sugar, the baking powder and salt just until moistened (batter will be lumpy). Divide batter evenly among muffin cups.

2 In small bowl, mix remaining ¼ cup sugar and 1¼ teaspoons orange peel; sprinkle over batter in cups.

3 Bake 10 to 15 minutes or until light golden brown. Cool 5 minutes; remove from pan to cooling rack.

1 Mini Muffin: Calories 70 (Calories from Fat 20); Total Fat 2.5g (Saturated Fat 0g; Trans Fat 0g); Cholesterol 5mg; Sodium 60mg; Total Carbohydrate 11g (Dietary Fiber 0g); Protein 1g **Exchanges:** ½ Starch, ½ Fat **Carbohydrate Choices:** 1

mini maraschino cherry muffins

prep time: 15 minutes ❖ start to finish: 30 minutes ❖ 24 MINI MUFFINS

muffins

- ¼ cup granulated sugar
- ¼ cup butter, melted
- ½ cup milk
- 1 egg
- 1 cup all-purpose flour
- 1 teaspoon baking powder
- ¼ teaspoon salt
- ⅓ cup chopped well-drained maraschino cherries
- ¼ cup chopped blanched almonds

glaze

- ½ cup powdered sugar
- 3 to 4 teaspoons maraschino cherry juice

1 Heat oven to 400°F. Grease bottoms only of 24 mini muffin cups or 12 regular-size muffin cups with shortening or cooking spray, or line with paper baking cups.

2 In medium bowl, beat granulated sugar, butter, milk and egg with whisk or spoon until well blended. Stir in flour, baking powder and salt just until moistened. Fold in cherries and almonds. Divide batter evenly among muffin cups (cups will be full).

3 Bake 10 to 15 minutes or until golden brown.

4 Meanwhile, in small bowl, mix all glaze ingredients until smooth and thin enough to drizzle. Immediately remove muffins from pan to cooling rack. Drizzle glaze over warm muffins. Serve warm if desired.

1 Mini Muffin: Calories 70 (Calories from Fat 25); Total Fat 3g (Saturated Fat 1.5g; Trans Fat 0g); Cholesterol 15mg; Sodium 65mg; Total Carbohydrate 10g (Dietary Fiber 0g); Protein 1g **Exchanges:** ½ Starch, ½ Fat **Carbohydrate Choices:** ½

bake smart Did you end up with empty cups in your muffin pan? If you've greased them, fill the empty ones half full with water. It keeps the grease from burning, and all the cups will bake more evenly.

coconut and lime mini muffins

prep time: 20 minutes ✛ start to finish: 1 hour ✛ **16 MINI MUFFINS**

muffins

¼ cup granulated sugar

3 tablespoons vegetable oil

1 egg

½ cup canned coconut milk (not cream of coconut)

2 teaspoons grated lime peel

¾ cup all-purpose flour

¾ teaspoon baking powder

¼ teaspoon salt

¼ cup flaked coconut

glaze

½ cup powdered sugar

2½ teaspoons lime juice

garnish

2 tablespoons flaked coconut

1 teaspoon grated lime peel

1 Heat oven to 375°F. Place paper baking cup in each of 16 mini muffin cups or grease bottoms only with shortening or spray with cooking spray.

2 In medium bowl, stir granulated sugar, oil and egg until blended. Stir in coconut milk and 2 teaspoons lime peel until blended. Stir in flour, baking powder, salt and ¼ cup coconut just until dry ingredients are moistened. Divide batter evenly among muffin cups.

3 Bake 14 to 18 minutes or until tops just begin to turn golden brown. Cool 2 to 3 minutes; remove from pan to cooling rack. Cool completely, about 20 minutes.

4 In small bowl, stir powdered sugar and lime juice until smooth. If necessary, stir in water, a few drops at a time, until glazing consistency; set aside.

5 In small bowl, toss 2 tablespoons coconut with 1 teaspoon lime peel. Dip the top of each muffin in glaze and let excess drip off; immediately sprinkle with coconut mixture.

1 Mini Muffin: Calories 100 (Calories from Fat 45); Total Fat 5g (Saturated Fat 2.5g; Trans Fat 0g); Cholesterol 15mg; Sodium 70mg; Total Carbohydrate 13g (Dietary Fiber 0g); Protein 1g **Exchanges:** ½ Starch, ½ Other Carbohydrate, 1 Fat **Carbohydrate Choices:** 1

bake smart If you have only one 12-cup mini muffin pan, simply place the bowl of remaining batter in the refrigerator while the first batch of muffins bakes. Cool the pan completely before baking remaining muffins. The cold batter might need an extra minute of bake time.

These adorable mini muffins are the perfect treat for a wedding or baby shower.

cinnamon-orange mini muffins

prep time: 15 minutes + start to finish: 30 minutes + **24 MINI MUFFINS**

2 cups Original Bisquick mix

¼ cup sugar

¼ cup butter, softened

½ cup milk

1 teaspoon grated orange peel

1 egg

⅔ cup sugar

1 teaspoon ground cinnamon

½ cup butter, melted

1 Heat oven to 400°F. Grease bottoms only of 24 mini muffin cups with shortening or cooking spray, or line with paper baking cups.

2 In medium bowl, stir Bisquick mix, ¼ cup sugar, the softened butter, milk, orange peel and egg until blended; beat vigorously with spoon 30 seconds. Divide batter evenly among muffin cups.

3 Bake 10 to 12 minutes or until light golden brown. In small bowl, stir ⅔ cup sugar and the cinnamon until mixed. Immediately roll tops of muffins in melted butter, then in cinnamon-sugar mixture. Cool 5 to 10 minutes. Serve warm.

1 Mini Muffin: Calories 130 (Calories from Fat 70); Total Fat 7g (Saturated Fat 4g; Trans Fat 0.5g); Cholesterol 25mg; Sodium 170mg; Total Carbohydrate 15g (Dietary Fiber 0g); Protein 1g **Exchanges:** ½ Starch, ½ Other Carbohydrate, 1½ Fat **Carbohydrate Choices:** 1

mini beer–pimiento cheese muffins

prep time: 10 minutes ✛ start to finish: 35 minutes ✛ 48 MINI MUFFINS

1 bottle (12 oz) beer, room temperature

1 jar (4 oz) diced pimientos, drained

1 egg

1 teaspoon finely grated onion

4 cups Original Bisquick mix

2 cups shredded sharp Cheddar cheese (8 oz)

1 Heat oven to 400°F. Lightly spray 48 mini muffin cups with cooking spray.

2 In large bowl, mix beer, pimientos, egg and onion. Stir in Bisquick mix just until blended. (Batter may be lumpy.) Stir in cheese. Divide batter evenly among muffin cups.

3 Bake 13 to 15 minutes or until lightly browned. Remove from pan to cooling rack. Cool 10 minutes. Serve warm.

1 Mini Muffin: Calories 65 (Calories from Fat 0); Total Fat 3g (Saturated Fat 1g; Trans Fat 0g); Cholesterol 0mg; Sodium 156mg; Total Carbohydrate 7g (Dietary Fiber 0g); Protein 2g **Exchanges:** ½ Starch, ½ Fat **Carbohydrate Choices:** ½

bake smart These little muffins are a great snack or appetizer, or serve them alongside a bowl of soup or stew.

sesame-cheddar mini muffins

prep time: 15 minutes ✛ start to finish: 30 minutes ✛ 18 MINI MUFFINS

1 tablespoon butter

1 small sweet onion, finely chopped (⅓ cup)

1½ cups Original Bisquick mix

1 cup shredded sharp Cheddar cheese (4 oz)

1 egg

½ cup milk

1 teaspoon sesame seed, toasted*

2 tablespoons butter, melted

1 Heat oven to 400°F. Spray 18 mini muffin cups with cooking spray. In 7-inch skillet, melt 1 tablespoon butter over medium-high heat. Cook onion in butter 2 minutes, stirring frequently, until tender. Remove from heat; set aside.

2 In large bowl, stir Bisquick mix and ½ cup of the cheese. In small bowl, stir egg, milk and onion with whisk or spoon until well blended. Make well in center of Bisquick mixture; stir in egg mixture just until dry ingredients are moistened.

3 Divide batter evenly among muffin cups. Sprinkle evenly with remaining ½ cup cheese and the sesame seed; drizzle with 2 tablespoons butter.

4 Bake 12 to 14 minutes or until golden. Serve warm.

*To toast sesame seed, sprinkle in ungreased heavy skillet. Cook over medium-low heat 5 to 7 minutes, stirring frequently until browning begins, then stirring constantly until golden brown.

1 Mini Muffin: Calories 90 (Calories from Fat 50); Total Fat 6g (Saturated Fat 3g; Trans Fat 0.5g); Cholesterol 25mg; Sodium 180mg; Total Carbohydrate 7g (Dietary Fiber 0g); Protein 3g **Exchanges:** ½ Starch, 1 Fat **Carbohydrate Choices:** ½

indian-spiced mini muffins

prep time: 15 minutes ÷ start to finish: 45 minutes ÷ 24 MINI MUFFINS

⅓ cup butter

½ cup sugar

1 egg

1½ cups all-purpose flour

1½ teaspoons baking powder

½ teaspoon salt

¼ teaspoon ground nutmeg

¼ teaspoon ground ginger

½ cup milk

1 cup sugar

1 teaspoon ground cinnamon

1 teaspoon garam masala

¼ teaspoon ground cardamom

½ cup butter, melted

1 Heat oven to 350°F. Grease 24 mini muffin cups.

2 In large bowl, beat ⅓ cup butter, ½ cup sugar and the egg with electric mixer on medium speed until blended. In medium bowl, mix flour, baking powder, salt, nutmeg and ginger. Add alternately with milk to butter mixture until blended. Divide batter evenly among muffin cups.

3 Bake 15 to 18 minutes or until light golden brown. Cool 5 minutes. Remove from pan to cooling rack.

4 In large resealable food-storage plastic bag, mix 1 cup sugar, the cinnamon, garam masala and cardamom. Roll hot muffins in melted butter, then toss in sugar mixture to coat. Serve warm.

1 Mini Muffin: Calories 140 (Calories from Fat 60); Total Fat 7g (Saturated Fat 4g; Trans Fat 0g); Cholesterol 25mg; Sodium 130mg; Total Carbohydrate 19g (Dietary Fiber 0g); Protein 1g **Exchanges:** 1½ Other Carbohydrate, 1 Fat **Carbohydrate Choices:** 1

bake smart If you've never tried garam masala, here is your chance. This Indian spice mixture can contain up to 12 different spices and will often include cinnamon, cloves, cumin, coriander, cardamom, black pepper and fennel.

bake smart To easily cook the sweet potato, pierce with a fork and place on a paper towel in the microwave. Microwave on High 5 to 7 minutes or until tender. Cool until it's easy enough to handle. Slit the potato skin and peel it away from the flesh. Mash the flesh with a fork and let cool to room temperature.

To easily drizzle rolls, place the glaze in a resealable food-storage plastic bag. Cut off a tiny corner of the bag and squeeze the bag to drizzle the glaze over rolls.

mini sweet potato–cinnamon rolls

prep time: 40 minutes ✛ start to finish: 2 hours 40 minutes ✛ **24 MINI ROLLS**

cinnamon rolls

1½ to 1¾ cups all-purpose or bread flour
2 tablespoons granulated sugar
½ teaspoon salt
¼ teaspoon ground cinnamon
1¼ teaspoons fast-acting dry yeast
¼ cup very warm milk (120°F to 130°F)
⅓ cup mashed cooked sweet potato, cooled
3 tablespoons butter, softened
1 egg yolk

filling

2 tablespoons butter, softened
2 tablespoons packed brown sugar
2 teaspoons ground cinnamon
½ teaspoon ground ginger
½ teaspoon ground nutmeg
¼ teaspoon ground cardamom
⅛ teaspoon ground cloves

glaze

2 tablespoons butter, melted
1 tablespoon plus 1 to 2 teaspoons milk
1 cup powdered sugar

1 In large bowl, mix 1 cup of the flour, 2 tablespoons granulated sugar, the salt, ¼ teaspoon cinnamon and the yeast. Add warm milk, sweet potato, 3 tablespoons butter and the egg yolk. Beat with electric mixer on low speed 1 minute, scraping bowl frequently. Beat on medium speed 1 minute, scraping bowl frequently. Stir in enough remaining flour, ¼ cup at a time, to make dough easy to handle.

2 Place dough on lightly floured surface, Knead dough 3 to 5 minutes or until dough is smooth and springy. Grease medium bowl with shortening. Place dough in bowl, turning dough to grease all sides. Cover bowl loosely with plastic wrap sprayed with cooking spray; let rise in warm place about 1 hour 15 minutes or until doubled in size. Dough is ready if indentation remains when touched.

3 In small bowl, mix 1 tablespoon of the butter and all remaining filling ingredients; set aside.

4 Grease bottoms and sides of 24 mini muffin cups with shortening or spray with cooking spray. Gently push fist into dough to deflate. On lightly floured surface, roll dough into 12×9-inch rectangle. Cut dough in half to form 2 (9×6-inch) rectangles. Spread rectangles with remaining 1 tablespoon butter; sprinkle with filling, covering entire surface. Starting with 9-inch side, roll up tightly. Pinch edges to seal. Stretch and shape until even. Using dental floss or serrated knife, cut each roll into 12 (¾-inch) slices.

5 Place slice in each muffin cup, cut side up. Cover loosely with plastic wrap sprayed with cooking spray; let rise in warm place 30 minutes.

6 Heat oven to 350°F. Bake 10 to 12 minutes or until light golden brown. Immediately remove from pan to cooling rack.

7 Meanwhile, in small bowl, stir melted butter, 1 tablespoon milk and the powdered sugar. Stir in additional milk, 1 teaspoon at a time, until glaze is smooth and consistency of thick syrup. Drizzle over rolls. Serve warm.

1 Mini Roll: Calories 100 (Calories from Fat 35); Total Fat 3.5g (Saturated Fat 2.5g; Trans Fat 0g); Cholesterol 20mg; Sodium 75mg; Total Carbohydrate 14g (Dietary Fiber 0g); Protein 1g **Exchanges:** ½ Starch, ½ Other Carbohydrate, ½ Fat **Carbohydrate Choices:** 1

bourbon-orange mini loaves

prep time: 30 minutes ✛ start to finish: 2 hours 25 minutes ✛ 4 LOAVES (4 SLICES EACH)

mini loaves

- ½ cup milk
- ¼ cup bourbon
- ¼ cup butter, melted
- 1 egg
- 2 teaspoons grated orange peel
- 1½ cups all-purpose flour
- ½ cup granulated sugar
- 2 teaspoons baking powder
- ¾ teaspoon salt
- ½ cup plus 2 tablespoons chopped pecans, toasted*

caramel-bourbon glaze

- 2 tablespoons butter
- ¼ cup packed brown sugar
- 1 tablespoon plus 1 to 2 teaspoons milk
- ½ cup powdered sugar
- 2 teaspoons bourbon

1 Heat oven to 350°F. Grease bottoms only of 4 (4½×2½-inch) mini loaf pans with shortening or cooking spray.

2 In large bowl, stir ½ cup milk, ¼ cup bourbon, the melted butter, egg and orange peel until blended. Stir in flour, granulated sugar, baking powder and salt just until moistened. Stir in ½ cup of the pecans. Divide batter evenly among pans, about ½ cup each. Place pans on cookie sheet at least 2 inches apart.

3 Bake 30 to 35 minutes or until toothpick inserted in center comes out clean and tops begin to turn golden brown. Cool 10 minutes.

4 Loosen sides of loaves from pans; remove from pans and place top side up on cooling rack. Cool completely, about 40 minutes.

5 Meanwhile, in 1-quart saucepan, melt 2 tablespoons butter over medium heat. Stir in brown sugar. Heat to boiling, stirring constantly; reduce heat to low. Boil and stir 2 minutes. Remove from heat; stir in 1 tablespoon milk. Increase heat to medium; cook, stirring constantly until mixture returns to a boil. Remove from heat. Place saucepan in bowl of ice water; cool to lukewarm, stirring constantly about 2 minutes.

6 Remove pan from ice water. Stir in powdered sugar and 2 teaspoons bourbon. Beat until smooth, adding additional milk as needed for drizzling consistency. Drizzle glaze over loaves; sprinkle with remaining 2 tablespoons pecans. Let stand 30 minutes for glaze to set. Wrap tightly and store at room temperature up to 4 days, or refrigerate.

✱To toast pecans, bake in ungreased shallow pan at 350°F for 5 to 7 minutes, stirring occasionally, until light brown.

1 Slice: Calories 180 (Calories from Fat 70); Total Fat 8g (Saturated Fat 3g; Trans Fat 0g); Cholesterol 25mg; Sodium 230mg; Total Carbohydrate 24g (Dietary Fiber 0g); Protein 2g **Exchanges:** ½ Starch, 1 Other Carbohydrate, 1½ Fat **Carbohydrate Choices:** 1½

bake smart These tiny pans don't sit well on an oven rack by themselves, so putting them on a cookie sheet ensures they won't tip over.

mini pumpkin-date bread

prep time: 15 minutes ✛ start to finish: 1 hour 30 minutes ✛ 11 MINI LOAVES (5 SLICES EACH)

1⅔ cups sugar

⅔ cup vegetable oil

2 teaspoons vanilla

4 eggs

1 can (15 oz) pumpkin (not pie filling mix)

3 cups all-purpose flour

2 teaspoons baking soda

1 teaspoon ground cinnamon

¾ teaspoon salt

½ teaspoon baking powder

½ teaspoon ground cloves

1 cup chopped dates

1 Heat oven to 350°F. Grease bottoms only of 11 (4½×2¾×1¼-inch) loaf pans.

2 In large bowl, mix sugar, oil, vanilla, eggs and pumpkin. Stir in all remaining ingredients except dates. Stir in dates. Pour into pans (about ½ cup each).

3 Bake 25 to 35 minutes or until toothpick inserted in center comes out clean. Cool 10 minutes. Loosen sides of loaves from pans; remove from pans and place top side up on cooling rack. Cool completely before slicing.

1 Slice: Calories 90 (Calories from Fat 30); Total Fat 3g (Saturated Fat 0.5g; Trans Fat 0g); Cholesterol 15mg; Sodium 90mg; Total Carbohydrate 14g (Dietary Fiber 0g); Protein 1g **Exchanges:** ½ Starch, ½ Other Carbohydrate, ½ Fat **Carbohydrate Choices:** 1

bake smart To make regular-size loaves, grease bottoms only of two 8- or 9-inch loaf pans. Bake 50 to 60 minutes.

For a crunchy praline topping, mix ⅓ cup packed brown sugar, ⅓ cup chopped pecans and 1 tablespoon softened butter until crumbly; sprinkle over the batter before baking.

mini rosemary scones

prep time: 25 minutes ✛ start to finish: 1 hour 5 minutes ✛ **18 MINI SCONES**

1 cup all-purpose flour

1 cup whole wheat flour

2 tablespoons sugar

2 teaspoons baking powder

½ teaspoon baking soda

½ teaspoon salt

2 teaspoons grated lemon peel

1 tablespoon finely chopped fresh or 1 teaspoon dried rosemary leaves, crushed

3 tablespoons cold butter

½ cup fat-free sour cream

¼ cup vegetable oil

1 tablespoon fresh lemon juice

1 Heat oven to 400°F. Spray cookie sheet with cooking spray.

2 In medium bowl, mix flours, sugar, baking powder, baking soda, salt, lemon peel and rosemary. Cut in butter, using pastry blender or fork, until mixture looks like fine crumbs. Stir in sour cream, oil and lemon juice.

3 On lightly floured surface, knead dough lightly 10 times. Divide dough into thirds. On cookie sheet, pat each third of dough into 5-inch round. Using sharp knife, cut each round into 6 wedges, but do not separate wedges.

4 Bake 12 to 17 minutes or until edges are golden brown. Immediately remove from cookie sheet to cooling rack. Carefully separate wedges. Cool 5 to 10 minutes. Serve warm.

1 Mini Scone: Calories 110 (Calories from Fat 45); Total Fat 5g (Saturated Fat 1.5g; Trans Fat 0g); Cholesterol 5mg; Sodium 180mg; Total Carbohydrate 13g (Dietary Fiber 1g); Protein 2g **Exchanges:** 1 Starch, 1 Fat **Carbohydrate Choices:** 1

stir 'n scoop mini rolls

prep time: 15 minutes + start to finish: 30 minutes + 18 MINI ROLLS

rolls

2 cups all-purpose flour

1 tablespoon sugar

2½ teaspoons baking powder

½ teaspoon salt

⅓ cup butter, softened

⅔ cup milk

savory italian cheese topping

2 tablespoons Caesar or Italian dressing

¼ teaspoon Italian seasoning

2 teaspoons grated Parmesan cheese

1 Heat oven to 400°F. Grease cookie sheet or line with cooking parchment paper. In medium bowl, mix flour, sugar, baking powder and salt. Cut in butter, using pastry blender or fork, until mixture is crumbly. Stir in ⅔ cup milk until dough leaves side of bowl and forms a ball. Stir in additional milk, if necessary, 1 tablespoon at a time, until dough is soft and slightly sticky. Beat 25 strokes.

2 Onto cookie sheet, drop dough by rounded tablespoonfuls about 1 inch apart. In small bowl, mix dressing and seasoning. Brush over tops of rolls. Sprinkle with cheese.

3 Bake 12 minutes or until golden brown. Serve warm.

1 Mini Roll: Calories 100 (Calories from Fat 45); Total Fat 4.5g (Saturated Fat 2.5g; Trans Fat 0g); Cholesterol 10mg; Sodium 180mg; Total Carbohydrate 12g (Dietary Fiber 0g); Protein 2g **Exchanges:** 1 Starch, ½ Fat **Carbohydrate Choices:** 1

bake smart For Crunchy Almond Butter Topping, in small bowl, mix 1½ tablespoons chopped sliced almonds, 1 tablespoon softened butter and 1 tablespoon light corn syrup. Spread over tops of unbaked rolls; sprinkle with 2 teaspoons sugar. Bake as directed.

Other ideas for topping the rolls before baking include sprinkling with shredded cheese, any herb, caraway or sesame seed or miniature chocolate chips.

miniature brioche

prep time: 20 minutes ✛ start to finish: 7 hours 30 minutes ✛ 12 MINI BRIOCHE

¼ cup water

3 tablespoons butter, softened

2 eggs

2½ cups bread flour

¼ cup sugar

¾ teaspoon salt

1 teaspoon grated orange or lemon peel

2½ teaspoons bread machine yeast

1 tablespoon milk

1 egg yolk

Coarse sugar crystals

1 Measure carefully, placing all ingredients except milk, egg yolk and sugar crystals in bread machine pan in the order recommended by the manufacturer.

2 Select Dough/Manual cycle. Do not use delay cycle.

3 Grease medium bowl. Place dough in bowl, turning dough to grease all sides. Cover with plastic wrap; refrigerate at least 4 hours but no longer than 24 hours.

4 Grease 12 regular-size muffin cups. Punch down dough. Divide dough into 16 equal pieces. Roll each piece into a ball. Cut 4 balls into 3 pieces each; roll into small balls. Place 12 large balls in muffin cups. Flatten and make an indentation in center of each with thumb. Place 1 small ball in each indentation. Cover and let rise in warm place 50 to 60 minutes or until doubled in size.

5 Heat oven to 350°F. Mix milk and egg yolk; gently brush over tops of rolls. Sprinkle with sugar crystals. Bake 15 to 20 minutes or until golden brown. Remove from pan to cooling rack. Serve warm.

1 Mini Brioche: Calories 170 (Calories from Fat 40); Total Fat 4.5g (Saturated Fat 2.5g; Trans Fat 0g); Cholesterol 60mg; Sodium 180mg; Total Carbohydrate 27g (Dietary Fiber 1g); Protein 5g **Exchanges:** 1½ Starch, ½ Other Carbohydrate, ½ Fat **Carbohydrate Choices:** 2

mini cheese 'n chive popovers

prep time: 10 minutes ✛ start to finish: 40 minutes ✛ **18 MINI POPOVERS**

2 eggs, room temperature

⅔ cup milk, room temperature

⅔ cup all-purpose flour

3 tablespoons finely shredded Cheddar cheese

1 tablespoon chopped fresh or 1 teaspoon freeze-dried chives

⅛ teaspoon garlic powder

⅛ teaspoon salt

1 Heat oven to 450°F. Generously spray 18 mini muffin cups with cooking spray. In small bowl, beat eggs with whisk or egg beater until lemon-colored and foamy. Add milk; blend well. Add flour and remaining ingredients; beat just until batter is smooth and foamy on top. Divide batter evenly among muffin cups, filling to within ¼ inch of top.

2 Bake 10 minutes. DO NOT OPEN OVEN. Reduce oven temperature to 350°F; bake 10 to 20 minutes longer or until popovers are high and deep golden brown. Remove from oven; insert sharp knife into each popover to allow steam to escape. Remove from pan. Serve hot.

2 Mini Popovers: Calories 70 (Calories from Fat 20); Total Fat 2.5g (Saturated Fat 1g; Trans Fat 0g); Cholesterol 50mg; Sodium 70mg; Total Carbohydrate 8g (Dietary Fiber 0g); Protein 3g **Exchanges:** ½ Starch, ½ Fat **Carbohydrate Choices:** ½

bake smart Chives are a fragrant herb with slender, vivid green hollow stems. Fresh chives can be snipped with scissors to the desired length. They have a mild onion flavor and are available year-round.

rosemary and garlic mini focaccias

prep time: 15 minutes ✛ start to finish: 25 minutes ✛ **24 MINI FOCACCIAS**

2¼ cups Original Bisquick mix

⅔ cup milk

2 teaspoons olive or vegetable oil

½ teaspoon dried rosemary leaves, crumbled

½ teaspoon garlic powder

1 Heat oven to 450°F. In medium bowl, stir Bisquick mix and milk until soft dough forms; beat 30 seconds. If dough is too sticky, gradually mix in enough additional Bisquick mix (up to ¼ cup) to make dough easy to handle.

2 Place dough on surface generously sprinkled with additional Bisquick mix, gently roll dough in Bisquick mix to coat. Shape into a ball; knead 10 times.

3 Roll out dough to ¼-inch thickness. Cut with 2-inch round cutter dipped in Bisquick mix. On ungreased cookie sheet, place about 2 inches apart. Brush with oil; sprinkle with rosemary and garlic powder.

4 Bake 8 to 10 minutes or until golden brown. Serve warm.

1 Mini Focaccia: Calories 50 (Calories from Fat 20); Total Fat 2g (Saturated Fat 0.5g; Trans Fat 0g); Cholesterol 0mg; Sodium 150mg; Total Carbohydrate 8g (Dietary Fiber 0g); Protein 1g **Exchanges:** ½ Starch, ½ Fat **Carbohydrate Choices:** ½

French Bread
(page 219)

chapter five

yeast breads

artisan semolina and rosemary bread

prep time: 20 minutes ✛ start to finish: 4 hours 40 minutes ✛ 1 LOAF (12 SLICES)

bread

- 2 to 2½ cups all-purpose flour
- 1 tablespoon sugar
- 1½ teaspoons table salt
- 1 package regular active dry yeast (2¼ teaspoons)
- 1¼ cups very warm water (120°F to 130°F)
- 1 tablespoon olive oil
- 1 cup semolina flour
- 1 tablespoon chopped fresh rosemary leaves
- 1 tablespoon cornmeal

topping

- 2 teaspoons olive oil
- 1 tablespoon chopped fresh rosemary leaves
- ½ teaspoon coarse (kosher or sea) salt

1 In large bowl, mix 2 cups of the all-purpose flour, the sugar, table salt and yeast. Stir in warm water and 1 tablespoon olive oil until well mixed, about 1 minute. Beat with wooden spoon 2 minutes.

2 Stir in semolina flour and 1 tablespoon rosemary. Stir in additional all-purpose flour, 1 tablespoon at a time, until dough leaves side of bowl, flour is incorporated and dough is not sticky. Cover tightly with plastic wrap; refrigerate at least 2 hours but no longer than 24 hours.

3 Line cookie sheet with cooking parchment paper. Sprinkle parchment with cornmeal. Place dough on lightly floured surface; turn dough to lightly coat with flour. With floured hands, shape dough into 6×4-inch oval by stretching surface of dough around to bottom on all 4 sides; pinch bottom to seal. Place on cookie sheet. Cover loosely with plastic wrap sprayed with cooking spray; let rise in warm place about 1 hour or until doubled in size.

4 Meanwhile, about 20 minutes before baking, place pizza stone on oven rack. Heat oven to 400°F. Brush dough with 2 teaspoons olive oil; sprinkle with 1 tablespoon rosemary and the sea salt. Slide dough and parchment paper from cookie sheet onto pizza stone.

5 Bake 20 to 25 minutes or until golden brown. Cool on cooling rack, about 1 hour.

1 Slice: Calories 150 (Calories from Fat 20); Total Fat 2.5g (Saturated Fat 0g; Trans Fat 0g); Cholesterol 0mg; Sodium 390mg; Total Carbohydrate 28g (Dietary Fiber 1g); Protein 4g **Exchanges:** 1½ Starch, ½ Other Carbohydrate **Carbohydrate Choices:** 2

bake smart This bread can also be baked without a pizza stone—simply bake the loaf as directed on a cookie sheet.

bake smart Baked in small batches, artisan breads are made with age-old bread-baking techniques. They're crafted with few ingredients, sometimes as few as five. The texture of artisan bread is firm and moist but crusty outside. This no-knead version of artisan bread was developed to be very much like a bakery bread. It's simply delicious!

no-knead artisan bread

prep time: **15 minutes** ✛ start to finish: **4 hours 5 minutes** ✛ 2 (6-INCH) LOAVES (12 SLICES EACH)

3 to 3½ cups all-purpose flour

1 tablespoon sugar

1½ teaspoons salt

1 package regular active dry yeast (2¼ teaspoons)

1¼ cups very warm water (120°F to 130°F)

1 tablespoon olive oil

Cornmeal

1 In large bowl, mix 2 cups of the flour, the sugar, salt and yeast. Stir in warm water and oil until well mixed, about 1 minute. Beat with wooden spoon 2 minutes.

2 Stir in 1 cup of the remaining flour. Stir in additional flour, 2 tablespoons at a time, until dough leaves side of bowl, flour is incorporated and dough is not sticky. Cover tightly with plastic wrap; refrigerate at least 2 hours but no longer than 24 hours.

3 Grease large cookie sheet with shortening or cooking spray; sprinkle with cornmeal, shaking off excess. Divide dough in half.

4 With floured hands, shape each half of dough into smooth ball by stretching surface of dough around to bottom on all 4 sides; pinch bottom to seal. Place dough balls on cookie sheet about 5 inches apart. Cover loosely with plastic wrap; let rise in warm place about 1hour 30 minutes or until doubled in size.

5 Heat oven to 375°F. Place 8- or 9-inch pan on bottom rack of oven; add hot water until about ½ inch from top. Uncover dough; using serrated knife, carefully slash tic-tac-toe pattern on each loaf top. Bake 15 to 20 minutes or until loaves are dark golden brown and sound hollow when tapped. Remove from cookie sheet to cooling rack; cool.

1 Slice: Calories 70 (Calories from Fat 5); Total Fat 1g (Saturated Fat 0g; Trans Fat 0g); Cholesterol 0mg; Sodium 150mg; Total Carbohydrate 15g (Dietary Fiber 0g); Protein 2g **Exchanges:** 1 Starch **Carbohydrate Choices:** 1

no-knead basil and sun-dried tomato bread: Fold ¼ cup well-drained sun-dried tomatoes in oil (from 7-oz jar) and 1 tablespoon fresh basil leaves (or 1 teaspoon dried basil leaves) into each dough half with hands in step 3 before shaping. Continue as directed.

no-knead kalamata olive–rosemary bread: Fold ¼ cup pitted and sliced kalamata olives and 1 tablespoon chopped fresh rosemary leaves (or 1 teaspoon dried rosemary leaves) into each dough half with hands in step 3 before shaping. Continue as directed.

artisan asiago bread

prep time: **25 minutes** ✛ start to finish: **4 hours 15 minutes** ✛ 1 LARGE LOAF (24 SLICES)

3½ to 3¾ cups bread flour

1 teaspoon sugar

1 package regular active or fast-acting dry yeast (2¼ teaspoons)

1¼ cups very warm water (120°F to 130°F)

2 tablespoons olive or vegetable oil

2 teaspoons dried rosemary or thyme leaves, if desired

1 teaspoon salt

1¼ cups diced Asiago, Swiss or other firm cheese

1 In large bowl, mix 1½ cups of the flour, the sugar and yeast. Add warm water. Beat with whisk or electric mixer on low speed 1 minute, scraping bowl frequently. Cover tightly with plastic wrap; let stand about 1 hour or until bubbly.

2 Stir in oil, rosemary and salt. Stir in enough remaining flour, ½ cup at a time, until a soft, smooth dough forms. Let stand 15 minutes.

3 Place dough on lightly floured surface. Knead 5 to 10 minutes or until dough is smooth and springy. Knead in 1 cup of the cheese. Grease large bowl with shortening. Place dough in bowl, turning dough to grease all sides. Cover bowl tightly with plastic wrap; let rise in warm place 45 to 60 minutes or until doubled in size. Dough is ready if indentation remains when touched.

4 Lightly grease uninsulated cookie sheet with shortening or cooking spray. Place dough on lightly floured surface. Gently shape into football-shaped loaf, about 12 inches long, by stretching sides of dough downward to make a smooth top. Place loaf with smooth side up on cookie sheet. Coat loaf generously with flour. Cover loosely with plastic wrap; let rise in warm place 45 to 60 minutes or until almost doubled in size.

5 Place 8- or 9-inch square pan on bottom rack of oven; add hot water to pan until about ½ inch from the top. Heat oven to 450°F.

6 Spray loaf with cool water; sprinkle with flour. Using serrated knife, carefully cut ½-inch-deep slash lengthwise down center of loaf. Sprinkle remaining ¼ cup cheese into slash.

7 Bake 10 minutes. Reduce oven temperature to 400°F. Bake 20 to 25 minutes longer or until loaf is deep golden and sounds hollow when tapped. Remove from cookie sheet to cooling rack; cool.

1 Slice: Calories 110 (Calories from Fat 30); Total Fat 3g (Saturated Fat 1.5g; Trans Fat 0g); Cholesterol 5mg; Sodium 115mg; Total Carbohydrate 16g (Dietary Fiber 0g); Protein 4g **Exchanges:** 1 Starch, ½ Fat **Carbohydrate Choices:** 1

bake smart This large, flour-sprinkled loaf looks and tastes like it came from a bakery. When you slice it, you'll find pockets of cheese scattered throughout.

whole-grain artisan bread

prep time: 25 minutes + start to finish: 4 hours 35 minutes + 1 LOAF (12 SLICES)

1¼ cups warm water
(110°F to 115°F)

1 teaspoon regular active
dry yeast

½ teaspoon sugar

1½ cups whole wheat flour

½ cup rye flour

1½ teaspoons salt

1½ to 1¾ cups bread flour

1 teaspoon cornmeal

1 In large bowl, stir warm water, yeast and sugar until yeast is dissolved. Stir in whole wheat flour and rye flour with whisk until mixture is smooth. Cover and let stand in warm place 1 hour or until mixture is bubbly and has doubled in size.

2 Stir in salt and 1½ cups of the bread flour, gradually adding additional bread flour as necessary to make dough easy to handle.

3 Place dough on lightly floured surface. Knead 10 minutes or until dough is smooth and springy. Grease large bowl with oil. Place dough in bowl, turning dough to grease all sides. Cover bowl loosely with plastic wrap; let rise in warm place about 1 hour or until doubled in size. Dough is ready if indentation remains when touched.

4 Line cookie sheet with cooking parchment paper and sprinkle center with cornmeal. Gently push fist into dough to deflate. Shape dough into round ball by tightly pulling edges under to form smooth top. Place on cookie sheet and press dough to flatten slightly. Cover with a clean towel or plastic wrap that has been sprayed with cooking spray and let rise in warm place 45 minutes or until doubled in size.

5 Meanwhile, about 20 minutes before baking, place pizza stone on oven rack. Heat oven to 425°F.

6 Using small strainer, sprinkle 1 teaspoon bread flour over top of dough. Using serrated knife, cut 4 (¼-inch-deep) slashes on top of loaf, then make 4 diagonal cuts to create crisscross pattern. Slide dough and parchment paper from cookie sheet onto pizza stone.

7 Bake 25 to 30 minutes or until crisp golden brown and bottom sounds hollow when tapped. Cool completely on cooling rack, about 1 hour.

1 Slice: Calories 130 (Calories from Fat 5); Total Fat 0.5g (Saturated Fat 0g; Trans Fat 0g); Cholesterol 0mg; Sodium 300mg; Total Carbohydrate 27g (Dietary Fiber 3g); Protein 4g **Exchanges:** 1½ Starch, ½ Other Carbohydrate **Carbohydrate Choices:** 2

bake smart While a pizza stone helps create a crisp crust, this loaf can also be baked on a cookie sheet.

The rye flour adds a hint of sourdough flavor to this bakery-style bread.

classic white bread

prep time: **35 minutes** ✛ start to finish: **2 hours 55 minutes** ✛ 2 LOAVES (16 SLICES EACH)

6 to 7 cups all-purpose or bread flour

3 tablespoons sugar

1 tablespoon salt

2 tablespoons shortening or softened butter

2 packages regular active or fast-acting dry yeast (4½ teaspoons)

2¼ cups very warm water (120°F to 130°F)

2 tablespoons butter, melted, if desired

1 In large bowl, stir 3½ cups of the flour, the sugar, salt, shortening and yeast until well mixed. Add warm water. Beat with electric mixer on low speed 1 minute, scraping bowl frequently. Beat on medium speed 1 minute, scraping bowl frequently. Stir in enough remaining flour, 1 cup at a time, to make dough easy to handle.

2 Place dough on lightly floured surface. Knead 10 minutes or until dough is smooth and springy. Grease large bowl with shortening. Place dough in bowl, turning dough to grease all sides. Cover bowl loosely with plastic wrap; let rise in warm place 40 to 60 minutes or until doubled in size. Dough is ready if indentation remains when touched.

3 Grease bottoms and sides of 2 (8×4- or 9×5-inch) loaf pans with shortening or cooking spray.

4 Gently push fist into dough to deflate. Divide dough in half. On lightly floured surface, flatten each half with hands or rolling pin into 18×9-inch rectangle. Roll dough up tightly, beginning at 9-inch side. Press with thumbs to seal after each turn. Pinch edge of dough into roll to seal. Pinch each end of roll to seal. Fold ends under loaf. Place loaves seam side down in pans. Brush loaves lightly with 1 tablespoon of the melted butter. Cover loosely with plastic wrap; let rise in warm place 35 to 50 minutes or until doubled in size.

5 Move oven rack to low position so that tops of pans will be in center of oven. Heat oven to 425°F. Bake 25 to 30 minutes or until loaves are deep golden brown and sound hollow when tapped. Remove from pans to cooling rack. Brush loaves with remaining 1 tablespoon melted butter; cool.

1 Slice: Calories 100 (Calories from Fat 10); Total Fat 1g (Saturated Fat 0g; Trans Fat 0g); Cholesterol 0mg, Sodium 220mg; Total Carbohydrate 21g (Dietary Fiber 0g); Protein 3g **Exchanges:** 1 Starch **Carbohydrate Choices:** 1½

making bread dough

After the first addition of flour has been beaten in, dough will be very soft and fall in "sheets" off rubber spatula.

Knead by folding dough toward you. With heels of your hands, push dough away from you with short rocking motion. Rotate dough one-quarter turn; repeat. Dough will feel springy and smooth.

Dough should rise until doubled in size. Press fingertips about ½ inch into dough. If indentations remain, dough has risen enough.

Gently push fist into dough to deflate. This releases large air bubbles to produce a finer texture in traditional loaves.

french bread

prep time: **25 minutes** ✛ start to finish: **8 hours** ✛ 2 LOAVES (16 SLICES EACH)

1½ cups all-purpose flour
1 package regular active dry yeast (2¼ teaspoons)
1 cup very warm water (120°F to 130°F)
1 teaspoon salt
1⅓ to 1⅔ cups all-purpose or bread flour

cheesy herbed french bread: Stir in ¼ cup grated Parmesan cheese and 1 teaspoon dried basil leaves with the flour in step 2.

garlic bread: Heat oven to 400°F. In small bowl, stir ¼ teaspoon garlic powder with ⅓ cup softened butter. Slice 1 loaf French bread into 1-inch slices. Spread each slice with butter mixture. Wrap in foil. Bake 10 to 15 minutes or until hot.

1 In large bowl, mix 1½ cups all-purpose flour and the yeast. Add warm water. Beat with whisk or electric mixer on low speed 1 minute, scraping bowl frequently, until batter is very smooth. Cover tightly with plastic wrap; let stand about 1 hour or until bubbly.

2 Stir in salt and enough flour, ½ cup at a time, until a soft dough forms. Place dough on lightly floured surface. Knead 5 to 10 minutes or until dough is smooth and springy (dough will be soft). Grease large bowl with shortening. Place dough in bowl, turning dough to grease all sides. Cover bowl loosely with plastic wrap; let rise in warm place 1 hour to 1 hour 15 minutes or until doubled in size. Dough is ready if indentation remains when touched.

3 Grease uninsulated cookie sheet with shortening or cooking spray. Place dough on lightly floured surface; form dough into an oval-shaped mound. Sprinkle top of dough with flour. With a straight-edged knife, press straight down on dough lengthwise to divide it into 2 equal parts (the parts will be elongated in shape). Gently shape each part into a narrow loaf, about 16 inches long, stretching the top of the loaf slightly to make it smooth. Place loaves, smooth side up, on cookie sheet about 4 inches apart.

4 Cover loaves loosely, but airtight, with plastic wrap. (Loaves will expand slightly in refrigerator.) Refrigerate at least 4 hours but no longer than 24 hours. (This step can be omitted, but refrigerating develops the flavor and texture of the bread. If omitted, continue with next step.)

5 Uncover loaves and spray with cool water; let rise in warm place about 1 hour or until refrigerated loaves have come to room temperature.

6 Place 8- or 9-inch square pan on bottom rack of oven; add hot water to pan until about ½ inch from the top. Heat oven to 450°F.

7 Using serrated knife, carefully cut ¼-inch-deep slashes diagonally across loaves at 2-inch intervals. Spray loaves with cool water. Place loaves in oven and spray again.

8 Bake 18 to 20 minutes or until loaves are deep golden brown with crisp crust and sound hollow when tapped. Remove from cookie sheet to cooling rack; cool.

1 Slice: Calories 40 (Calories from Fat 0); Total Fat 0g (Saturated Fat 0g; Trans Fat 0g); Cholesterol 0mg; Sodium 75mg; Total Carbohydrate 9g (Dietary Fiber 0g); Protein 1g **Exchanges:** ½ Starch **Carbohydrate Choices:** ½

ciabatta

prep time: **25 minutes** ✛ start to finish: **18 hours 20 minutes** ✛ 2 LOAVES (12 SLICES EACH)

starter

- ¼ teaspoon regular active dry yeast
- ½ cup water
- 1 cup bread flour

bread

- ¾ cup water
- 2 teaspoons olive or vegetable oil
- 2¼ cups bread flour
- ¾ teaspoon regular active dry yeast
- 1½ teaspoons salt
- Cornmeal

1 In small bowl, stir all starter ingredients until well blended. Cover with plastic wrap; let stand at room temperature 12 to 24 hours.

2 In large bowl, mix starter and all bread ingredients except cornmeal with heavy-duty electric mixer using dough hook on medium speed 4 minutes or in food processor fitted with metal blade for 1 minute. Dough will be very sticky.

3 Grease medium bowl with shortening or cooking spray. Place dough in bowl, turning dough to grease all sides. Cover bowl loosely with plastic wrap; let rise at room temperature about 1 hour 30 minutes or until doubled in size. Dough is ready if indentation remains when touched. Gently stir down dough with rubber spatula. Cover with plastic wrap; let rise 1 hour longer.

4 On generously floured surface, divide dough in half. Gently press each half with floured fingers into 10×4-inch rectangle. Sprinkle cornmeal over large cookie sheet; place loaves about 3 inches apart on cornmeal. Using spray bottle with fine mist, spray tops of loaves with cool water. Cover loosely with plastic wrap; let rise 1 hour 30 minutes to 2 hours or until almost doubled in size.

5 Heat oven to 425°F. Using spray bottle with fine mist, spray tops of loaves with cool water. Bake 18 to 22 minutes or until loaves sound hollow when tapped. Remove from cookie sheet to cooling rack. Cool completely, about 1 hour.

1 Slice: Calories 70 (Calories from Fat 5); Total Fat 0.5g (Saturated Fat 0g; Trans Fat 0g); Cholesterol 0mg; Sodium 150mg; Total Carbohydrate 14g (Dietary Fiber 0g); Protein 2g **Exchanges:** 1 Starch **Carbohydrate Choices:** 1

bake smart To let dough rise, set the covered bowl in a warm, draft-free place. You can also place the covered bowl on a cooling rack over a bowl of hot water.

country loaf

prep time: **25 minutes** ✛ start to finish: **4 hours 5 minutes** ✛ 1 LARGE LOAF (32 SLICES)

5 to 5½ cups bread flour

1 teaspoon sugar

1 package regular active or fast-acting dry yeast (2¼ teaspoons)

2 cups very warm water (120°F to 130F°)

2 tablespoons olive or vegetable oil

2 teaspoons salt

1 In large bowl, mix 2 cups of the flour, the sugar and yeast. Add warm water. Beat with whisk or electric mixer on low speed 1 minute, scraping bowl frequently. Cover tightly with plastic wrap; let stand about 1 hour or until bubbly.

2 Stir in oil and salt. Stir in enough remaining flour, ½ cup at a time, until a soft, smooth dough forms. Place dough on lightly floured surface. Knead 10 minutes, adding flour as necessary to keep dough from sticking, or until dough is smooth and springy.

3 Grease large bowl with shortening. Place dough in bowl, turning dough to grease all sides. Cover bowl loosely with plastic wrap; let rise in warm place about 1 hour or until doubled in size. Dough is ready if indentation remains when touched.

4 Grease uninsulated cookie sheet with shortening. Place dough on lightly floured surface. Gently shape into an even, round ball, without releasing all of the bubbles in the dough. Stretch sides of dough downward to make a smooth top. Place loaf with smooth side up on cookie sheet. Spray loaf with cool water. Cover loosely with plastic wrap; let rise in warm place 45 to 60 minutes or until almost double.

5 Place 8- or 9-inch square pan on bottom rack of oven; add hot water to pan until about ½ inch from top. Heat oven to 425°F.

6 Spray loaf with cool water; sprinkle lightly with flour. Using serrated knife, carefully cut 3 (¼-inch-deep) slashes on top of loaf.

7 Bake 35 to 40 minutes or until loaf is deep golden brown with crisp crust and sounds hollow when tapped. Remove from cookie sheet to cooling rack; cool.

1 Slice: Calories 80 (Calories from Fat 10); Total Fat 1g (Saturated Fat 0g; Trans Fat 0g); Cholesterol 0mg; Sodium 150mg; Total Carbohydrate 16g (Dietary Fiber 0g); Protein 2g **Exchanges:** 1 Starch **Carbohydrate Choices:** 1

bake smart For Whole Wheat Country Loaf, substitute 2 cups whole wheat flour for 2 cups of the bread flour.

This large, crusty loaf gains a country quality when sprinkled with flour before baking.

braided pumpkin wreaths

prep time: **50 minutes** + start to finish: **3 hours 45 minutes** + 2 WREATHS (24 SLICES EACH)

bread

5¾ to 6½ cups all-purpose flour

⅓ cup sugar

1½ teaspoons salt

2 packages regular active dry yeast (4½ teaspoons)

1 cup canned pumpkin (not pie filling mix)

¼ cup butter

1½ cups apple cider or apple juice

topping

1 egg

1 tablespoon water

2 teaspoons sesame seed, if desired

2 teaspoons poppy seed, if desired

1 In large bowl, stir 2 cups of the flour, the sugar, salt and yeast. In 2-quart saucepan, heat pumpkin, butter and cider over medium heat until very warm (120°F to 130°F). Add to flour mixture; beat with electric mixer on medium speed 3 minutes, scraping bowl occasionally.

2 Stir in enough of the remaining flour to make a soft dough. On floured surface, knead dough 3 to 5 minutes or until smooth and springy. Place dough in greased bowl, turning to grease top. Cover with plastic wrap and cloth towel; let rise in warm place until doubled in size, about 1 hour.

3 Grease large cookie sheet. Punch down dough. Divide in half; divide each half into 3 pieces. On lightly floured surface, roll each piece into 24-inch rope. On cookie sheet, place 3 ropes close together. Braid loosely; pinch ends together, forming a circle. Repeat with remaining dough. Cover and let rise in warm place 20 to 30 minutes or until almost doubled in size.

4 Heat oven to 375°F. In small bowl, beat egg and water until well blended; brush over braids; sprinkle with sesame and poppy seed.

5 Bake 18 to 24 minutes or until golden brown. Remove from cookie sheet to cooling racks. Cool about 1 hour.

1 Slice: Calories 80 (Calories from Fat 10); Total Fat 1.5g (Saturated Fat 0.5g; Trans Fat 0g); Cholesterol 5mg; Sodium 85mg; Total Carbohydrate 14g (Dietary Fiber 0g); Protein 2g **Exchanges:** 1 Starch **Carbohydrate Choices:** 1

bake smart Knead in only enough flour, about 2 tablespoons at a time, to make the dough smooth, elastic and easy to handle. Too much flour will create a heavy, dense bread.

swiss cheese soufflé bread

prep time: 25 minutes + start to finish: 2 hours 20 minutes + 1 LOAF (24 SLICES)

1⅓ cups all-purpose flour

1 tablespoon sugar

½ teaspoon salt

1 package regular active or fast-acting dry yeast (2¼ teaspoons)

⅓ cup butter

¼ cup water

¼ cup milk

1 egg

1 cup shredded Swiss cheese (4 oz)

1 clove garlic, finely chopped

Butter, softened

Grated Parmesan cheese, if desired

Freshly cracked pepper, if desired

1 In medium bowl, mix 1 cup of the flour, the sugar, salt and yeast. In 1-quart saucepan, heat ⅓ cup butter, the water and milk over medium heat, stirring frequently, until very warm (120°F to 130°F). Pour over flour mixture; beat with electric mixer on low speed about 30 seconds or until blended. Beat in egg on medium speed; continue beating 3 minutes, scraping bowl occasionally.

2 Stir in remaining ⅓ cup flour, the Swiss cheese and garlic. (If dough is sticky, stir in 1 to 2 tablespoons additional flour.) Cover and let rise in warm place about 45 minutes or until doubled in size.

3 Grease 1-quart casserole with shortening or cooking spray. Stir down dough; shape into a ball. Place in casserole. Brush top with softened butter; sprinkle with Parmesan cheese and pepper. Cover and let rise in warm place about 35 minutes or until doubled in size. (If using fast-acting yeast, do not let rise 35 minutes; cover and let rest on floured surface 10 minutes.)

4 Heat oven to 375°F. Bake 30 to 35 minutes or until loaf is golden brown and sounds hollow when tapped. (If loaf browns too quickly, cover loosely with foil during last 15 minutes of baking.) Immediately remove from casserole to cooling rack. Serve warm.

1 Slice: Calories 70 (Calories from Fat 40); Total Fat 4.5g (Saturated Fat 2.5g; Trans Fat 0g); Cholesterol 20mg; Sodium 80mg; Total Carbohydrate 6g (Dietary Fiber 0g); Protein 2g Exchanges: ½ Starch, 1 Fat Carbohydrate Choices: ½

easy no-knead wheat bread

prep time: **15 minutes** ✛ start to finish: **4 hours 10 minutes** ✛ 2 LOAVES (12 SLICES EACH)

2 cups whole wheat flour

½ cup sugar

1 teaspoon salt

2 packages regular active dry yeast (2¼ teaspoons)

1 cup very warm water (120°F to 130°F)

½ cup butter, melted

3 eggs

2 to 2½ cups all-purpose flour

Cornmeal

1 In large bowl, mix whole wheat flour, sugar, salt and yeast. Add warm water, butter and eggs; beat with electric mixer on low speed 1 minute to moisten ingredients. Beat on medium speed 2 minutes. Stir in enough all-purpose flour to make a stiff dough. Cover tightly with plastic wrap; refrigerate at least 2 hours or up to 4 days.

2 Grease large cookie sheet with shortening or cooking spray; sprinkle with cornmeal, shaking off excess. Divide dough in half. (One half of dough can be shaped and baked; other half can be shaped and baked at another time.)

3 With floured hands, shape each half of dough into a smooth ball by stretching surface of dough around to bottom on all 4 sides; pinch bottom to seal. Place on cookie sheet. (If baking both loaves at same time, place on same cookie sheet about 5 inches apart.) Cover loosely with plastic wrap; let rise in warm place about 1 hour 30 minutes or until doubled in size.

4 Heat oven to 375°F. Uncover dough; using serrated knife, carefully slash tic-tac-toe pattern on each loaf top. Sprinkle loaf lightly with flour. Bake 20 to 25 minutes or until loaves are golden brown. Immediately remove from cookie sheet to cooling rack; cool.

1 Slice: Calories 140 (Calories from Fat 45); Total Fat 5g (Saturated Fat 2.5g; Trans Fat 0g); Cholesterol 35mg; Sodium 135mg; Total Carbohydrate 20g (Dietary Fiber 1g); Protein 3g **Exchanges:** 1 Starch, 1 Fat **Carbohydrate Choices:** 1

bake smart You can make the dough and refrigerate up to 4 days before baking, or bake one loaf and refrigerate remaining dough to bake later.

four-grain batter bread

prep time: 15 minutes ✛ start to finish: 1 hour 10 minutes ✛ 2 LOAVES (16 SLICES EACH)

Cornmeal

4½ to 4¾ cups all-purpose or bread flour

2 tablespoons sugar

1 teaspoon salt

¼ teaspoon baking soda

2 packages regular active or fast-acting dry yeast (4½ teaspoons)

2 cups milk

½ cup water

½ cup whole wheat flour

½ cup wheat germ

½ cup quick-cooking oats

1 Grease bottoms and sides of 2 (8×4-inch) loaf pans with shortening or cooking spray; sprinkle with cornmeal.

2 In large bowl, mix 3½ cups of the all-purpose flour, the sugar, salt, baking soda and yeast. In 1-quart saucepan, heat milk and water over medium heat, stirring occasionally, until very warm (120°F to 130°F). Add milk mixture to flour mixture. Beat with electric mixer on low speed until moistened. Beat on medium speed 3 minutes, scraping bowl occasionally.

3 Stir in whole wheat flour, wheat germ, oats and enough remaining all-purpose flour to make a stiff batter. Divide batter evenly between pans. Round tops of loaves by patting with floured hands. Sprinkle with cornmeal. Cover loosely with plastic wrap; let rise in warm place about 30 minutes or until batter is about 1 inch below tops of pans.

4 Heat oven to 400°F. Bake 25 minutes or until tops of loaves are light brown. Remove from pans to cooling rack; cool.

1 Slice: Calories 100 (Calories from Fat 5); Total Fat 1g (Saturated Fat 0g; Trans Fat 0g); Cholesterol 0mg; Sodium 90mg; Total Carbohydrate 19g (Dietary Fiber 1g); Protein 4g **Exchanges:** 1 Starch **Carbohydrate Choices:** 1

whole wheat–raisin batter bread: Increase whole wheat flour to 2 cups. Omit wheat germ and oats. Stir in 1 cup raisins with the second addition of all-purpose flour.

bake smart Homemade bread doesn't get much easier than this! It's called batter bread because the dough is soft and doesn't require kneading. Just mix it, put it in the pan, let it rise and bake.

fresh herb batter bread

prep time: **10 minutes** ✚ start to finish: **1 hour 35 minutes** ✚ 1 LOAF (20 SLICES)

3 cups all-purpose flour

1 tablespoon sugar

1 teaspoon salt

1 package regular active or fast-acting dry yeast (2¼ teaspoons)

1¼ cups very warm water (120°F to 130°F)

2 tablespoons chopped fresh parsley

2 tablespoons shortening or softened butter

1½ teaspoons chopped fresh or ½ teaspoon dried rosemary leaves

½ teaspoon chopped fresh or ¼ teaspoon dried thyme leaves

Butter, melted, if desired

1 Grease bottom and sides of 8×4- or 9×5-inch loaf pan with shortening or cooking spray.

2 In large bowl, mix 2 cups of the flour, the sugar, salt and yeast. Add warm water, parsley, shortening, rosemary and thyme. Beat with electric mixer on low speed 1 minute, scraping bowl frequently. Beat on medium speed 1 minute, scraping bowl frequently. Stir in remaining 1 cup flour until smooth.

3 Spread batter evenly in pan. Round top of loaf by patting with floured hands. Cover loosely with plastic wrap lightly sprayed with cooking spray; let rise in warm place about 40 minutes or until doubled in size.

4 Heat oven to 375°F. Bake 40 to 45 minutes or until loaf sounds hollow when tapped. Immediately remove from pan to cooling rack. Brush top of loaf with melted butter; sprinkle with additional chopped fresh herbs if desired. Cool.

1 Slice: Calories 80 (Calories from Fat 15); Total Fat 1.5g (Saturated Fat 0g; Trans Fat 0g); Cholesterol 0mg; Sodium 120mg; Total Carbohydrate 15g (Dietary Fiber 0g); Protein 2g **Exchanges:** 1 Starch **Carbohydrate Choices:** 1

bake smart We've flavored this loaf with rosemary and thyme, but you can vary the herbs to your taste. Basil, tarragon, dill or parsley would all be good to try.

wheat 'n flax bread

prep time: 30 minutes ✛ start to finish: 5 hours 35 minutes ✛ 1 LOAF (16 SLICES)

½ cup milk

½ cup water

1 tablespoon butter, softened

1¾ to 2 cups all-purpose flour

1 teaspoon salt

1 package regular active or fast-acting dry yeast (2¼ teaspoons)

3 tablespoons honey

1 cup whole wheat flour

¼ cup old-fashioned or quick-cooking oats

¼ cup ground flaxseed

Additional butter, melted, if desired

1 In 1-quart saucepan, heat milk, water and 1 tablespoon softened butter over medium heat until very warm (120°F to 130°F; butter will not melt). In large bowl, mix 1½ cups of the all-purpose flour, the salt and yeast. Add milk mixture and honey. Beat with electric mixer on low speed 1 minute, scraping bowl frequently. Beat on medium speed 1 minute, scraping bowl frequently. Stir in whole wheat flour, oats, flaxseed and enough remaining all-purpose flour to make dough easy to handle.

2 On lightly floured surface, knead dough about 5 minutes or until smooth and springy. Grease medium bowl with shortening or cooking spray. Place dough in bowl, turning dough to grease all sides. Cover bowl loosely with plastic wrap; let rise in warm place 1 hour to 1 hour 30 minutes or until doubled in size. Dough is ready if indentation remains when touched.

3 Grease bottom and sides of 8×4-inch loaf pan with shortening or cooking spray. On lightly floured surface, roll dough into 12×8-inch rectangle. Starting with 8-inch side, roll up tightly. Pinch edge of dough into roll to seal. Pinch each end of roll to seal; fold ends under loaf. Place seam side down in pan. Cover and let rise in warm place 45 to 60 minutes or until doubled in size.

4 Heat oven to 375°F. Uncover loaf. Bake 30 to 35 minutes or until loaf is golden brown and sounds hollow when tapped. Remove from pan to cooling rack. Brush top of loaf with melted butter. Cool completely, about 2 hours.

1 Slice: Calories 120 (Calories from Fat 20); Total Fat 2g (Saturated Fat 0.5g; Trans Fat 0g); Cholesterol 0mg; Sodium 160mg; Total Carbohydrate 21g (Dietary Fiber 2g); Protein 3g **Exchanges:** 1½ Starch **Carbohydrate Choices:** 1½

bake smart Toast slices of this bread and top with peanut butter and honey for an especially delicious treat.

triple-seed wheat bread

prep time: 30 minutes ✛ start to finish: 2 hours 35 minutes ✛ 1 LOAF (16 SLICES)

1½ to 2 cups all-purpose flour

2 tablespoons sugar

1½ teaspoons salt

1½ teaspoons poppy seed

1½ teaspoons sesame seed

1 teaspoon fennel seed

1 package regular active or fast-acting dry yeast (2¼ teaspoons)

1 cup water

2 tablespoons butter, softened

1½ to 2 cups whole wheat flour

1 egg white, beaten

1 teaspoon poppy seed

1 teaspoon sesame seed

1 teaspoon fennel seed

1 In large bowl, mix 1½ cups of the all-purpose flour, the sugar, salt, 1½ teaspoons poppy seed, 1½ teaspoons sesame seed, 1 teaspoon fennel seed and the yeast. In 1-quart saucepan, heat water and butter over medium heat, stirring frequently, until very warm (120°F to 130°F); stir into flour mixture until blended. Stir in remaining ½ cup all-purpose flour and enough of the whole wheat flour to make dough easy to handle.

2 Place dough on lightly floured surface; gently roll in flour to coat. Knead 8 minutes or until smooth and springy. Grease large bowl with shortening or cooking spray. Place dough in bowl, turning dough to grease all sides. Cover and let rise in warm place about 1 hour or until doubled in size. (If using fast-acting yeast, do not let rise 1 hour; cover and let rest on floured surface 10 minutes.)

3 Grease large cookie sheet with shortening or cooking spray. Roll dough into 20-inch rope. Place on cookie sheet. Curl each end of rope in the opposite direction to form a coiled S shape. Cover and let rise in warm place 30 to 40 minutes or until almost double.

4 Heat oven to 375°F. Brush egg white over dough; sprinkle with 1 teaspoon each poppy seed, sesame seed and fennel seed. Bake 20 to 25 minutes or until loaf is golden brown and sounds hollow when tapped. Remove from cookie sheet to cooling rack; cool.

1 Slice: Calories 110 (Calories from Fat 20); Total Fat 2.5g (Saturated Fat 1g; Trans Fat 0g); Cholesterol 0mg; Sodium 240mg; Total Carbohydrate 19g (Dietary Fiber 2g); Protein 3g **Exchanges:** 1 Starch, ½ Fat **Carbohydrate Choices:** 1

sun-dried tomato and olive bread

prep time: 40 minutes ✛ start to finish: 4 hours 10 minutes ✛ 1 LOAF (16 SLICES)

1½ teaspoons regular active dry yeast

½ teaspoon sugar

1⅓ cups warm water (105°F to 115°F)

1½ teaspoons salt

1 cup white whole wheat flour

½ cup cornmeal

1½ to 1¾ cups bread flour or all-purpose flour

⅓ cup sun-dried tomatoes in oil, drained, chopped and patted dry

⅓ cup pitted kalamata olives, quartered, patted dry

2 teaspoons olive oil

1 In large bowl, combine yeast and sugar; add ⅓ cup of the warm water. Let stand 10 minutes or until yeast is dissolved and foamy.

2 Add remaining 1 cup warm water and the salt. Stir in white whole wheat flour, cornmeal and 1½ cups of the bread flour, slowly adding additional flour as necessary to make dough easy to handle.

3 Place dough on lightly floured surface. Knead 10 minutes or until dough is smooth and springy. Gently knead in sun-dried tomatoes and olives. Grease large bowl with oil. Place dough in bowl, turning dough to grease all sides. Cover bowl loosely with plastic wrap sprayed with cooking spray; let rise in warm place about 1 hour or until doubled in size. Dough is ready if indentation remains when touched.

4 Line cookie sheet with cooking parchment paper. Gently push fist into dough to deflate. Place dough on lightly floured surface; press into 10×8-inch oval. Fold 1 long side up to the center; press edge into dough. Fold other long side over to center; press edge into dough (seam will be visible on top). Pinch and press each end to form point. Place dough on cookie sheet. Cover loosely with plastic wrap sprayed with cooking spray; let rise in warm place 45 to 60 minutes or until doubled in size.

5 Heat oven to 400°F. Brush loaf with oil. Bake 30 to 35 minutes or until golden brown and bottom sounds hollow when tapped. Cool completely on cooling rack, about 1 hour.

1 Slice: Calories 110 (Calories from Fat 15); Total Fat 1.5g (Saturated Fat 0g; Trans Fat 0g); Cholesterol 0mg; Sodium 250mg; Total Carbohydrate 20g (Dietary Fiber 1g); Protein 3g **Exchanges:** 1 Starch, ½ Other Carbohydrate **Carbohydrate Choices:** 1

bake smart Substitute green olives for the kalamata olives in this bread. Also, if basil plentiful in your garden, add 2 tablespoons of the chopped fresh herb to the dough when you knead in the olives and tomatoes.

This bread can be baked on a pizza stone for a crisper crust, if desired. For the best results, heat pizza stone at least 20 minutes before baking the bread.

no-knead oatmeal-molasses bread

prep time: 15 minutes ✛ start to finish: 2 hours 40 minutes ✛ 1 LOAF (16 SLICES)

¾ cup boiling water

½ cup old-fashioned or quick-cooking oats

3 tablespoons shortening

¼ cup light molasses

2 teaspoons salt

1 package regular active or fast-acting dry yeast (2¼ teaspoons)

¼ cup warm water (105°F to 115°F)

1 egg

2¾ cups all-purpose flour

1 Grease 9×5- or 8×4-inch loaf pan with shortening or cooking spray. In large bowl, mix boiling water, oats, shortening, molasses and salt; cool to lukewarm. In small bowl, dissolve yeast in warm water. Add yeast mixture, egg and 1½ cups of the flour to oat mixture. Beat with electric mixer on medium speed 2 minutes, scraping bowl frequently. Stir in remaining flour until completely mixed.

2 Spread batter evenly in pan (batter will be sticky; smooth and pat into shape with floured hands). Cover and let rise in warm place about 1 hour 30 minutes or until batter is 1 inch from top of 9×5-inch pan or reaches top of 8×4-inch pan.

3 Heat oven to 375°F. Bake 50 to 55 minutes or until loaf is brown and sounds hollow when tapped. (If loaf browns too quickly, cover loosely with foil during last 15 minutes of baking.) Remove from pan to cooling rack; cool. For a soft, shiny crust, brush top with butter if desired.

1 Slice: Calories 130 (Calories from Fat 30); Total Fat 3g (Saturated Fat 1g; Trans Fat 0g); Cholesterol 15mg; Sodium 300mg; Total Carbohydrate 22g (Dietary Fiber 1g); Protein 3g **Exchanges:** 1 Starch, ½ Other Carbohydrate, ½ Fat **Carbohydrate Choices:** 1½

gluten-free sandwich bread

prep time: 30 minutes ÷ start to finish: 3 hours 45 minutes ÷ 1 LOAF (16 SLICES)

- ¾ cup warm water (105°F to 115°F)
- 1 tablespoon fast-acting dry yeast
- ¾ cup plus 1 tablespoon tapioca flour
- ½ cup white rice flour
- ¼ cup sweet white sorghum flour
- ¼ cup garbanzo and fava flour
- ½ cup plus 2 tablespoons potato starch
- 1½ teaspoons salt
- 1½ teaspoons gluten-free baking powder
- 1 teaspoon xanthan gum
- 2 eggs
- ¼ cup sugar
- ¼ cup sunflower oil
- 1 teaspoon guar gum
- ½ teaspoon apple cider vinegar
- Cooking spray without flour

1 Spray bottom and sides of 8×4-inch loaf pan with cooking spray without flour. In small bowl, mix warm water and yeast; set aside.

2 In another small bowl, stir together all flours, the potato starch, salt, baking powder and xanthan gum; set aside.

3 In medium bowl, beat all remaining ingredients except cooking spray with electric mixer on medium speed 1 to 2 minutes. Beat in yeast mixture. Add flour mixture; beat on medium speed until thoroughly mixed. Pour into pan. Spray top of dough with cooking spray; if necessary, smooth top of dough with spatula. Cover with plastic wrap; let rise in warm place 1 hour to 1 hour 30 minutes or until dough rises to top of pan.

4 Heat oven to 375°F. Carefully remove plastic wrap from pan; bake 30 minutes. Reduce oven temperature to 350°F. Cover loaf with parchment paper; bake 25 to 30 minutes longer or until instant-read thermometer inserted in center of loaf reads 207°F. Cool 5 minutes. Remove from pan to cooling rack. Cool completely, about 40 minutes.

1 Slice: Calories 140 (Calories from Fat 40); Total Fat 4.5g (Saturated Fat 0.5g; Trans Fat 0g); Cholesterol 25mg; Sodium 280mg; Total Carbohydrate 22g (Dietary Fiber 1g); Protein 2g **Exchanges:** 1 Starch, ½ Other Carbohydrate, 1 Fat **Carbohydrate Choices:** 1½

Jean Duane, Alternative Cook { www.alternativecook.com }

bake smart Cooking gluten free? Always read labels to make sure each recipe ingredient is gluten free. Products and ingredient sources can change.

Gluten-free bread looks "done" long before it is done, so don't be afraid to bake it for an hour.

Don't omit the xanthan gum! It's necessary to hold the bread together. Look for it in the gluten-free section of your grocery store or a natural foods store.

sourdough bread

prep time: **45 minutes** + start to finish: **3 days 12 hours** + 2 LOAVES (16 SLICES EACH)

sourdough starter

- 1 teaspoon regular active dry yeast
- ¼ cup warm water (105°F to 115°F)
- ¾ cup milk
- 1 cup all-purpose flour

bread

- 1 cup sourdough starter
- 2½ cups all-purpose or bread flour
- 2 cups warm water (105°F to 115°F)
- 3¾ to 4¼ cups all-purpose or bread flour
- 3 tablespoons sugar
- 1 teaspoon salt
- 3 tablespoons vegetable oil

1 MAKE SOURDOUGH STARTER 3 DAYS BEFORE MAKING BREAD. In 3-quart glass bowl, dissolve yeast in ¼ cup warm water. Stir in milk. Gradually stir in 1 cup flour; beat until smooth. Cover with towel or cheesecloth; let stand in warm, draft-free place (80°F to 85°F) about 24 hours or until starter begins to ferment (bubbles will appear on surface of starter). If starter has not begun fermentation after 24 hours, discard and begin again. If fermentation has begun, stir well; cover tightly with plastic wrap and return to warm, draft-free place. Let starter stand 2 to 3 days or until foamy.

2 When starter has become foamy, stir well; pour into 1-quart crock or glass jar with tight-fitting cover. Store in refrigerator. Starter is ready to use when a clear liquid has risen to top. Stir before using.

3 TO MAKE SOURDOUGH BREAD, in 3-quart glass bowl, mix 1 cup sourdough starter, 2½ cups flour and 2 cups warm water with wooden spoon until smooth. Cover and let stand in warm, draft-free place 8 hours.

4 Add 3¾ cups flour, the sugar, salt and oil to mixture in bowl. Stir with wooden spoon until dough is smooth and flour is completely absorbed. (Dough should be just firm enough to gather into a ball. If necessary, gradually add remaining ½ cup flour, stirring until all flour is absorbed.)

5 On heavily floured surface, knead dough about 10 minutes or until smooth and springy. Grease large bowl with shortening. Place dough in bowl, turning to grease all sides. Cover bowl with plastic wrap; let rise in warm place about 1 hour 30 minutes or until doubled in size. Dough is ready if indentation remains when touched.

6 Grease large cookie sheet with shortening. Gently push fist into dough several times to remove air bubbles. Divide dough in half. Shape each half into a round, slightly flat loaf. Do not tear dough by pulling. Place loaves at opposite corners on cookie sheet. With serrated knife, make 3 (¼-inch-deep) slashes in top of each loaf. Cover and let rise about 45 minutes or until doubled in size.

7 Heat oven to 375°F. Brush loaves with cold water. Place in middle of oven. Bake 35 to 45 minutes, brushing occasionally with water, until loaves sound hollow when tapped. Remove from cookie sheet to cooling rack. Cool completely, about 1 hour.

1 Slice: Calories 110 (Calories from Fat 25); Total Fat 2.5g (Saturated Fat 0g; Trans Fat 0g); Cholesterol 0mg; Sodium 220mg; Total Carbohydrate 20g (Dietary Fiber 0g); Protein 3g **Exchanges:** 1½ Starch **Carbohydrate Choices:** 1

bake smart Use 1 cup starter in the Sourdough Bread recipe; reserve remaining starter for more bread recipes. To remaining starter, add ¾ cup milk and ¾ cup flour. Store covered at room temperature about 12 hours or until bubbles appear. Store in refrigerator.

Use starter regularly, every week or so. If the volume of the breads you bake begins to decrease, dissolve 1 teaspoon active dry yeast in ¼ cup warm water. Stir in ½ cup milk, ¾ cup flour and the remaining starter.

leftover bread magic

Do you have some bread that is left over after a meal? Don't throw it away—try using it in one of these delicious recipes. We've included two easy French toast recipes that are perfect for breakfast and two decadent bread pudding recipes for dessert. Plus, the recipe for croutons makes a great topper for a salad or casserole any time. And remember that it's easy to substitute the type of bread that you might have on hand for what is called for in the recipe—it's all good! So go ahead and use your imagination to transform leftover bread into magically delicious recipes.

cinnamon-raisin bread pudding

prep time: 10 minutes ✛ start to finish: 2 hours 40 minutes ✛ 8 SERVINGS

6 cups cinnamon-raisin bread cubes (12 to 14 slices bread)

½ cup raisins

1 can (14 oz) sweetened condensed milk

1 cup fat-free egg product

¾ cup warm water (110°F to 115°F)

1 teaspoon vanilla

½ teaspoon ground cinnamon

1 Spray inside of 3½- to 6-quart slow cooker with cooking spray.

2 Place bread cubes in cooker. Sprinkle with raisins. In medium bowl, mix remaining ingredients; pour over bread cubes and raisins.

3 Cover and cook on High heat setting 2½ to 3 hours or until toothpick inserted in center comes out clean. Serve warm.

1 Serving: Calories 280 (Calories from Fat 50); Total Fat 6g (Saturated Fat 3g; Trans Fat 0g); Cholesterol 15mg; Sodium 220mg; Total Carbohydrate 49g (Dietary Fiber 2g); Protein 9g **Exchanges:** 3 Starch, 1 Fat **Carbohydrate Choices:** 3

bake smart Using bread that is a day or two old is best because it will be firmer and drier than fresh bread. Bread that is too fresh and soft will give you a bread pudding that is too moist and soggy. We use an egg substitute because it is pasteurized, making it safe for long, slow cooking.

Cinnamon-raisin bread adds a little more flavor to the pudding, but cubed French bread also makes an excellent pudding. If using French bread, you may want to increase the raisins to ¾ cup and the cinnamon to ¾ teaspoon.

bread pudding with whiskey sauce

prep time: 25 minutes ✛ start to finish: 2 hours 20 minutes ✛ 12 SERVINGS

bread pudding

- 4 whole eggs
- 1 egg yolk
- ¾ cup sugar
- 2½ cups milk
- 2½ cups whipping cream
- 1 tablespoon vanilla
- 1 teaspoon ground cinnamon
- 12 oz French or other firm bread, cut into ½-inch slices, then cut into 1½-inch pieces (10 cups)
- ½ cup raisins, if desired
- 2 tablespoons sugar
- ½ teaspoon ground cinnamon
- 2 tablespoons butter, melted

whiskey sauce

- ½ cup butter
- 2 tablespoons water
- 1 egg
- 1 cup sugar
- 2 tablespoons whiskey or bourbon or 1 teaspoon brandy extract

1 Heat oven to 325°F. Grease bottom and sides of 13×9-inch (3-quart) glass baking dish with shortening or spray with cooking spray.

2 In large bowl, beat 4 whole eggs, 1 egg yolk and ¾ cup sugar with whisk until well blended. Beat in milk, whipping cream, vanilla and 1 teaspoon cinnamon until well blended. Stir in 7 cups of the bread pieces and the raisins. Let stand 20 minutes. Pour into baking dish. Lightly press remaining 3 cups bread pieces on top of mixture in baking dish.

3 In small bowl, stir 2 tablespoons sugar and ½ teaspoon cinnamon until well blended. Brush top of bread mixture with 2 tablespoons melted butter; sprinkle with cinnamon-sugar. Bake uncovered 55 to 65 minutes or until top is puffed and light golden brown (center will jiggle slightly). Cool 30 minutes.

4 Meanwhile, in 1-quart saucepan, melt ½ cup butter over low heat; do not allow to simmer. Remove from heat; cool 10 minutes. In small bowl, mix water and 1 egg; stir into butter until blended. Stir in 1 cup sugar. Cook over medium-low heat, stirring constantly, until sugar is dissolved and mixture begins to boil; remove from heat. Stir in whiskey. Cool at least 10 minutes before serving.

5 Serve sauce over warm bread pudding. Store remaining dessert and sauce covered in refrigerator.

1 Serving: Calories 500 (Calories from Fat 270); Total Fat 30g (Saturated Fat 16g; Trans Fat 1.5g); Cholesterol 190mg; Sodium 300mg; Total Carbohydrate 50g (Dietary Fiber 0g); Protein 8g **Exchanges:** 2 Starch, 1½ Other Carbohydrate, 5½ Fat **Carbohydrate Choices:** 3

croutons

prep time: 10 minutes + start to finish: 55 minutes +
16 SERVINGS

10 slices (½ inch thick) firm white
    or whole-grain bread
½ cup butter, melted

1 Heat oven to 300°F. Cut bread slices into ½-inch
cubes. Spread in single layer in 15×10×1-inch pan.
Drizzle butter evenly over bread cubes; toss to coat.

2 Bake 30 to 35 minutes, stirring occasionally, or until
golden brown, dry and crisp. Cool completely. Store
tightly covered at room temperature up to 2 days.

1 Serving: Calories 90 (Calories from Fat 60); Total Fat 6g (Saturated Fat 4g; Trans Fat 0g);
Cholesterol 15mg; Sodium 150mg; Total Carbohydrate 8g (Dietary Fiber 0g); Protein 1g
Exchanges: ½ Starch, 1 Fat **Carbohydrate Choices:** ½

garlic croutons: Add 3 cloves garlic, very finely
chopped, or ¼ teaspoon garlic powder to butter before
drizzling over bread cubes.

herbed croutons: Drizzle bread cubes with olive oil
instead of butter. Sprinkle with 2 teaspoons Italian seasoning and ½ teaspoon salt; toss to coat.

french toast

prep time: 5 minutes + start to finish: 25 minutes +
8 SLICES

3 eggs
¾ cup milk
1 tablespoon sugar
¼ teaspoon vanilla
⅛ teaspoon salt
8 slices firm-textured sandwich bread, Texas
    toast or 1-inch-thick slices French bread

1 In medium bowl, beat eggs, milk, sugar, vanilla
and salt with whisk until well mixed. Pour into
shallow bowl.

2 Heat griddle or skillet over medium heat or to 375°F.
(To test griddle, sprinkle with a few drops of water.
If bubbles jump around, heat is just right.) Grease
griddle with vegetable oil if necessary (or spray with
cooking spray before heating).

3 Dip bread into egg mixture. Place on griddle. Cook
about 4 minutes on each side or until golden brown.

1 Slice: Calories 230 (Calories from Fat 30); Total Fat 3.5g (Saturated Fat 1g; Trans Fat 0g);
Cholesterol 80mg; Sodium 490mg; Total Carbohydrate 39g (Dietary Fiber 1g); Protein 10g
Exchanges: 2 Starch, ½ Other Carbohydrate, ½ Medium-Fat Meat **Carbohydrate Choices:** 2½

oven french toast: Heat oven to 450°F. Generously butter 15×10×1-inch pan. Heat pan in oven 1 minute; remove from oven. Arrange dipped bread in hot pan.
Drizzle any remaining egg mixture over bread. Bake 5 to
8 minutes or until bottoms are golden brown; turn bread.
Bake 2 to 4 minutes longer or until golden brown.

bake smart Olive oil can be
substituted for the butter. After drizzling
bread cubes with oil, sprinkle evenly with
½ teaspoon coarse (kosher or sea) salt;
toss to coat.

bake smart To lighten the nutritional
profile to 2 grams of fat and 95 calories per
serving, substitute 1 whole egg and 2 egg whites
for the 3 eggs and use ⅔ cup fat-free (skim) milk.
Increase vanilla to ½ teaspoon.

apricot-stuffed french toast

prep time: 15 minutes ✛ start to finish: 1 hour 10 minutes ✛ 6 SERVINGS (2 SLICES EACH)

1 loaf (8 oz) or ½ loaf (1-lb size) day-old French bread

1 package (3 oz) cream cheese, softened

3 tablespoons apricot preserves

¼ teaspoon grated lemon peel

3 eggs

¾ cup half-and-half or milk

2 tablespoons granulated sugar

1 teaspoon vanilla

⅛ teaspoon salt

⅛ teaspoon ground nutmeg, if desired

2 tablespoons butter, melted

Powdered sugar, if desired

1 Spray 13×9-inch pan with cooking spray. Cut bread crosswise into 12 (1-inch) slices. Cut horizontal slit in the side of each bread slice, cutting to, but not through, the other edge.

2 In medium bowl, beat cream cheese, preserves and lemon peel with electric mixer on medium speed about 1 minute or until well mixed. Spread about 2 teaspoons of cream cheese mixture inside slit in each bread slice. Place stuffed bread slices in pan.

3 In medium bowl, beat eggs, half-and-half, granulated sugar, vanilla, salt and nutmeg with fork or whisk until well mixed. Pour egg mixture over bread slices in pan; turn slices carefully to coat. Cover and refrigerate at least 30 minutes but no longer than 24 hours.

4 Heat oven to 425°F. Uncover French toast; drizzle with butter. Bake 20 to 25 minutes or until golden brown. Sprinkle with powdered sugar.

1 Serving: Calories 310 (Calories from Fat 150); Total Fat 16g (Saturated Fat 8g; Trans Fat 1g); Cholesterol 145mg; Sodium 380mg; Total Carbohydrate 32g (Dietary Fiber 1g); Protein 9g **Exchanges:** 1 Starch, 1 Other Carbohydrate, 1 High-Fat Meat, 1½ Fat **Carbohydrate Choices:** 2

walnut-gorgonzola baguettes

prep time: 25 minutes ✛ start to finish: 5 hours ✛ 2 LOAVES (12 SLICES EACH)

2½ to 3 cups bread flour

1 package regular active dry yeast (2¼ teaspoons)

1 cup very warm water (120°F to 130°F)

1 teaspoon salt

⅓ cup chopped walnuts

⅓ cup crumbled Gorgonzola cheese

1 In large bowl, mix 1½ cups of the flour and the yeast. Add warm water. Beat with electric mixer on low speed 1 minute, scraping bowl frequently. Cover tightly with plastic wrap; let stand about 1 hour or until bubbly.

2 Stir in salt and enough remaining flour to form a soft dough. On lightly floured surface, knead dough 5 to 10 minutes or until dough is smooth and springy (dough will be soft). Grease large bowl with shortening or cooking spray. Place dough in bowl, turning dough to grease all sides. Sprinkle walnuts and cheese over dough. Cover bowl loosely with plastic wrap; let rise in warm place 1 hour to 1 hour 15 minutes or until doubled in size. Dough is ready if indentation remains when touched.

3 Grease large cookie sheet with shortening or cooking spray. On lightly floured surface, knead dough until nuts and cheese are worked into dough. Sprinkle top of dough with flour. Divide dough in half. Gently shape each half into a narrow loaf, about 12 inches long. Place about 4 inches apart on cookie sheet. Using spray bottle with fine mist, spray loaves with cool water. Let rise uncovered in warm place about 1 hour or until doubled in size.

4 Place 8- or 9-inch square pan on bottom rack in oven; add hot water to pan until about ½ inch from top. Heat oven to 425°F.

5 Using serrated knife, carefully cut ¼-inch-deep slashes diagonally across loaves at 2-inch intervals. Spray tops of loaves with cool water. Place loaves in oven and spray again.

6 Bake 15 to 20 minutes or until loaves are deep golden with crisp crust and sound hollow when tapped. Remove from cookie sheet to cooling rack. Cool completely, about 1 hour.

1 Slice: Calories 70 (Calories from Fat 15); Total Fat 2g (Saturated Fat 0g; Trans Fat 0g); Cholesterol 0mg; Sodium 125mg; Total Carbohydrate 11g (Dietary Fiber 0g); Protein 3g **Exchanges:** 1 Starch **Carbohydrate Choices:** 1

pumpernickel bread

prep time: **10 minutes** ✛ start to finish: **3 hours 40 minutes** ✛ 1 LOAF (12 SLICES)

1 cup plus 2 tablespoons water

1½ teaspoons salt

⅓ cup molasses

2 tablespoons vegetable oil

1 cup plus 1 tablespoon rye flour

1 cup plus 2 tablespoons whole wheat flour

1½ cups bread flour

3 tablespoons unsweetened baking cocoa

1½ teaspoons instant coffee granules or crystals

1 tablespoon caraway seed

1 teaspoon bread machine or fast-acting dry yeast

1 Measure carefully, placing all ingredients in bread machine pan in the order recommended by the manufacturer.

2 Select Whole Wheat or Basic/White cycle. Use Medium or Light crust color. Remove baked bread from pan; cool on cooling rack.

1 Slice: Calories 190 (Calories from Fat 30); Total Fat 3g (Saturated Fat 0g; Trans Fat 0g); Cholesterol 0mg; Sodium 300mg; Total Carbohydrate 36g (Dietary Fiber 3g); Protein 5g **Exchanges:** 1½ Starch, 1 Other Carbohydrate, ½ Fat **Carbohydrate Choices:** 2½

bake smart Here's your chance to make a great deli corned beef sandwich: Spread slices of pumpernickel bread with a spicy mustard. Pile one slice high with slices of corned beef, drained canned sauerkraut and Swiss cheese, and add the other slice. Serve with big, crisp kosher dill pickles.

Pumpernickel bread is a heavier dark bread. This recipe uses both rye and whole wheat flours. The molasses, cocoa and coffee not only add flavor, but they also increase the deep brown color.

beer and pretzel bread

prep time: 10 minutes ✛ start to finish: 3 hours 40 minutes ✛ 1 LOAF (12 SLICES)

¾ cup regular or
   nonalcoholic beer

⅓ cup water

2 tablespoons butter,
   softened

3 cups bread flour

1 tablespoon packed
   brown sugar

1 teaspoon ground
   mustard

1 teaspoon salt

1½ teaspoons bread
   machine yeast

½ cup bite-size pretzel
   pieces, about 1×¾ inch,
   or pretzel rods, cut into
   1-inch pieces

1 Measure carefully, placing all ingredients except pretzels in bread machine pan in order recommended by the manufacturer.

2 Select Basic/White cycle. Use Medium or Light crust color. Do not use delay cycle.

3 Add pretzels 5 minutes before the last kneading cycle ends. Remove baked bread from pan; cool on cooling rack.

1 Slice: Calories 150 (Calories from Fat 20); Total Fat 2.5g (Saturated Fat 1.5g; Trans Fat 0g); Cholesterol 5mg; Sodium 250mg; Total Carbohydrate 28g (Dietary Fiber 1g); Protein 3g **Exchanges:** 2 Starch **Carbohydrate Choices:** 2

bread machine tips

You might choose to use your bread machine for making bread. Here are some special techniques to help ensure your success.

✛ Follow the directions in the manual that comes with your machine, and add ingredients in the order they recommend.

✛ Carefully measure ingredients using standard measuring cups and spoons. Even small variations can affect the finished bread.

✛ Use bread machine yeast unless directed otherwise. The finer granules in this product disperse more thoroughly during mixing and kneading.

✛ Opening the machine during rising or baking can cause the loaf to collapse, so don't check the progress except during mixing and kneading.

✛ Don't use the delay cycle with recipes using eggs, dairy products (except butter), honey, meat or fresh fruits and vegetables because bacteria can grow during that cycle.

✛ Keep the area around the machine open for good ventilation.

tomato-peppercorn-cheese bread

prep time: 20 minutes + **start to finish: 3 hours 5 minutes** + 1 LOAF (16 SLICES)

1 cup boiling water

1 cup Fiber One original bran cereal

½ cup dry-pack sun-dried tomatoes, diced

2 packages regular active dry yeast (4½ teaspoons)

1 tablespoon sugar

¼ cup warm water (105°F to 115°F)

2 tablespoons vegetable oil

1 teaspoon salt

2 teaspoons black peppercorns, ground

½ cup shredded Cheddar cheese (2 oz)

2¼ to 2½ cups all-purpose flour

1 In small bowl, pour boiling water over cereal and tomatoes; let stand 5 minutes or until mixture is lukewarm.

2 In large bowl, dissolve yeast and sugar in warm water. Stir in cereal mixture, oil, salt, ground peppercorns, cheese and enough of the flour to make a soft dough. Place dough on lightly floured surface. Knead 5 minutes or until smooth and springy. Place dough in greased bowl and turn greased side up. Cover and let rise in warm place 1 hour to 1 hour 30 minutes or until doubled in size.

3 Grease large cookie sheet with shortening or cooking spray. Gently push fist into dough to deflate. Shape dough into 10-inch loaf. Place on cookie sheet. Cover and let rise in warm place 30 to 40 minutes or until almost doubled in size.

4 Heat oven to 350°F. Using serrated knife, make ¼-inch-deep slits in top of loaf. Bake 35 minutes or until loaf sounds hollow when tapped on bottom.

1 Slice: Calories 120 (Calories from Fat 30); Total Fat 3.5g (Saturated Fat 1g; Trans Fat 0g); Cholesterol 0mg; Sodium 220mg; Total Carbohydrate 19g (Dietary Fiber 2g); Protein 4g **Exchanges:** 1 Starch, ½ Other Carbohydrate, ½ Fat **Carbohydrate Choices:** 1

bake smart Add more flavor, not more cheese. An aged or jalapeño-Cheddar cheese will boost the flavor without increasing calories.

sage-raisin wheat bread

prep time: **15 minutes** ✛ start to finish: **3 hours 20 minutes** ✛ 1 LOAF (16 SLICES)

1¼ cups water
  2 tablespoons butter, softened
1½ cups bread flour
1½ cups whole wheat flour
  2 tablespoons sugar
1½ teaspoons salt
  ¾ teaspoon crumbled dried sage leaves
1¾ teaspoons bread machine or fast-acting dry yeast
  ¾ cup golden raisins
  1 egg, beaten

1 Measure carefully, placing all ingredients except raisins and egg in bread machine pan in the order recommended by the manufacturer. Add raisins at the Raisin/Nut signal.

2 Select Dough/Manual cycle. Do not use delay cycle.

3 Remove dough from pan, using lightly floured hands. Cover and let rest 10 minutes on lightly floured surface.

4 Grease large cookie sheet. Cut off one-third of the dough; shape into small ball (about 3 inches). Shape remaining dough into large ball (about 5 inches). Place large ball on cookie sheet; place small ball on large ball. Holding thumb and first two fingers together, push into the middle of the small ball, pushing through center of dough until almost touching cookie sheet. Cover and let rise in warm place 30 to 45 minutes or until doubled in size. Dough is ready if indentation remains when touched.

5 Heat oven to 400°F. Brush egg over loaf. Using serrated knife, cut ¼-inch-deep vertical slashes on sides of each ball about 2 inches apart. Bake 18 to 20 minutes or until loaf is deep golden brown and sounds hollow when tapped. Remove from cookie sheet to cooling rack; cool.

1 Slice: Calories 130 (Calories from Fat 20); Total Fat 2.5g (Saturated Fat 1g; Trans Fat 0g); Cholesterol 15mg; Sodium 240mg; Total Carbohydrate 25g (Dietary Fiber 2g); Protein 4g **Exchanges:** 1½ Starch, ½ Fat **Carbohydrate Choices:** 1½

bake smart If your bread machine doesn't have a Raisin/Nut signal, add the raisins 5 to 10 minutes before the last kneading cycle ends. Check your bread machine's use-and-care book for how long the last cycle runs.

caramelized-onion bread

prep time: 15 minutes ✛ **start to finish: 3 hours 45 minutes** ✛ 1 LOAF (1½ LB); 12 SLICES

caramelized onions

- 1 tablespoon butter
- 2 medium onions, sliced

bread

- 1 cup water
- 1 tablespoon olive or vegetable oil
- 3 cups bread flour
- 2 tablespoons sugar
- 1 teaspoon salt
- 1¼ teaspoons bread machine or fast-acting dry yeast

1 In 10-inch skillet, melt butter over medium-low heat. Cook onions in butter 10 to 15 minutes, stirring occasionally, until onions are brown and caramelized; remove from heat.

2 Measure carefully, placing all ingredients except onions in bread machine pan in the order recommended by the manufacturer.

3 Select Basic/White cycle. Use Medium or Light crust color. Do not use delay cycle. Add ½ cup of the onions at the Raisin/Nut signal or 5 to 10 minutes before last kneading cycle ends. (Reserve any remaining onions for another use.) Remove baked bread from pan; cool on cooling rack.

1 Slice: Calories 160 (Calories from Fat 20); Total Fat 2.5g (Saturated Fat 1g; Trans Fat 0g); Cholesterol 0mg; Sodium 210mg; Total Carbohydrate 30g (Dietary Fiber 2g); Protein 4g **Exchanges:** 2 Starch **Carbohydrate Choices:** 2

bake smart The onions need to cook slowly so the natural sugar in them can caramelize and develop that delicious, delicate sweet flavor. So be patient, and don't increase the heat to make the onions brown more quickly.

If your bread machine doesn't have a Raisin/Nut signal, add the caramelized onions 5 to 10 minutes before the last kneading cycle ends. Check your bread machine's use-and-care book to find out how long the last cycle runs.

stollen

prep time: 35 minutes ✛ start to finish: 12 hours ✛ 2 LOAVES (16 SLICES EACH)

stollen

- 1 package regular active or fast-acting dry yeast (2¼ teaspoons)
- ¾ cup warm water (105°F to 115°F)
- ½ cup granulated sugar
- ½ teaspoon salt
- 3 eggs
- 1 egg, separated
- ½ cup butter, softened
- 3½ cups all-purpose flour or bread flour
- ½ cup blanched almonds
- ¼ cup chopped candied citron
- ¼ cup chopped candied cherries, if desired
- ¼ cup raisins
- 1 tablespoon grated lemon peel
- 1 tablespoon butter, softened
- 1 tablespoon water

glaze

- 1⅓ cups powdered sugar
- 2 tablespoons milk

1 In large bowl, dissolve yeast in ¾ cup warm water. Beat in granulated sugar, the salt, eggs, egg yolk, ½ cup butter and 1¾ cups of the flour with electric mixer on medium speed 10 minutes, scraping bowl constantly. Stir in remaining 1¾ cups flour, the almonds, citron, cherries, raisins and lemon peel. Scrape batter from side of bowl. Cover and let rise in warm place 1 hour 30 minutes to 2 hours or until doubled in size. Dough is ready if indentation remains when touched. Cover and refrigerate egg white.

2 Stir down batter by beating about 25 strokes. Cover tightly and refrigerate at least 8 hours or overnight.

3 Grease cookie sheet. Place dough on generously floured surface; gently roll in flour to coat. Divide dough in half; press each half into 10×7-inch oval. Spread with 1 tablespoon butter. Fold ovals lengthwise in half; press only folded edge firmly. Place on cookie sheet. Beat egg white and 1 tablespoon water; brush over folded ovals. Cover and let rise in warm place 45 to 60 minutes or until doubled in size.

4 Heat oven to 375°F. Bake 20 to 25 minutes or until golden brown.

5 In medium bowl, mix powdered sugar and milk until smooth. Spread glaze over warm stollen.

1 Slice: Calories 280 (Calories from Fat 90); Total Fat 10g (Saturated Fat 4.5g; Trans Fat 0g); Cholesterol 55mg; Sodium 140mg; Total Carbohydrate 42g (Dietary Fiber 1g); Protein 5g **Exchanges:** 1½ Starch, 1½ Other Carbohydrate, 2 Fat **Carbohydrate Choices:** 3

bake smart Tuck one or two of these baked loaves in the freezer for up to 2 months.

Instead of making the glaze, you can sprinkle the top of the stollen with powdered sugar.

cinnamon swirl raisin bread

prep time: 35 minutes ✛ start to finish: 3 hours 10 minutes ✛ 2 LOAVES (16 SLICES EACH)

6 to 6½ cups all-purpose flour

1 cup sugar

1 tablespoon salt

2 packages regular active or fast-acting dry yeast (4½ teaspoons)

2 cups water

¼ cup vegetable oil

2 eggs

1 cup raisins

1 tablespoon vegetable oil

1 tablespoon ground cinnamon

Vegetable oil

1 tablespoon butter, softened

1 In large bowl, mix 3 cups of the flour, ½ cup of the sugar, the salt and yeast. In 1-quart saucepan, heat water and oil until very warm (120°F to 130°F); stir into flour mixture. Stir in eggs; beat until smooth. Stir in enough remaining flour to make dough easy to handle.

2 Place dough on lightly floured surface; gently roll in flour to coat. Knead 8 to 10 minutes or until smooth and springy. Grease large bowl with shortening or cooking spray. Place dough in bowl, turning dough to grease all sides. (If desired, at this point, dough can be refrigerated up to 4 days.) Cover and let rise in warm place about 1 hour or until doubled in size. (If using fast-acting yeast, do not let rise 1 hour; cover and let rest on floured surface 10 minutes.)

3 Grease 2 (9×5-inch) loaf pans with shortening or cooking spray. Gently push fist into dough to deflate; divide in half. Knead ½ cup of the raisins into each half. Roll each half into 18×9-inch rectangle. Brush 1 tablespoon oil over rectangles.

4 In small bowl, mix remaining ½ cup sugar and the cinnamon; sprinkle each rectangle with half of cinnamon-sugar mixture. Starting with 9-inch side, roll up each rectangle. Pinch edge of dough into roll to seal. Press each end with side of hand to seal; fold ends under loaf. Place loaves, seam sides down, in pans. Brush oil over loaves. Cover and let rise in warm place about 1 hour or until doubled in size.

5 Move oven rack to lowest position. Heat oven to 375°F. Bake 30 to 35 minutes or until loaves are deep golden brown and sound hollow when tapped. Remove from pans to cooling rack. Brush butter over loaves; cool.

1 Slice: Calories 160 (Calories from Fat 30); Total Fat 3.5g (Saturated Fat 0.5g; Trans Fat 0g); Cholesterol 15mg; Sodium 230mg; Total Carbohydrate 28g (Dietary Fiber 1g); Protein 3g **Exchanges:** 1 Starch, 1 Other Carbohydrate, ½ Fat **Carbohydrate Choices:** 2

cinnamon, raisin and walnut wheat bread

prep time: **25 minutes** ✛ start to finish: **3 hours 20 minutes** ✛ 1 LARGE LOAF (24 SLICES)

2 **cups whole wheat flour**

1 **package regular active or fast-acting dry yeast (2¼ teaspoons)**

2 **cups very warm water (120°F to 130°F)**

2 **tablespoons packed brown sugar**

2 **tablespoons olive or vegetable oil**

2 **teaspoons salt**

2 **teaspoons ground cinnamon**

2 **to 2½ cups bread flour**

1 **cup coarsely chopped walnuts, toasted if desired**＊

1 **cup raisins, dried cherries or dried cranberries**

Cornmeal

1 In large bowl, mix whole wheat flour and yeast. Add warm water. Beat with whisk or electric mixer on low speed 1 minute, scraping bowl frequently. Cover tightly with plastic wrap; let stand 15 minutes.

2 Stir in brown sugar, oil, salt, cinnamon and 1 cup of the bread flour; beat until smooth. Stir in enough remaining bread flour, ½ cup at a time, until a soft, smooth dough forms.

3 Place dough on lightly floured surface. Knead 5 to 10 minutes or until dough is smooth and springy. Knead in walnuts and raisins. Grease large bowl with shortening. Place dough in bowl, turning dough to grease all sides. Cover bowl loosely with plastic wrap; let rise in warm place about 1 hour or until doubled in size. Dough is ready if indentation remains when touched.

4 Grease uninsulated cookie sheet with shortening or cooking spray; sprinkle with cornmeal. Place dough on lightly floured surface. Gently shape into an even, round ball, without releasing all of the bubbles in dough. Stretch sides of dough downward to make a smooth top. Place loaf with smooth side up on cookie sheet. Spray loaf with cool water. Cover loosely with plastic wrap; let rise in warm place 45 to 60 minutes or until almost doubled in size.

5 Heat oven to 375°F. Spray loaf with cool water. Using serrated knife, carefully cut ¼-inch-deep slashes in tic-tac-toe pattern on top of loaf.

6 Place in oven; spray with cool water. Bake 35 to 40 minutes or until loaf is dark brown and sounds hollow when tapped. Remove from cookie sheet to cooling rack; cool.

＊To toast walnuts, bake in ungreased shallow pan at 350°F for 6 to 10 minutes, stirring occasionally, until light brown.

1 Slice: Calories 150 (Calories from Fat 40); Total Fat 4.5g (Saturated Fat 0.5g; Trans Fat 0g); Cholesterol 0mg; Sodium 200mg; Total Carbohydrate 24g (Dietary Fiber 2g); Protein 4g **Exchanges:** 1 Starch, ½ Other Carbohydrate, ½ Fat **Carbohydrate Choices:** 1½

fruit and almond bread: Omit cinnamon. Substitute chopped almonds for the walnuts and diced dried fruit for the raisins.

apple-pecan bread: Substitute chopped pecans for the walnuts and chopped dried apples for the raisins.

s'more swirl bread

prep time: **20 minutes** ✛ start to finish: **2 hours 40 minutes** ✛ 1 LOAF (16 SLICES)

filling

¼	cup finely crushed graham crackers (4 squares)
2	teaspoons sugar
¾	cup miniature marshmallows
1½	bars (1.55 oz each) milk chocolate candy, finely chopped

bread

2	cups whole wheat flour
1	cup all-purpose flour
⅓	cup sugar
1	teaspoon salt
1	package regular active or fast-acting dry yeast (2¼ teaspoons)
1¼	cups very warm milk (120°F to 130°F)
2	tablespoons vegetable oil
1	egg
2	teaspoons butter, melted

1 Grease bottom and sides of 9×5- or 8×4-inch loaf pan with shortening or cooking spray. In small bowl, mix graham cracker crumbs and 2 teaspoons sugar. Reserve 2 teaspoons mixture for topping baked bread.

2 In large bowl, mix flours, ⅓ cup sugar, the salt and yeast. Add warm milk, oil and egg; stir until flour is completely moistened and stiff batter forms. Spoon half of batter into pan, spreading completely to sides of pan.

3 In the following order, sprinkle batter with marshmallows, graham cracker mixture and chocolate, keeping at least a ½-inch border of uncovered batter on all sides. Spoon remaining batter as evenly as possible over filling; carefully and gently spread batter to sides of pan. Cover loosely with plastic wrap lightly sprayed with cooking spray and let rise in warm place 1 hour to 1 hour 10 minutes or until doubled in size.

4 Heat oven to 350°F. Bake 35 to 40 minutes or until top of loaf is deep golden brown and loaf sounds hollow when tapped. Immediately remove from pan to cooling rack. Brush top of loaf with melted butter; sprinkle with reserved 2 teaspoons graham cracker mixture. Cool 30 minutes.

1 Slice: Calories 170 (Calories from Fat 40); Total Fat 4.5g (Saturated Fat 1.5g; Trans Fat 0g); Cholesterol 15mg; Sodium 180mg; Total Carbohydrate 28g (Dietary Fiber 2g); Protein 4g **Exchanges:** ½ Starch, 1½ Other Carbohydrate, 1 Fat **Carbohydrate Choices:** 2

dried cherry and walnut bread

prep time: 20 minutes ✛ start to finish: 3 hours 40 minutes ✛ 1 LOAF (16 SLICES)

3¼ to 3¾ cups bread flour

2 tablespoons sugar

1 package fast-acting dry yeast (2¼ teaspoons)

1¼ cups very warm water (120°F to 130°F)

2 tablespoons vegetable oil

1 cup walnuts, coarsely chopped

1 cup dried cherries

1 tablespoon orange peel

1 teaspoon salt

1 tablespoon cornmeal

1 teaspoon milk

1 In large bowl, mix 1½ cups of the flour, the sugar and yeast. Add warm water and oil. Beat with electric mixer on low speed 1 minute, scraping bowl frequently. Beat on medium speed 1 minute, scraping bowl frequently.

2 Stir in 1¾ cups of the remaining flour, the walnuts, cherries, orange peel and salt using wooden spoon until dough pulls away from side of bowl and forms sticky ball. Place dough on lightly floured surface. Knead 2 to 3 minutes or until dough is smooth and springy, using enough of the remaining ½ cup flour as necessary to form into smooth ball.

3 Grease large bowl with oil. Place dough in bowl, turning dough to grease all sides. Cover bowl loosely with plastic wrap; let rise in warm place 1 hour or until doubled in size.

4 Lightly grease large cookie sheet with shortening or cooking spray; sprinkle with cornmeal. Gently push fist into dough to deflate. Place dough on lightly floured surface. Gently shape into smooth ball by stretching surface of dough around to bottom on all sides; pinch bottom to seal. Place on cookie sheet. Cover dough loosely with plastic wrap sprayed with cooking spray; let rise in warm place 30 to 40 minutes or until doubled in size.

5 Heat oven to 350°F. Brush top of loaf with milk. Using serrated knife, cut 3 (¼-inch-deep) slashes across top of dough. Bake 35 to 40 minutes or until loaf is deep golden brown and sounds hollow when tapped. Cool completely on cooling rack, about 1 hour.

1 Slice: Calories 210 (Calories from Fat 60); Total Fat 7g (Saturated Fat 1g; Trans Fat 0g); Cholesterol 0mg; Sodium 150mg; Total Carbohydrate 32g (Dietary Fiber 2g); Protein 5g **Exchanges:** 1½ Starch, ½ Other Carbohydrate, 1½ Fat **Carbohydrate Choices:** 2

monkey bread

prep time: 35 minutes ✛ start to finish: 3 hours 25 minutes ✛ 16 SERVINGS

3½ to 4 cups all-purpose flour

⅓ cup granulated sugar

1 teaspoon salt

1 package regular active or fast-acting dry yeast (2¼ teaspoons)

1 cup water

⅓ cup butter, room temperature

1 egg

¾ cup granulated sugar

½ cup finely chopped nuts

1 teaspoon ground cinnamon

½ cup butter, melted

1 In large bowl, stir 2 cups of the flour, ⅓ cup sugar, the salt and yeast with spoon until well mixed. In 1-quart saucepan, heat water and ⅓ cup butter over medium-low heat, stirring frequently, until very warm (120°F to 130°F). Add water mixture and egg to flour mixture. Beat with whisk or electric mixer on low speed 1 minute, until smooth. Beat on medium speed 1 minute. Using spoon, stir in enough of the remaining flour, 1 cup at a time, until dough is soft, leaves side of bowl and is easy to handle (dough may be slightly sticky).

2 Place dough on lightly floured surface; turn to coat with flour. Knead dough about 10 minutes, until dough is smooth and springy.

3 Spray large bowl with cooking spray. Place dough in bowl, turning dough to grease all sides. Cover bowl loosely with plastic wrap; let rise in warm place 1 hour to 1 hour 30 minutes or until doubled in size. Dough is ready if indentation remains when touched.

4 Spray 10-inch angel food (tube) cake pan or 12-cup fluted tube cake pan with baking spray with flour. (If angel food cake pan has removable bottom, line pan with foil before spraying to help prevent the sugar mixture from dripping into the oven during baking.) In small bowl, mix ¾ cup sugar, the nuts and cinnamon.

5 Gently push fist into dough to deflate. Shape dough into about 25 balls, 1½ inches in diameter. Dip each ball into melted butter, then into cinnamon-sugar mixture. Place balls in single layer in pan so they just touch. Top with another layer of balls. Cover pan loosely with plastic wrap; let rise in warm place about 40 minutes or until doubled in size. Remove plastic wrap.

6 Move oven rack to low position so that top of pan will be in center of oven. Heat oven to 375°F. Bake 35 to 40 minutes or until golden brown. (If bread browns too quickly, cover loosely with foil.) Run a metal spatula or knife around edge of pan to loosen bread. Place heatproof serving plate upside down on pan; holding plate and pan with pot holders, turn plate and pan over together. Let pan remain 1 minute so butter-sugar mixture can drizzle over bread, then remove pan. Serve bread warm, pulling it apart using 2 forks or your fingers.

1 Serving: Calories 270 (Calories from Fat 110); Total Fat 13g (Saturated Fat 6g; Trans Fat 0g); Cholesterol 40mg; Sodium 220mg; Total Carbohydrate 35g (Dietary Fiber 1g); Protein 4g **Exchanges:** 1 Starch, 1½ Other Carbohydrate, 2½ Fat **Carbohydrate Choices:** 2

whole wheat–cranberry bread

prep time: **10 minutes** ✛ start to finish: **3 hours 40 minutes** ✛ 1 LOAF (1½ LB); 12 SLICES

bread

- 1 cup plus 2 tablespoons water
- ¼ cup honey
- 2 tablespoons butter, softened
- 2 cups bread flour
- 1¼ cups whole wheat flour
- 1½ teaspoons salt
- ¾ teaspoon ground mace
- 2 teaspoons bread machine or fast-acting dry yeast
- ½ cup sweetened dried cranberries or raisins

cranberry-orange butter

- ½ cup butter, softened
- 2 tablespoons cranberry-orange relish or sauce

1 Measure carefully, placing all bread ingredients except cranberries in bread machine pan in the order recommended by the manufacturer. Add cranberries at the Raisin/Nut signal or 5 to 10 minutes before last kneading cycle ends.

2 Select Whole Wheat or Basic/White cycle. Use Medium or Light crust color. Do not use delay cycle. Remove baked bread from pan; cool on cooling rack.

3 In small bowl, mix butter and cranberry-orange relish until well blended. Serve with bread. Store butter in refrigerator.

1 Slice: Calories 260 (Calories from Fat 90); Total Fat 10g (Saturated Fat 6g; Trans Fat 0.5g); Cholesterol 25mg; Sodium 370mg; Total Carbohydrate 38g (Dietary Fiber 3g); Protein 4g **Exchanges:** 1½ Starch, 1 Other Carbohydrate, 2 Fat **Carbohydrate Choices:** 2½

bake smart You'll get a deeper flavor if you use molasses instead of honey. You can also use 2 tablespoons honey and 2 tablespoons molasses instead of the ¼ cup honey.

caramel apple and pecan bread

prep time: **10 minutes** ✛ start to finish: **3 hours 40 minutes** ✛ 1 LOAF (1½ LBS); 12 SLICES

1 cup water

2 tablespoons butter, softened

3 cups bread flour

¼ cup packed brown sugar

¾ teaspoon ground cinnamon

1 teaspoon salt

2 teaspoons bread machine or fast-acting dry yeast

½ cup chopped unpeeled apple

⅓ cup coarsely chopped pecans, toasted*

1 Measure carefully, placing all ingredients except apple and pecans in bread machine pan in the order recommended by the manufacturer. Add apple and pecans at the Raisin/Nut signal or 5 to 10 minutes before last kneading cycle ends.

2 Select Sweet or Basic/White cycle. Use Light crust color. Do not use delay cycle. Remove baked bread from pan; cool on cooling rack.

✳To toast pecans, bake in ungreased shallow pan at 400°F for 4 to 6 minutes, stirring occasionally, until light brown.

1 Slice: Calories 190 (Calories from Fat 45); Total Fat 5g (Saturated Fat 1.5g; Trans Fat 0g); Cholesterol 5mg; Sodium 220mg; Total Carbohydrate 31g (Dietary Fiber 1g); Protein 4g **Exchanges:** 1½ Starch, ½ Other Carbohydrate, 1 Fat **Carbohydrate Choices:** 2

bake smart You'll probably have part of an apple left after making the bread. Dice the remaining apple and stir into peanut butter—along with raisins and sunflower nuts—for a yummy, satisfying spread.

cranberry-cornmeal bread

prep time: 10 minutes ✛ start to finish: 3 hours 40 minutes ✛ 1 LOAF (1½ LB), 12 SLICES

- 1 cup plus 1 tablespoon water
- 3 tablespoons molasses or honey
- 2 tablespoons butter, softened
- 3 cups bread flour
- ⅓ cup cornmeal
- 1½ teaspoons salt
- 2 teaspoons bread machine yeast
- ½ cup sweetened dried cranberries

1 Measure carefully, placing all ingredients except cranberries in bread machine pan in the order recommended by the manufacturer. Add cranberries at the Raisin/Nut signal or 5 to 10 minutes before last kneading cycle ends.

2 Select Basic/White cycle. Use Medium or Light crust color. Do not use delay cycle. Remove baked bread from pan; cool on cooling rack.

1 Slice: Calories 170 (Calories from Fat 20); Total Fat 2g (Saturated Fat 1g; Trans Fat 0g); Cholesterol 5mg; Sodium 310mg; Total Carbohydrate 34g (Dietary Fiber 1g); Protein 4g **Exchanges:** 1½ Starch, 1 Other Carbohydrate **Carbohydrate Choices:** 2

bake smart Change the look of this bread by using white cornmeal instead of yellow and replacing the dried cranberries with dried blueberries.

Use leftover slices to make French toast. A sprinkle of powdered sugar and a drizzle of warm maple syrup make it an irresistible breakfast treat!

make-ahead raisin brioche

prep time: 30 minutes ✛ start to finish: 10 hours 25 minutes ✛ 12 BRIOCHE

1 package regular active or fast-acting dry yeast (2¼ teaspoons)

3 tablespoons warm water (105° F to 115°F)

2 tablespoons sugar

3½ cups all-purpose or bread flour

½ cup sugar

1 teaspoon ground cinnamon

½ teaspoon salt

¾ cup cold butter, cut into small pieces

⅓ cup milk

3 eggs

1½ cups golden raisins

1 egg white, beaten

1 In small bowl, mix yeast, warm water and 2 teaspoons sugar; set aside. Place flour, ½ cup sugar, the cinnamon and salt in food processor; cover and process until mixed. Add butter; process until well blended.

2 Beat milk and 3 eggs into yeast mixture with whisk; slowly add to flour mixture and process until well blended. Stir in raisins. (Dough will be sticky.)

3 Place dough on generously floured surface; gently roll in flour to coat. Knead 1 minute or until dough is smooth and springy, adding more flour if necessary. Place dough in greased large bowl, turning dough to grease all sides. Cover tightly and let rise in warm place 40 minutes.

4 Grease 12 large muffin cups, 3×1½ inches. Gently push fist into dough to deflate. Using about ¼ cup dough each, make 12 balls; place in muffin cups. Using about 1 tablespoon dough each, make 12 smaller balls; place on top of each large ball. Cover and refrigerate at least 8 hours or overnight.

5 Remove rolls from refrigerator. Cover; let rise in warm place 40 to 45 minutes or until almost double.

6 Heat oven to 350°F. Brush rolls with beaten egg white. Bake 22 to 26 minutes or until golden brown. Immediately remove from pan to cooling rack. Serve warm, or cool on cooling rack.

1 Brioche: Calories 360 (Calories from Fat 120); Total Fat 13g (Saturated Fat 8g; Trans Fat 0g); Cholesterol 85mg; Sodium 210mg; Total Carbohydrate 54g (Dietary Fiber 2g); Protein 6g **Exchanges:** 2 Starch, 1½ Other Carbohydrate, 2½ Fat **Carbohydrate Choices:** 3½

bake smart These individual French yeast breads, pronounced bree-OHSH, are light yet rich with butter and eggs.

Tuck these baked rolls in the freezer wrapped tightly for up to 2 months.

european golden raisin wheat rolls

prep time: **40 minutes** ✛ start to finish: **4 hours** ✛ 18 ROLLS

5½ to 6½ cups bread flour

1 package regular active dry yeast (2¼ teaspoons)

2½ cups warm water (105°F to 115°F)

¾ cup golden raisins

¾ cup whole wheat flour

2½ teaspoons salt

¾ cup walnuts, toasted, coarsely chopped✳

¾ cup coarsely chopped hazelnuts (filberts)

1 In medium bowl, combine 2 cups of the bread flour and the yeast; mix well. Stir in 1½ cups of the warm water to form a loose starter dough. Let rest 15 to 30 minutes. In small bowl, combine raisins and remaining 1 cup warm water. Let stand 15 minutes.

2 Meanwhile, grease cookie sheets. In large bowl, combine 3½ cups of the remaining bread flour, the whole wheat flour and salt; mix well.

3 Stir raisins with water into starter dough until well mixed. Add starter mixture to whole wheat flour mixture; stir until soft dough forms. Place dough on floured surface. Knead 10 to 12 minutes, adding ½ to 1 cup bread flour until dough is smooth and springy. Dough will be slightly sticky. Knead walnuts and hazelnuts into dough.

4 Spray large bowl with cooking spray. Place dough in bowl; cover loosely with plastic wrap sprayed with cooking spray and cloth towel. Let rise in warm place 1 hour 30 minutes or until doubled in size.

5 Punch down dough several times to remove all air bubbles. Divide dough into 18 pieces. Shape each piece into a ball; place on greased cookie sheets. Cover and let rise 1 hour or until doubled in size.

6 Heat oven to 425°F. Uncover dough; brush tops of rolls lightly with water. Bake 17 to 22 minutes or until golden brown.

✳To toast walnuts, bake in ungreased shallow pan at 400°F for 4 to 6 minutes, stirring occasionally, until light brown.

1 Roll: Calories 250 (Calories from Fat 60); Total Fat 7g (Saturated Fat 0.5g; Trans Fat 0g); Cholesterol 0mg; Sodium 330mg; Total Carbohydrate 40g (Dietary Fiber 2g); Protein 7g **Exchanges:** 2½ Starch, 1 Fat **Carbohydrate Choices:** 2½

bake smart This recipe is inspired by the little raisin-walnut rolls sold in Parisian *boulangeries*. Nourishing, just-sweet and with a bit of nutty crunch, these rolls are perfect at breakfast with steaming bowls of café au lait. They also make a nice teatime snack. Bake them for guests who don't care for sugary pastries.

To simulate the steamy interior of a *boulangerie* oven, place several ice cubes in a shallow pan. Set the pan on the lowest oven rack beneath the rolls. Shut the oven door and let the steam give the rolls more spring. The initial moisture, followed by dry heat once the ice cubes have evaporated, will make the crust extra crunchy.

sweet potato–cranberry knots

prep time: 30 minutes ✛ start to finish: 3 hours ✛ 12 ROLLS

2¼ to 2¾ cups bread flour

¼ cup sugar

1 teaspoon salt

½ teaspoon ground cinnamon

1 package fast-acting dry yeast (2¼ teaspoons)

¼ cup butter, softened

¾ cup lukewarm water (95°F)

¾ cup mashed drained sweet potatoes packed in syrup (from 23-oz can)

½ cup sweetened dried cranberries

Butter, melted

1 In large bowl, mix 1 cup of the flour, the sugar, salt, cinnamon and yeast. Add ¼ cup butter and the warm water. Beat with electric mixer on low speed 1 minute, scraping bowl frequently. Add sweet potatoes. Beat on medium speed 1 minute, scraping bowl frequently. Stir in cranberries and enough remaining flour, ½ cup at a time, to make dough easy to handle.

2 Place dough on lightly floured surface. Knead 5 minutes or until smooth and springy. Grease large bowl with shortening. Place dough in bowl, turning dough to grease all sides. Cover and let rise in warm place 1 hour to 1 hour 30 minutes or until doubled in size. Dough is ready if indentation remains when touched.

3 Heat oven to 375°F. Spray cookie sheet with cooking spray. Gently push fist into dough to deflate. Divide dough into 12 equal pieces. Roll each piece into 8-inch rope; tie into knot. Place on cookie sheet.

4 Brush knots with melted butter. Cover and let rise in warm place about 40 minutes or until doubled in size. Bake 14 to 20 minutes or until golden brown.

1 Roll: Calories 150 (Calories from Fat 50); Total Fat 6g (Saturated Fat 3.5g; Trans Fat 0g); Cholesterol 15mg; Sodium 240mg; Total Carbohydrate 22g (Dietary Fiber 1g); Protein 2g **Exchanges:** ½ Starch, 1 Other Carbohydrate, 1 Fat **Carbohydrate Choices:** 1½

bake smart For a citrus twist, add 1 teaspoon freshly grated orange peel with the sweet potatoes.

Rolls can be made up to a day ahead of time. Reheat in the microwave just before serving.

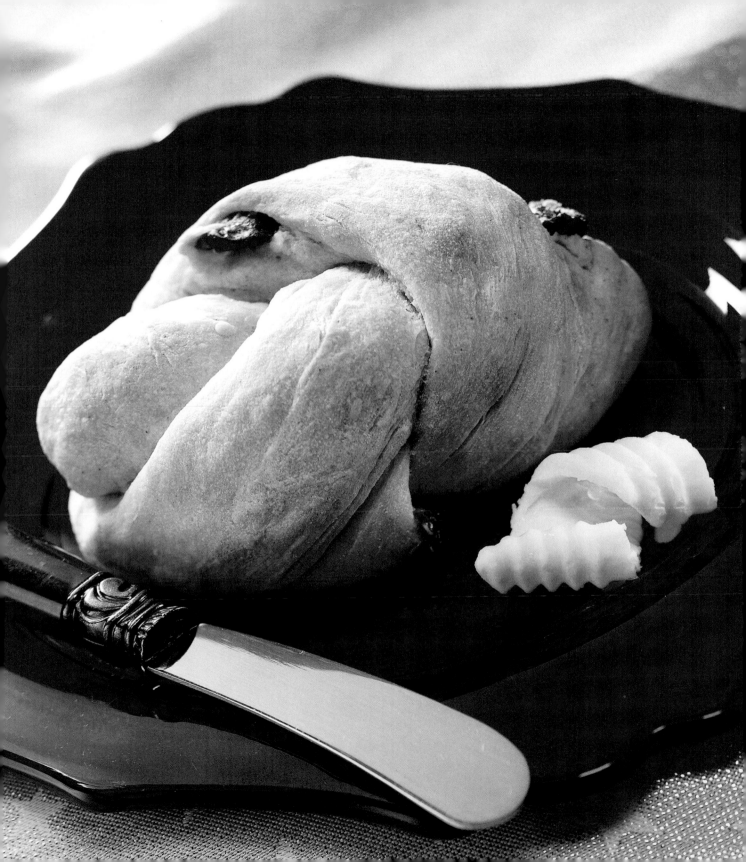

caramel sticky rolls

prep time: 40 minutes ✛ start to finish: 3 hours 15 minutes ✛ 15 ROLLS

rolls

3½ to 4 cups all-purpose or bread flour

⅓ cup granulated sugar

1 teaspoon salt

2 packages regular active or fast-acting dry yeast (4½ teaspoons)

1 cup very warm milk (120°F to 130°F)

¼ cup butter, softened

1 egg

caramel topping

1 cup packed brown sugar

½ cup butter, softened

¼ cup light corn syrup

1 cup pecan halves, if desired

filling

½ cup chopped pecans or raisins, if desired

¼ cup granulated sugar or packed brown sugar

1 teaspoon ground cinnamon

2 tablespoons butter, softened

1 In large bowl, mix 2 cups of the flour, ⅓ cup granulated sugar, the salt and yeast. Add warm milk, ¼ cup butter and the egg. Beat with electric mixer on low speed 1 minute, scraping bowl frequently. Beat on medium speed 1 minute, scraping bowl frequently. Stir in enough remaining flour, ½ cup at a time, to make dough easy to handle.

2 Place dough on lightly floured surface. Knead 5 minutes or until dough is smooth and springy. Grease large bowl with shortening. Place dough in bowl, turning dough to grease all sides. Cover bowl loosely with plastic wrap; let rise in warm place about 1 hour 30 minutes or until doubled in size. Dough is ready if indentation remains when touched.

3 In 2-quart saucepan, heat brown sugar and ½ cup butter to boiling, stirring constantly; remove from heat. Stir in corn syrup. Pour into 13×9-inch pan. Sprinkle with pecan halves.

4 In small bowl, mix all filling ingredients except 2 tablespoons butter; set aside.

5 Gently push fist into dough to deflate. On lightly floured surface, roll dough into 15×10-inch rectangle. Spread with 2 tablespoons butter; sprinkle with filling. Starting with 15-inch side, roll up tightly. Pinch edges to seal. With fingers, shape until even. Using dental floss or serrated knife, cut roll into 15 (1-inch) slices.

6 Place slices slightly apart in pan. Cover loosely with plastic wrap; let rise in warm place about 30 minutes or until doubled in size.

7 Heat oven to 350°F. Bake 30 to 35 minutes or until golden brown. Let stand 2 to 3 minutes. Place heatproof tray or serving plate upside down on pan; immediately turn tray and pan over. Let pan remain 1 minute so caramel can drizzle over rolls; remove pan. Serve warm.

1 Roll: Calories 320 (Calories from Fat 110); Total Fat 12g (Saturated Fat 6g; Trans Fat 0.5g); Cholesterol 45mg; Sodium 250mg; Total Carbohydrate 50g (Dietary Fiber 1g); Protein 4g **Exchanges:** 1 Starch, 2½ Other Carbohydrate, 2 Fat **Carbohydrate Choices:** 3

lighter caramel sticky rolls: For Caramel Rolls weighing in at 4 grams of fat and 255 calories per serving, make recipe as directed—except omit caramel topping and pecan halves. Line pan with foil; spray with cooking spray. Drizzle 1 cup caramel ice-cream topping over foil (heat topping slightly if it is stiff). Continue as directed—except omit chopped pecans from filling.

cinnamon rolls: Omit caramel topping and pecan halves. Grease bottom and sides of 13×9-inch pan with shortening or cooking spray. Place dough slices in pan. Let rise and bake as directed in steps 6 and 7—except do not turn pan upside down. Remove rolls from pan to cooling rack. Cool 10 minutes. Drizzle rolls with a powdered sugar glaze, if desired.

bake smart To make ahead, after placing slices in pan, cover tightly with plastic wrap or foil; refrigerate 4 to 24 hours. Before baking, remove from refrigerator; remove plastic wrap or foil and cover loosely with plastic wrap. Let rise in warm place about 2 hours or until doubled in size. If some rising has occurred in the refrigerator, rising time may be less than 2 hours. Bake as directed.

orange-cardamom artisan rolls

prep time: 20 minutes ✛ start to finish: 4 hours 10 minutes ✛ 15 ROLLS

2 packages regular
active dry yeast
(4½ teaspoons)

1 tablespoon sugar

1½ cups warm water
(105°F to 115°F)

½ cup sugar

1 teaspoon salt

1 teaspoon ground
cardamom

2 teaspoons grated
orange peel

2½ teaspoons vanilla

3½ to 4 cups all-purpose
flour

2 tablespoons butter,
melted

7½ teaspoons sugar

1 In large bowl, dissolve yeast and 1 tablespoon sugar in warm water. Let stand 10 minutes or until mixture is foamy. Add ½ cup sugar, the salt, cardamom, orange peel and vanilla; stir until well mixed, about 1 minute. Gradually add flour, until mixture begins to pull away from sides of bowl. Mixture will be slightly sticky.

2 Cover bowl loosely with plastic wrap; let rise in warm place about 2 hours or until doubled in size. Refrigerate at least 30 minutes or up to 24 hours.

3 Spray 13×9-inch pan with cooking spray. On lightly floured surface, divide dough evenly into 15 pieces. With floured hands, shape each piece into a ball by stretching surface of dough around to bottom on all 4 sides; pinch bottom to seal. Place in pan.

4 Heat oven to 375°F. Cover pan loosely with plastic wrap; let stand 30 minutes at room temperature. Lightly brush tops of rolls with melted butter; sprinkle ½ teaspoon sugar over each roll.

5 Bake 25 to 30 minutes or until tops are golden brown. Cool 10 minutes; remove from pan to cooling rack. Serve warm.

1 Roll: Calories 160 (Calories from Fat 15); Total Fat 2g (Saturated Fat 1g; Trans Fat 0g); Cholesterol 0mg; Sodium 170mg; Total Carbohydrate 32g (Dietary Fiber 1g); Protein 3g **Exchanges:** 1 Starch, 1 Other Carbohydrate, ½ Fat **Carbohydrate Choices:** 2

hot cross buns

prep time: **25 minutes** + start to finish: **3 hours 15 minutes** + 16 BUNS

dough

2 eggs plus enough water to equal 1⅓ cups

½ cup butter, softened

4 cups bread flour

¾ teaspoon ground cinnamon

¼ teaspoon ground nutmeg

1½ teaspoons salt

2 tablespoons granulated sugar

1½ teaspoons bread machine or fast-acting dry yeast

½ cup raisins

½ cup golden raisins

1 egg

2 tablespoons cold water

icing

1 cup powdered sugar

1 tablespoon milk or water

½ teaspoon vanilla

1 Measure carefully, placing all dough ingredients except raisins, 1 egg and the cold water in bread machine pan in the order recommended by the manufacturer. Add raisins at the Raisin/Nut signal.

2 Select Dough/Manual cycle. Do not use delay cycle.

3 Remove dough from pan, using lightly floured hands. Cover and let rest 10 minutes on lightly floured surface.

4 Grease cookie sheet or 2 (9-inch) round pans. Divide dough in half. Divide each half into 8 equal pieces. Shape each piece into a smooth ball. Place balls about 2 inches apart on cookie sheet or 1 inch apart in pans. Using scissors, snip a cross shape in top of each ball. Cover and let rise in warm place about 40 minutes or until doubled in' size.

5 Heat oven to 375°F. Beat egg and cold water slightly; brush on buns. Bake 18 to 20 minutes or until golden brown. Remove from cookie sheet to cooling rack. Cool slightly.

6 In small bowl, mix all icing ingredients until smooth and spreadable. Make a cross on top of each bun with icing.

1 Bun: Calories 260 (Calories from Fat 70); Total Fat 7g (Saturated Fat 4g; Trans Fat 0g); Cholesterol 55mg; Sodium 280mg; Total Carbohydrate 42g (Dietary Fiber 1g); Protein 5g **Exchanges:** 1½ Starch, 1½ Other Carbohydrate, 1½ Fat **Carbohydrate Choices:** 3

bake smart If your bread machine doesn't have a Raisin/Nut signal, add the raisins 5 to 10 minutes before the last kneading cycle ends. Check your bread machine's use-and-care book for how long the last cycle runs.

To make ahead, after you have shaped the dough into buns and snipped the cross in the top of each, cover with plastic wrap. You can refrigerate them from 4 to 24 hours. Before baking, remove the buns from the refrigerator and remove the plastic wrap. Cover with a kitchen towel and let rise in a warm place about 2 hours or until doubled in size. Then brush the tops and bake as directed.

festive raspberry rolls

prep time: **20 minutes** ✛ start to finish: **3 hours 5 minutes** ✛ 12 ROLLS

⅓ cup milk

⅓ cup water

3 tablespoons butter, softened

1 egg

2 cups bread flour

⅓ cup sugar

½ teaspoon salt

1¾ teaspoons bread machine or fast-acting dry yeast

3 tablespoons raspberry preserves

1 Measure carefully, placing all ingredients except preserves in bread machine pan in the order recommended by the manufacturer.

2 Select Dough/Manual cycle. Do not use delay cycle.

3 Remove dough from pan, using lightly floured hands. Cover and let rest 10 minutes on lightly floured surface.

4 Grease 12 regular-size muffin cups. Roll or pat dough into 15×10-inch rectangle. Spread preserves over dough to within ¼ inch of edges. Starting with 15-inch side, roll up dough; pinch edge of dough into roll to seal. Stretch and shape roll to make even.

5 Cut roll into 12 equal slices. Place slices, cut side up, in muffin cups. Using kitchen scissors, snip through each slice twice, cutting into fourths. Gently spread dough pieces open. Cover and let rise in warm place about 25 minutes or until doubled in size. Dough is ready if indentation remains when touched.

6 Heat oven to 375°F. Bake 15 to 20 minutes or until golden brown. Immediately remove from pan to cooling rack. Serve warm or cool.

1 Roll: Calories 150 (Calories from Fat 35); Total Fat 4g (Saturated Fat 1g; Trans Fat 0.5g); Cholesterol 20mg; Sodium 135mg; Total Carbohydrate 26g (Dietary Fiber 0g); Protein 3g **Exchanges:** 1 Starch, 1 Other Carbohydrate, ½ Fat **Carbohydrate Choices:** 2

bake smart To make ahead, after you have snipped each slice and opened the dough pieces, cover with plastic wrap. You can refrigerate the rolls from 4 to 24 hours. Before baking, remove the rolls from the refrigerator and remove the plastic wrap. Cover with a kitchen towel and let rise in a warm place about 2 hours or until doubled in size. Bake the rolls as directed.

maple-walnut twists

prep time: 25 minutes ✛ start to finish: 4 hours 5 minutes ✛ 16 TWISTS

dough

1	cup water
¼	butter, softened
1	egg
3½	cups bread flour
⅓	cup granulated sugar
1	teaspoon salt
1½	teaspoons bread machine or fast-acting dry yeast

filling

¼	cup finely chopped walnuts
2	tablespoons maple-flavored syrup
2	tablespoons butter, softened
½	teaspoon ground cinnamon

icing

1	cup powdered sugar
½	teaspoon maple extract
	About 1 tablespoon milk

1 Measure carefully, placing all dough ingredients in bread machine pan in the order recommended by the manufacturer.

2 Select Dough/Manual cycle. Do not use delay cycle.

3 Remove dough from pan, using lightly floured hands. Cover and let rest 10 minutes on lightly floured surface. In small bowl, mix all filling ingredients.

4 Grease 13×9-inch pan. Roll or pat dough into 16×10-inch rectangle on lightly floured surface. Spread half of the filling lengthwise down center third of rectangle. Fold one outer third of dough over filling; spread remaining filling over folded dough. Fold remaining third of dough over filling; pinch edge to seal.

5 Cut crosswise into sixteen 1-inch strips. Holding a strip at each end, twist in opposite directions. Place strips about 1 inch apart in pan, forming 2 rows of 8 strips each. Cover and let rise in warm place 50 to 60 minutes or until doubled in size. Dough is ready if indentation remains when touched.

6 Heat oven to 350°F. Bake 35 to 40 minutes or until golden brown. In small bowl, mix all icing ingredients until smooth and thin enough to drizzle. Drizzle icing over warm twists. Serve warm.

1 Twist: Calories 220 (Calories from Fat 60); Total Fat 6g (Saturated Fat 1g; Trans Fat 1g); Cholesterol 15mg; Sodium 190mg; Total Carbohydrate 36g (Dietary Fiber 1g); Protein 4g **Exchanges:** 1½ Starch, 1 Other Carbohydrate, 1 Fat **Carbohydrate Choices:** 2½

pull-apart bread

prep time: 30 minutes ✛ start to finish: 1 hour 35 minutes ✛ 1 LOAF (12 SERVINGS)

3½ to 3¾ cups all-purpose or bread flour

2 tablespoons sugar

½ teaspoon salt

1 package regular active or fast-acting dry yeast (2¼ teaspoons)

1 cup milk

½ cup butter

1 egg

1 Spray 12-cup fluted tube cake pan or 10-inch angel food (tube) cake pan with cooking spray. In large bowl, stir 1½ cups of the flour, the sugar, salt and yeast until well mixed.

2 In 1-quart saucepan, heat milk and ¼ cup of the butter over medium-low heat, stirring frequently, until very warm (120°F to 130°F). Add milk mixture and the egg to the flour mixture. Beat with electric mixer on low speed 1 minute, scraping bowl frequently, until flour mixture is moistened. Beat on medium speed 3 minutes, scraping bowl frequently. With wooden spoon, stir in enough of the remaining flour, 1 cup at a time, until dough is soft, leaves side of bowl and is easy to handle (dough may be slightly sticky).

3 Place dough on lightly floured surface. Knead 5 to 10 minutes or until dough is smooth and springy.

4 In small microwavable bowl, microwave remaining ¼ cup butter on l ligh 30 to 50 seconds or until melted.

5 Shape dough into 24 balls. Dip each ball into melted butter. Layer balls evenly in pan. Cover pan loosely with plastic wrap; let rise in warm place 20 to 30 minutes or until doubled in size. Dough is ready if indentation remains when touched. Remove plastic wrap.

6 Move oven rack to low position so that top of pan will be in center of oven. Heat oven to 350°F.

7 Bake 25 to 30 minutes or until golden brown. Cool in pan 2 minutes. Place heatproof serving plate upside down on pan; holding plate and pan with pot holders, turn plate and pan over together; remove pan. Serve warm, pulling bread apart with 2 forks or with fingers.

1 Serving: Calories 230 (Calories from Fat 80); Total Fat 9g (Saturated Fat 5g; Trans Fat 0g); Cholesterol 40mg; Sodium 170mg; Total Carbohydrate 31g (Dietary Fiber 1g); Protein 5g **Exchanges:** 2 Starch, 1½ Fat **Carbohydrate Choices:** 2

garlic-and-chive mashed potato rolls

prep time: 35 minutes ✛ start to finish: 2 hours 40 minutes ✛ 16 ROLLS

rolls

- ¼ cup warm water (105°F to 115°F)
- ¼ teaspoon sugar
- 1 package active dry yeast (2¼ teaspoons)
- 3 tablespoons butter
- 1 medium clove garlic, finely chopped
- ½ cup warm milk (105°F to 115°F)
- ½ cup mashed potatoes, room temperature
- ¼ cup finely chopped fresh chives
- 1 egg
- 1½ teaspoons salt
- 1½ cups white whole wheat flour
- 1¾ to 2 cups all-purpose flour

topping

- 2 tablespoons butter, melted
- 1 tablespoon finely chopped fresh chives

1 In small bowl, combine warm water, sugar and yeast. Let stand 10 minutes or until yeast is dissolved and foamy. Meanwhile, in small nonstick skillet, melt 3 tablespoons butter over medium heat. Add garlic; cook 1 minute or until softened, stirring constantly.

2 In large bowl, stir warm milk, potatoes, ¼ cup chives, the egg, salt and garlic mixture with whisk until blended. Stir in yeast mixture. Stir in white whole wheat flour and 1¾ cups of the all-purpose flour until soft dough forms, slowly adding additional flour as necessary to make dough easy to handle.

3 Place dough on lightly floured surface. Knead 10 minutes or until dough is smooth and springy. Grease large bowl with butter. Place dough in bowl, turning dough to grease all sides. Cover bowl loosely with plastic wrap; let rise in warm place about 1 hour or until doubled in size. Dough is ready if indentation remains when touched.

4 Line 2 cookie sheets with cooking parchment paper. Gently push fist into dough to deflate. Divide dough in half; cut each half into 8 pieces. Roll each piece into 12-inch rope. Loosely tie each rope into knot. Do not pull tight; dough should have room to expand during rising and baking. (If desired, press ends of knot together to form a locked-knot roll.) Cover loosely with plastic wrap lightly sprayed with cooking spray. Let rise 30 minutes or until doubled in size.

5 Heat oven to 375°F. Bake one cookie sheet at a time, leaving other sheet covered, 18 to 20 minutes or until light brown. Brush rolls with 2 tablespoons butter; sprinkle with 1 tablespoon chives. Serve warm or cool.

1 Roll: Calories 140 (Calories from Fat 40); Total Fat 4.5g (Saturated Fat 2.5g; Trans Fat 0g); Cholesterol 25mg; Sodium 250mg; Total Carbohydrate 21g (Dietary Fiber 2g); Protein 4g **Exchanges:** 1½ Starch, ½ Fat **Carbohydrate Choices:** 1½

bake smart Prepared mashed potato products such as refrigerated mashed potatoes or instant mashed potatoes (from potato flakes) can be used in this recipe.

To make your own mashed potato, place 1 small peeled, cubed russet potato in small saucepan; add water to cover. Bring to a boil over medium heat; cook 5 to 7 minutes or until tender, reducing heat to medium-low if cooking too quickly. Drain; place in small bowl; using potato masher or fork, mash until smooth. Measure out ½ cup to use in this recipe.

no-knead bran rolls

prep time: 20 minutes ✛ start to finish: 3 hours ✛ 24 ROLLS

3½ to 3¾ cups all-purpose flour

½ cup Fiber One original bran cereal

¼ cup packed brown sugar

1 teaspoon salt

1 package regular active or fast-acting dry yeast (2¼ teaspoons)

1 cup very warm water (120°F to 130°F)

3 tablespoons shortening

1 egg

1 In large bowl, mix 1¾ cups of the flour, the cereal, brown sugar, salt and yeast. Add warm water, shortening and egg. Beat with electric mixer on low speed 1 minute, scraping bowl frequently. Beat on medium speed 1 minute, scraping bowl frequently.

2 Stir in enough remaining flour to make dough easy to handle. Grease large bowl with shortening or cooking spray. Place dough in bowl, turning dough to grease all sides. Cover and let rise in warm place about 1 hour 30 minutes or until doubled in size.

3 Grease 2 (9-inch) round pans with shortening or cooking spray. Gently push fist into dough to deflate; divide dough into 24 equal pieces. With greased hands, shape each piece into a ball (dough will be slightly sticky). Place 12 balls in each pan. Cover and let rise in warm place about 45 minutes or until doubled in size.

4 Heat oven to 375°F. Bake 20 to 25 minutes or until golden brown. Serve warm or cool.

1 Roll: Calories 100 (Calories from Fat 20); Total Fat 2g (Saturated Fat 0.5g; Trans Fat 0g); Cholesterol 10mg; Sodium 105mg; Total Carbohydrate 17g (Dietary Fiber 1g); Protein 2g **Exchanges:** 1 Starch, ½ Fat **Carbohydrate Choices:** 1

bakery-style pumpernickel rolls

prep time: 25 minutes ✛ start to finish: 4 hours 25 minutes ✛ 12 ROLLS

2½ cups all-purpose flour

¾ cup rye flour

1 tablespoon regular active dry yeast

2 tablespoons unsweetened baking cocoa

1½ teaspoons coarse (kosher or sea) salt or 1 teaspoon table salt

1⅓ cups warm water (105°F to 115°F)

3 tablespoons dark molasses

1 tablespoon cornmeal

1 egg

1 tablespoon water

1 teaspoon caraway seed, if desired

1 In large bowl, mix flours, yeast, cocoa and salt. In small bowl, mix 1⅓ cups warm water and molasses. Add water mixture to flour mixture; stir with wooden spoon until dough is thoroughly mixed and no dry spots remain, about 1 to 2 minutes. Cover bowl loosely with plastic wrap. Let rise at room temperature 2 hours; refrigerate at least 1 hour but no longer than 24 hours.

2 Line large cookie sheet with cooking parchment paper; sprinkle with cornmeal. On generously floured surface, turn dough to lightly coat with flour. Form dough into ball; cut in half. Cut each half into 6 equal pieces, coating with flour as needed to prevent sticking. Shape each piece into a ball by stretching surface of dough around to bottom on all sides; pinch bottom to seal. Place balls on cookie sheet about 2 inches apart.

3 Loosely cover rolls with plastic wrap sprayed with cooking spray; let rise in warm place 40 minutes or until doubled in size.

4 Place empty broiler tray or cast-iron skillet on bottom rack of oven. Heat oven to 400°F.

5 Meanwhile, in small bowl, beat egg and 1 tablespoon water. Brush buns with egg mixture; sprinkle with caraway seed. Place cookie sheet in oven. Gently pull out bottom rack of oven and pour 1 cup hot water into broiler tray; gently slide rack back and quickly shut oven door.

6 Bake 12 to 15 minutes or until buns begin to slightly brown and sound hollow when tapped. Cool 5 minutes on cooling rack. Serve warm or cool.

1 Roll: Calories 150 (Calories from Fat 10); Total Fat 1g (Saturated Fat 0g; Trans Fat 0g); Cholesterol 20mg; Sodium 300mg; Total Carbohydrate 30g (Dietary Fiber 2g); Protein 4g **Exchanges:** 1½ Starch, ½ Other Carbohydrate **Carbohydrate Choices:** 2

bake smart These buns are great for pastrami and Swiss cheese sandwiches.

This no-knead dough will be sticky to handle. Be sure to coat the dough with flour and shaping will be a breeze.

bake smart To make ahead, after placing rolls in pan, cover tightly with foil and refrigerate from 4 to 24 hours. Before baking, remove from refrigerator; remove foil and cover loosely with plastic wrap. Let rise in warm place about 2 hours or until doubled in size. If some rising has occurred in the refrigerator, rising time may be less than 2 hours. Bake as directed.

dinner rolls

prep time: **30 minutes** + start to finish: **2 hours 15 minutes** +

3½ to 3¾ cups all-purpose or bread flour

¼ cup sugar

¼ cup butter, softened

1 teaspoon salt

1 package regular active or fast-acting dry yeast (2¼ teaspoons)

½ cup very warm water (120°F to 130°F)

½ cup very warm milk (120°F to 130°F)

1 egg

Butter, melted, if desired

1 In large bowl, stir 2 cups of the flour, the sugar, ¼ cup butter, the salt and yeast until well mixed. Add warm water, warm milk and egg. Beat with electric mixer on low speed 1 minute, scraping bowl frequently. Beat on medium speed 1 minute, scraping bowl frequently. Stir in enough remaining flour, ¼ cup at a time, to make dough easy to handle.

2 Place dough on lightly floured surface. Knead 5 minutes or until dough is smooth and springy. Grease large bowl with shortening. Place dough in bowl, turning dough to grease all sides. Cover bowl loosely with plastic wrap; let rise in warm place about 1 hour or until doubled in size. Dough is ready if indentation remains when touched.

3 Grease bottom and sides of 13×9-inch pan with shortening or cooking spray.

4 Gently push fist into dough to deflate. Divide dough into 15 equal pieces. Shape each piece into a ball; place balls in pan. Brush with melted butter. Cover loosely with plastic wrap; let rise in warm place about 30 minutes or until doubled in size.

5 Heat oven to 375°F. Bake 12 to 15 minutes or until golden brown. Serve warm or cool.

1 Roll: Calories 160 (Calories from Fat 35); Total Fat 4g (Saturated Fat 2g; Trans Fat 0g); Cholesterol 25mg; Sodium 190mg; Total Carbohydrate 26g (Dietary Fiber 1g); Protein 4g **Exchanges:** 2 Starch **Carbohydrate Choices:** 2

cloverleaf dinner rolls: Grease 24 regular-size muffin cups with shortening or cooking spray. Make dough as directed in recipe—except after pushing fist into dough, divide dough into 72 equal pieces. (To divide, cut dough in half, then continue cutting pieces in half until there are 72 pieces.) Shape each piece into a ball. Place 3 balls in each muffin cup. Brush with melted butter. Cover loosely with plastic wrap; let rise in warm place about 30 minutes or until doubled in size. Bake as directed. MAKES 24 ROLLS

crescent dinner rolls: Grease cookie sheet with shortening or cooking spray. Make dough as directed in recipe—except after pushing fist into dough, cut dough in half. On floured surface, roll each half into 12-inch round. Spread with softened butter. Cut each round into 16 wedges. Starting with rounded edge, roll up each wedge. Place rolls point side down on cookie sheet and curve slightly. Brush with melted butter. Cover loosely with plastic wrap; let rise in warm place about 30 minutes or until doubled in size. Bake as directed. MAKES 32 ROLLS

double-quick dinner rolls

prep time: **15 minutes** ✛ start to finish: **1 hour 35 minutes** ✛ 12 ROLLS

2¼ cups all-purpose flour

2 tablespoons sugar

1 teaspoon salt

1 package regular active or fast-acting dry yeast (2¼ teaspoons)

1 cup very warm water (120°F to 130°F)

2 tablespoons shortening

1 egg

1 In large bowl, mix 1¼ cups of the flour, the sugar, salt and yeast. Add warm water, shortening and egg; beat with spoon until smooth. Stir in remaining flour until smooth. Scrape batter from side of bowl. Cover and let rise in warm place about 30 minutes or until doubled in size.

2 Grease 12 regular-size muffin cups. Stir down batter by beating about 25 strokes. Divide batter evenly among muffin cups. Let rise 20 to 30 minutes or until batter rounds over tops of cups.

3 Heat oven to 400°F. Bake 15 to 20 minutes or until golden brown.

1 Roll: Calories 120 (Calories from Fat 25); Total Fat 3g (Saturated Fat 0.5g; Trans Fat 0g); Cholesterol 20mg; Sodium 200mg; Total Carbohydrate 20g (Dietary Fiber 1g); Protein 3g **Exchanges:** 1 Starch, ½ Other Carbohydrate, ½ Fat **Carbohydrate Choices:** 1

bake smart Add personality to these quick-fix rolls by sprinkling with toasted sesame seed.

Use leftover rolls as pizza "crusts" at another meal. Split and toast the rolls. Top them with pizza sauce and your favorite pizza toppings. Sprinkle with shredded cheese. Bake them until warm and the cheese is melted.

two-seed checkerboard dinner rolls

prep time: 40 minutes ✛ start to finish: 3 hours 5 minutes ✛ 15 ROLLS

2 cups bread flour
or all-purpose flour

¼ cup honey

1 teaspoon salt

1 package regular active
or fast-acting dry yeast
(2¼ teaspoons)

1 cup very warm water
(120°F to 130°F)

3 tablespoons butter,
softened

1 egg

1½ to 2 cups whole wheat
flour

1 egg white

1 teaspoon water

3 tablespoons sesame
seed

2 tablespoons poppy
seed

1 In large bowl, mix bread flour, honey, salt and yeast. Add warm water, butter and egg. Beat with electric mixer on low speed 1 minute, scraping bowl frequently. Beat on medium speed 1 minute, scraping bowl frequently. Stir in enough of the whole wheat flour to make dough easy to handle.

2 On lightly floured surface, knead dough about 5 minutes or until dough is smooth and springy. Grease large bowl with shortening or spray with cooking spray. Place dough in bowl, turning dough to grease all sides. Cover bowl loosely with plastic wrap; let rise in warm place about 1 hour or until doubled in size. Dough is ready if indentation remains when touched.

3 Grease bottom and sides of 13×9-inch pan with shortening or spray with cooking spray. In small bowl, mix egg white and 1 teaspoon water with fork. Gently push fist into dough to deflate. Divide dough into 15 equal pieces. Shape each piece into a ball. Brush top of each ball with egg white mixture. Dip tops of 8 balls into sesame seed and tops of 7 balls into poppy seed. Arrange seed side up in checkerboard pattern in pan. Cover pan loosely with plastic wrap; let rise in warm place 45 to 60 minutes or until balls are doubled in size.

4 Heat oven to 375°F. Bake 17 to 21 minutes or until golden brown. Remove from pan to cooling rack. Serve warm or cool.

1 Roll: Calories 170 (Calories from Fat 40); Total Fat 4.5g (Saturated Fat 2g; Trans Fat 0g); Cholesterol 20mg; Sodium 180mg; Total Carbohydrate 28g (Dietary Fiber 2g); Protein 5g **Exchanges:** 1½ Starch, ½ Other Carbohydrate, ½ Fat **Carbohydrate Choices:** 2

For great rolls every time, follow these easy tips:

✛ Follow recipe directions carefully.

✛ Heat milk to temperature within range indicated in recipe for yeast to grow properly.

✛ Knead dough until smooth and springy.

✛ Let dough rise in warm, draft-free area.

✛ Let dough rise until doubled so rolls rise properly.

✛ Stretch and shape dough until even for uniform rolls.

✛ Cut dough with unflavored dental floss or serrated knife.

gluten-free dinner rolls

prep time: **30 minutes** + start to finish: **2 hours 15 minutes** + 24 ROLLS

½ cup warm water
(105°F to 115°F)

1 teaspoon unflavored
gelatin

1 package fast-acting dry
yeast (2¼ teaspoons)

¾ cup cornstarch

¾ cup potato starch

½ cup sweet white
sorghum flour

½ cup brown rice flour

½ cup white rice flour

⅓ cup tapioca flour

⅓ cup garbanzo and fava
flour

2 eggs

½ cup almond milk,
soymilk or regular milk

¼ cup honey

3 tablespoons sunflower
oil or ghee (measured
melted)

1 teaspoon cider vinegar

2 teaspoons xanthan gum

1½ teaspoons salt

1 Spray 24 regular-size muffin cups with cooking spray (without flour). In small bowl, mix warm water, gelatin and yeast; set aside. In medium bowl, mix cornstarch and all flours; set aside.

2 In food processor, place eggs, milk, honey, oil, vinegar, xanthan gum and salt. Cover; process about 30 seconds or until well blended. Add flour mixture and yeast mixture. Cover; process about 30 seconds or until well blended.

3 Spray 2 teaspoons with cooking spray without flour. Spoon 3 balls of dough into each muffin cup, respraying spoons as necessary. Spray sheet of plastic wrap with cooking spray without flour; cover dough in pans. Let rise in warm place 1 hour to 1 hour 30 minutes or until doubled in size.

4 Heat oven to 375°F. Remove plastic wrap from rolls. Bake 14 to 16 minutes or until light golden brown. Immediately remove from pans to cooling racks. Serve warm.

1 Roll: Calories 120 (Calories from Fat 25); Total Fat 2.5g (Saturated Fat 0g; Trans Fat 0g); Cholesterol 20mg; Sodium 160mg; Total Carbohydrate 22g (Dietary Fiber 1g); Protein 2g **Exchanges:** 1½ Starch **Carbohydrate Choices:** 1½

Jean Duane, Alternative Cook { www.alternativecook.com }

bake smart Cooking gluten free? Always read labels to make sure that each recipe ingredient is gluten free. Products and ingredient sources can vary.

Although these are fantastic right out of the oven, they can also be baked and frozen in a tightly covered container. Just pop them into the toaster oven when you're ready to serve them.

sun-dried tomato rolls

prep time: 20 minutes + start to finish: 3 hours 5 minutes + 12 ROLLS

¾ cup warm milk
(105°F to 115°F)

2 cups bread flour

¼ cup chopped sun-dried
tomatoes in oil, drained,
1 tablespoon oil reserved

1 tablespoon sugar

1 teaspoon salt

1½ teaspoons bread
machine yeast

1 Measure carefully, placing all ingredients in bread machine pan in the order recommended by the manufacturer.

2 Select Dough/Manual cycle. Do not use delay cycle.

3 Remove dough from pan; place on lightly floured surface. Cover and let rest 10 minutes.

4 Lightly grease cookie sheet with shortening or spray with cooking spray. Gently push fist into dough to deflate. Divide dough into 12 equal pieces. Shape each piece into a ball. Place balls about 2 inches apart on cookie sheet. Cover and let rise in warm place 30 to 45 minutes or until almost doubled in size.

5 Heat oven to 350°F. Bake 12 to 16 minutes or until golden brown. Remove from cookie sheet to cooling rack. Serve warm or cool.

1 Roll: Calories 100 (Calories from Fat 15), Total Fat 2g (Saturated Fat 0g; Trans Fat 0g); Cholesterol 0mg; Sodium 210mg; Total Carbohydrate 17g (Dietary Fiber 0g); Protein 3g **Exchanges:** 1 Starch, ½ Fat **Carbohydrate Choices:** 1

bake smart If you like rolls that are golden brown on top but have soft sides, place the rolls closer together on the cookie sheet so they will rise and bake together.

The intense flavor of sun-dried tomatoes can bring out the best in soups, stews and breads. You'll find these flavor-packed gems sold either packed in oil, which keeps them a little softer, or dry packed in cellophane. The dry tomatoes need to be soaked before using to make them softer.

bagels

prep time: 20 minutes ✛ start to finish: 1 hour 35 minutes ✛ 10 BAGELS

1 cup plus 1 tablespoon water

1½ tablespoons honey

3 cups bread flour

1¼ teaspoons salt

1½ teaspoons bread machine or fast-acting dry yeast

Old-fashioned oats, instant minced onion, sesame seed or poppy seed, if desired

1 Measure carefully, placing all ingredients except oats in bread machine pan in the order recommended by the manufacturer.

2 Select Dough/Manual cycle. Do not use delay cycle. Stop cycle after 50 minutes; remove dough from pan, using lightly floured hands.

3 Grease cookie sheet. Cut dough into 10 equal pieces. Shape each piece into 3-inch round; poke 1-inch hole in center, using thumb. Smooth into bagel shape, using fingers. Place on cookie sheet. Cover and let rise in warm place about 20 minutes or until almost doubled in size.

4 Heat oven to 450°F. In Dutch oven, heat 2 quarts water to boiling. Lower 3 or 4 bagels at a time into boiling water. Boil 30 seconds, turning once after 15 seconds. Remove with slotted spoon; drain on paper towels. Sprinkle with oats. Place on cookie sheet. Bake 8 minutes or until light golden brown. Remove from cookie sheet to cooling rack; cool.

1 Bagel: Calories 160 (Calories from Fat 5); Total Fat 0.5g (Saturated Fat 0g; Trans Fat 0g); Cholesterol 0mg; Sodium 300mg; Total Carbohydrate 33g (Dietary Fiber 1g); Protein 5g **Exchanges:** 1½ Starch, ½ Other Carbohydrate **Carbohydrate Choices:** 2

berry bagels: Add ½ cup dried blueberries, cherries or cranberries at the Raisin/Nut signal or 5 to 10 minutes before the last kneading cycle ends.

cinnamon bagels: Add 1 teaspoon ground cinnamon with the salt.

garlic bagels: Add 1 teaspoon garlic powder with the salt.

wild rice breadsticks

prep time: 30 minutes + start to finish: 2 hours 5 minutes + 15 BREADSTICKS

2 to 2¼ cups all-purpose flour

¾ cup whole wheat flour

¾ cup cooked wild rice or brown rice

1 tablespoon vegetable oil

2 tablespoons molasses

1½ teaspoons fennel seed, if desired

1½ teaspoons salt

1½ teaspoons regular active or fast-acting dry yeast

1 cup very warm water (120°F to 130°F)

Additional vegetable oil, if desired

1 In large bowl, mix 1 cup of the all-purpose flour, the whole wheat flour, wild rice, 1 tablespoon oil, the molasses, fennel seed, salt and yeast. Stir in warm water until blended. Stir in enough remaining all-purpose flour to make dough easy to handle.

2 On lightly floured surface, knead dough about 5 minutes or until smooth and springy. Grease large bowl with shortening. Place dough in bowl, turning dough to grease all sides. Cover and let rise in warm place about 1 hour or until doubled in size. (If using fast-acting yeast, do not let rise 1 hour; cover and let rest on floured surface 10 minutes.)

3 Grease 2 cookie sheets. Punch down dough. Divide dough into 15 equal pieces. Roll each piece into 9-inch rope. Place on cookie sheets. Brush with additional oil. Cover and let rise in warm place 5 to 15 minutes or until slightly risen.

4 Heat oven to 375°F. Bake 15 to 20 minutes or until golden brown.

1 Breadstick: Calories 110 (Calories from Fat 10); Total Fat 1g (Saturated Fat 0g; Trans Fat 0g); Cholesterol 0mg; Sodium 240mg; Total Carbohydrate 21g (Dietary Fiber 1g); Protein 3g **Exchanges:** 1 Starch, ½ Other Carbohydrate **Carbohydrate Choices:** 1½

bake smart Use instant simmer-and-serve wild rice, and while you're at it, cook enough for another recipe or meal.

Warm breadsticks in the microwave. Microwave uncovered on a microwavable plate or in a napkin-lined basket. For 8 to 10 breadsticks, microwave on Medium (50%) 1 minute. Continue to microwave, checking at 15-second intervals, until warm.

black pepper 'n parmesan grissini

prep time: 30 minutes + start to finish: 3 hours + 32 GRISSINI

breadsticks

¾ cup warm water (105°F to 115°F)

1 teaspoon regular active dry yeast

½ teaspoon sugar

2 tablespoons olive oil

½ cup whole wheat flour

1¼ to 1¾ cups all-purpose flour

⅓ cup grated Parmesan cheese

1 teaspoon salt

½ teaspoon coarsely ground black pepper

topping

2 to 3 teaspoons olive oil

¼ cup grated Parmesan cheese

1 teaspoon coarsely ground black pepper

1 In large bowl, combine warm water, yeast and sugar; stir until yeast is dissolved. Add 2 tablespoons olive oil. Stir in whole wheat flour and ½ cup of the all-purpose flour with whisk until mixture is smooth. Cover and let stand in warm place 35 to 45 minutes or until mixture is light and bubbly.

2 Stir in ⅓ cup Parmesan cheese, the salt and ½ teaspoon pepper. Add ¾ cup of the all-purpose flour, gradually adding additional all-purpose flour as necessary to make dough easy to handle.

3 Place dough on lightly floured surface. Knead 10 minutes or until dough is smooth and springy. Grease large bowl with oil. Place dough in bowl, turning dough to grease all sides. Cover bowl loosely with plastic wrap; let rise in warm place about 1 hour or until dough has doubled in size. Dough is ready if indentation remains when touched.

4 Position one oven rack in lower third of oven and second oven rack in upper third of oven. Heat oven to 425°F. Line 2 cookie sheets with cooking parchment paper.

5 Gently push fist into dough to deflate. On lightly oiled surface, pat out dough to 8-inch square. Using pizza cutter or sharp knife, cut square in half. Cut each half crosswise into 16 strips. Roll each strip to 10- to 12-inch length; place on cookie sheet. Brush with 2 to 3 teaspoons olive oil; sprinkle with ¼ cup Parmesan cheese and 1 teaspoon pepper.

6 Bake 12 to 15 minutes or until golden brown and crisp, moving cookie sheets to other rack position halfway through baking. Remove from cookie sheets to cooling rack. Cool completely, about 30 minutes.

1 Grissini: Calories 280 (Calories from Fat 80); Total Fat 9g (Saturated Fat 5g; Trans Fat 0g); Cholesterol 50mg; Sodium 2300mg; Total Carbohydrate 37g (Dietary Fiber 1g); Protein 11g **Exchanges:** 2½ Starch, ½ Medium-Fat Meat, 1 Fat **Carbohydrate Choices:** 2½

bake smart *Grissini* is Italian for "breadsticks." They are a thin, crisp breadstick.

This dough uses the sponge method, where the yeast, water and some of the flour are combined into a batter-like mixture and allowed to rise before the remaining ingredients are added. This step kick-starts the rising process and gives the bread added flavor and texture.

bake smart   To reheat the pretzels, place on a cookie sheet in a 350°F oven for 5 to 7 minutes or until warm and slightly crisp.

To serve these pretzels Philly-style, generously brush them with unsalted melted butter as soon as they come out of the oven.

pretzels with cheese filling

prep time: 35 minutes ✛ start to finish: 1 hour 30 minutes ✛ 8 PRETZELS

pretzels

- 3 cups all-purpose flour
- 1 package fast-acting dry yeast (2¼ teaspoons)
- 1 teaspoon table salt
- ½ teaspoon sugar
- 1 to 1¼ cups very warm water (120°F to 130°F)

filling

- ¾ cup shredded sharp Cheddar cheese (3 oz)
- ½ cup shredded Swiss cheese (2 oz)
- 2 oz cream cheese (one-fourth of 8-oz package), softened
  Dash ground red pepper (cayenne)

topping

- 2 cups water
- ¼ cup baking soda
- 1 egg
- 1 tablespoon water
- 1 teaspoon coarse (kosher or sea) salt, if desired

1 In large bowl, stir flour, yeast, table salt and sugar with whisk. Add 1 cup warm water; stir to combine, slowly adding additional water as necessary to make dough easy to handle.

2 Place dough on lightly floured surface. Knead 10 minutes or until dough is smooth and springy. Grease large bowl with oil. Place dough in bowl, turning dough to grease all sides. Cover bowl loosely with plastic wrap sprayed with cooking spray; let rise in warm place about 30 minutes or until doubled in size. Dough is ready if indentation remains when touched.

3 Meanwhile, in small bowl, stir together all filling ingredients.

4 Heat oven to 425°F. Line 2 cookie sheets with cooking parchment paper. Gently push fist into dough to deflate. Place dough on lightly floured surface. Using floured rolling pin, roll to 16×12-inch rectangle. Using pizza cutter, cut dough crosswise into 8 (2×12-inch) strips. Spoon cheese mixture down center of each dough strip. Press dough over filling, pinching edges and ends to seal. Gently press or roll each strip to 15-inch rope.

5 To make pretzel shape, form each rope into U shape. Twist ends twice. Overlap twisted ends to form X shape; press together where dough touches. Pick ends up and place on rounded portion of U shape. Tuck one end under dough; place other end on top of dough.

6 In medium microwavable bowl, microwave 2 cups water on High 2 minutes or until hot. Add baking soda; stir until dissolved. Dip each pretzel, one at a time, into water mixture. Immediately remove from water with large pancake turner; place on cooling rack. Let stand at room temperature about 5 minutes.

7 Meanwhile, in small bowl, stir egg and 1 tablespoon water with fork. Brush pretzels with egg mixture; sprinkle with sea salt. Carefully transfer to cookie sheet. Bake 10 to 12 minutes or until golden brown. Remove from pan to cooling rack; cool 10 minutes. Serve warm or cool completely.

1 Pretzel: Calories 280 (Calories from Fat 80); Total Fat 9g (Saturated Fat 5g; Trans Fat 0g); Cholesterol 50mg; Sodium 2300mg; Total Carbohydrate 37g (Dietary Fiber 1g); Protein 11g **Exchanges:** 2½ Starch, ½ Medium-Fat Meat, 1 Fat **Carbohydrate Choices:** 2½

soft pretzels

prep time: **35 minutes** ✛ start to finish: **1 hour 40 minutes** ✛ 16 PRETZELS

3¾ to 4¼ cups all-purpose flour

1 tablespoon sugar

1½ teaspoons table salt

1 package regular active or fast-acting dry yeast (2¼ teaspoons)

1½ cups water

2 tablespoons vegetable oil

1 cup water

2 teaspoons baking soda

2 teaspoons coarse (kosher or sea) salt

1 In large bowl, stir 2 cups of the flour, the sugar, salt and yeast with wooden spoon until well mixed. In 1-quart saucepan, heat 1½ cups water over medium heat until very warm (120°F to 130°F). Add warm water and oil to flour mixture. Beat with electric mixer on low speed 1 minute, scraping bowl frequently. Beat on medium speed 1 minute, scraping bowl frequently. With wooden spoon, stir in enough of the remaining flour, about ½ cup at time, until dough is soft, leaves side of bowl and is easy to handle (dough may be slightly sticky).

2 Place dough on lightly floured surface. Knead 5 to 10 minutes or until dough is smooth and springy. Lightly spray a sheet of plastic wrap with cooking spray; cover dough. Let rest 10 minutes.

3 Heat oven to 425°F. Spray cookie sheets with cooking spray. In shallow bowl, stir 1 cup water and the baking soda to make pretzel "wash."

4 Divide dough into 16 equal pieces. Roll each piece into 24-inch rope (dip hands in pretzel wash to make rolling dough easier). To make pretzel shape, form rope into circle, crossing ends at top. Fold dough so crossed ends rest on bottom of circle. Stir pretzel wash; using a pastry brush, brush over both sides of pretzel. Place pretzel on cookie sheet. Repeat with remaining dough. Reserve remaining pretzel wash. Cover pretzels loosely with plastic wrap. To make thin pretzels, let rest about 5 minutes or until very slightly puffed. To make thicker pretzels, let rise in warm place 15 to 20 minutes or until puffed.

5 Just before baking, brush pretzels with reserved wash; sprinkle with coarse salt. Bake 1 cookie sheet at a time 10 to 13 minutes or until golden brown. Remove from cookie sheets to cooling racks; cool at least 15 minutes. Serve warm or cool.

1 Pretzel: Calories 120 (Calories from Fat 20); Total Fat 2g (Saturated Fat 0g; Trans Fat 0g); Cholesterol 0mg; Sodium 670mg; Total Carbohydrate 23g (Dietary Fiber 0g); Protein 3g **Exchanges:** 1 Starch, ½ Other Carbohydrate **Carbohydrate Choices:** 1½

parmesan-herb soft pretzels: Mix 2 tablespoons grated Parmesan cheese, ½ teaspoon dried basil leaves and ¼ teaspoon garlic powder. Brush hot baked pretzels with melted butter; sprinkle with cheese mixture.

Gluten-Free Pizza Crust
(page 313)

pizza, focaccia and flatbread

healthified fresh mozzarella and tomato pizza

prep time: 35 minutes ✛ start to finish: 3 hours 15 minutes ✛ 8 SERVINGS

italian-style pizza dough

- 1 package regular or fast-acting dry yeast (2¼ teaspoons)
- ½ cup warm water (105°F to 115°F)
- 1¼ to 1½ cups all-purpose flour
- 1 teaspoon olive oil
- ½ teaspoon salt
- ½ teaspoon sugar

toppings

- 4 oz fresh mozzarella cheese, well drained
- 2 plum (Roma) tomatoes, thinly sliced
- ¼ teaspoon salt
- Cracked black pepper
- ¼ cup thin strips fresh basil leaves
- 1 tablespoon chopped fresh oregano leaves
- 1 tablespoon small capers, if desired
- 1 tablespoon olive oil

1 In large bowl, dissolve yeast in warm water. Stir in half of the flour, 1 teaspoon oil, ½ teaspoon salt and the sugar. Stir in enough of the remaining flour to make dough easy to handle. Place dough on lightly floured surface. Knead 10 minutes or until smooth and springy. Grease large bowl with shortening. Place dough in bowl, turning dough to grease all sides. Cover and let rise in warm place 20 minutes.

2 Gently push fist into dough to deflate. Cover and refrigerate at least 2 hours but no longer than 48 hours. (If dough should double in size during refrigeration, gently push fist into dough to deflate.)

3 Move oven rack to lowest position. Heat oven to 425°F. Grease cookie sheet or 12-inch pizza pan with oil. Using floured fingers, press dough into 12-inch round on cookie sheet or pat in pizza pan. Press dough from center to edge so edge is slightly thicker than center.

4 Cut cheese into ¼-inch slices. Place cheese on dough to within ½ inch of edge. Arrange tomatoes on cheese. Sprinkle with ¼ teaspoon salt, the pepper, 2 tablespoons of the basil, the oregano and capers. Drizzle with 1 tablespoon oil.

5 Bake 20 minutes or until crust is golden brown and cheese is melted. Sprinkle with remaining 2 tablespoons basil.

1 Serving: Calories 140 (Calories from Fat 50); Total Fat 5g (Saturated Fat 2g; Trans Fat 0g); Cholesterol 10mg; Sodium 300mg; Total Carbohydrate 17g (Dietary Fiber 1g); Protein 6g **Exchanges:** 1 Starch, 1 Fat **Carbohydrate Choices:** 1

bake smart Fresh mozzarella is very different from the familiar blocks of mozzarella or shredded mozzarella. The fresh version is usually made with whole milk, is white colored and has a delicate, sweet, milky flavor and much softer texture. Some cheese shops, delis and large supermarkets may carry an Italian import called "buffalo mozzarella," which is made with water buffalo milk or a combination of cow and water buffalo milk. Fresh mozzarella is packed in water or whey and is often formed into balls.

bake smart For Cheese Pizza, top pizza sauce with 3 cups shredded mozzarella cheese (12 oz) and ¼ cup grated Parmesan cheese.

classic homemade pizza

prep time: 20 minutes ✛ start to finish: 3 hours ✛ 8 SERVINGS

1 package regular
   or fast-acting dry yeast
   (2¼ teaspoons)
½ cup warm water
   (105°F to 115°F)
1¼ to 1½ cups all-purpose
   flour or bread flour
1 teaspoon olive or
   vegetable oil
½ teaspoon salt
½ teaspoon sugar
1 can (8 oz) pizza sauce
   Toppings for desired
   pizza (below)

1 In large bowl, dissolve yeast in warm water. Stir in half of the flour and the oil, salt and sugar. Stir in enough of the remaining flour, ¼ cup at a time, to make dough easy to handle.

2 Place dough on lightly floured surface. Knead 10 minutes or until dough is smooth and springy. Spray large bowl with cooking spray. Place dough in bowl, turning dough to grease all sides. Cover bowl loosely with plastic wrap; let rise in warm place 20 minutes.

3 Gently push fist into dough to deflate. Cover bowl loosely with plastic wrap; refrigerate at least 2 hours but no longer than 48 hours. (If dough should double in size during refrigeration, gently push fist into dough to deflate.)

4 Move oven rack to middle position. Heat oven to 425°F. Place dough on center of ungreased cookie sheet or 12-inch pizza pan. Using floured fingers, press dough into 12-inch round. Press dough from center to edge so edge is slightly thicker than center. Spread pizza sauce over dough to within ½ inch of edge. Add toppings for either cheese, hamburger, Italian sausage or pepperoni pizza.

5 Bake 15 to 20 minutes or until crust is golden brown and cheeses are melted and lightly browned.

1 Serving (Crust and Sauce): Calories 80 (Calories from Fat 5); Total Fat 1g (Saturated Fat 0g; Trans Fat 0g); Cholesterol 0mg; Sodium 150mg; Total Carbohydrate 16g (Dietary Fiber 0g); Protein 2g **Exchanges:** 1 Starch **Carbohydrate Choices:** 1

hamburger pizza: In 10-inch skillet, cook 1 lb lean (at least 80%) ground beef, 1 cup chopped onion and 1 teaspoon Italian seasoning over medium heat 8 to 10 minutes, stirring occasionally, until beef is thoroughly cooked. Pour into paper towel–lined strainer to drain. Spread beef mixture over pizza sauce. Sprinkle with 2 cups shredded mozzarella cheese and ¼ cup grated Parmesan cheese.

italian sausage pizza: In 10-inch skillet, cook 1 lb bulk Italian pork sausage and 1 cup chopped green bell pepper (if desired) over medium heat 8 to 10 minutes, stirring occasionally, until pork is no longer pink. Pour into paper towel–lined strainer to drain. Spread sausage mixture over pizza sauce. Sprinkle with 2 cups shredded mozzarella cheese and ¼ cup grated Parmesan cheese.

pepperoni pizza: Arrange 1 package (3 oz) sliced pepperoni over pizza sauce. Sprinkle with 2 cups shredded mozzarella cheese and ¼ cup grated Parmesan cheese.

easy bisquick pizza

prep time: 15 minutes ÷ start to finish: 35 minutes ÷ 8 SERVINGS

2¼ cups Original Bisquick mix

¼ to ⅓ cup cornmeal

⅔ cup milk

1 jar (10 oz) basil pesto

1 plum (Roma) tomato, thinly sliced

2 cups shredded mozzarella cheese (8 oz)

½ cup shredded Parmesan cheese

¼ cup thinly sliced fresh basil leaves

1 tablespoon olive oil

1 Heat oven to 450°F. Spray large cookie sheet with cooking spray.

2 In large bowl, stir Bisquick mix, ¼ cup cornmeal and the milk until soft dough forms.

3 Press dough into 13×9-inch rectangle on cookie sheet, using additional cornmeal as needed. Using fork, pierce dough at 1-inch intervals. Bake 8 minutes, or until just beginning to brown.

4 Spread pesto over crust. Top with tomato and cheeses. Bake an additional 8 to 10 minutes or until cheese is melted. Sprinkle basil and olive oil over top. Cut into 2 rows by 4 rows.

1 Serving: Calories 480 (Calories from Fat 290); Total Fat 33g (Saturated Fat 10g; Trans Fat 1.5g); Cholesterol 30mg; Sodium 980mg; Total Carbohydrate 31g (Dietary Fiber 2g); Protein 17g **Exchanges:** 2 Starch, 1½ High-Fat Meat, 4 Fat **Carbohydrate Choices:** 2

bake smart In addition to the chopped fresh basil, sprinkle ¼ cup thinly sliced arugula over the baked pizza.

chicago-style deep-dish pizza

prep time: 45 minutes ✛ start to finish: 1 hour 15 minutes ✛ **12 SERVINGS**

2 packages regular active dry yeast (4½ teaspoons)

1½ cups warm water (105°F to 115°F)

6 cups Original Bisquick mix

¼ cup olive or vegetable oil

8 cups shredded mozzarella cheese (32 oz)

1 lb bulk Italian pork sausage, cooked, drained, or 2 packages (3½ oz each) sliced pepperoni

Vegetable toppings such as sliced fresh mushrooms, chopped green bell pepper or chopped onion, sliced green onions, sliced ripe olives, sliced pimiento-stuffed olives, if desired

2 cans (28 oz each) whole peeled tomatoes with basil, well drained

2 to 4 tablespoons chopped fresh or 2 teaspoons dried oregano leaves or Italian seasoning

½ to 1 cup grated Parmesan cheese

1 Move oven racks to lowest positions. Heat oven to 425°F. Grease 2 (15×10×1-inch) pans or 4 (9-inch) round cake pans with olive oil. In large bowl, dissolve yeast in warm water. Stir in Bisquick mix and ¼ cup oil; beat vigorously 20 strokes.

2 Place dough on surface generously sprinkled with Bisquick mix; gently roll in Bisquick to coat. Knead 60 times or until smooth and no longer sticky. Let rest 5 minutes. (At this point, dough can be covered and refrigerated for up to 24 hours. See tip below.)

3 Divide dough in half. Pat each half of dough in bottom and up sides of pans. Or divide dough into fourths and press in bottom and up sides of round pans.

4 Reserve 1 cup of the mozzarella cheese. Sprinkle remaining mozzarella cheese over crusts. Top with sausage, desired vegetable toppings and tomatoes. Sprinkle with oregano and Parmesan cheese. Sprinkle with the reserved mozzarella cheese.

5 Bake 20 to 25 minutes (switching top and bottom pans halfway through bake time) or until crust is brown and cheese is melted and bubbly. Immediately cut pizza into pieces. Let stand a few minutes for easier serving.

1 Serving: Calories 640 (Calories from Fat 320); Total Fat 36g (Saturated Fat 14g; Trans Fat 3g); Cholesterol 60mg; Sodium 1500mg; Total Carbohydrate 48g (Dietary Fiber 3g); Protein 31g **Exchanges:** 3 Starch, 3 Medium-Fat Meat, 3½ Fat **Carbohydrate Choices:** 3

bake smart Pass the grated Parmesan cheese and crushed red pepper—no Chicago-style pizza is complete without them!

You can make the pizza dough ahead of time. Place the dough in a lightly greased bowl, and turn it over to grease all sides. Cover tightly with plastic wrap and refrigerate up to 24 hours. For easier shaping, let the dough stand at room temperature at least 20 minutes.

chicken fajita pizza

prep time: 20 minutes ✛ start to finish: 2 hours 35 minutes ✛ **8 SERVINGS**

crust

- ½ cup water
- 1 tablespoon vegetable oil
- ¾ cup whole wheat flour
- ¾ cup all-purpose or bread flour
- ½ teaspoon salt
- ¼ teaspoon sugar
- 1¼ teaspoons bread machine or fast-acting dry yeast

toppings

- 1 teaspoon vegetable oil
- ½ lb boneless skinless chicken breasts, cut into ⅛- to ¼-inch strips
- 1 medium bell pepper, cut into ¼-inch strips
- 1 small onion, sliced
- 1 cup chunky-style salsa
- 2 teaspoons chopped fresh or 1½ teaspoons dried cilantro, if desired
- 1½ cups shredded Monterey Jack cheese (6 oz)

1 Measure carefully, placing all crust ingredients in bread machine pan in the order recommended by the manufacturer. Select Dough/Manual cycle. Do not use delay cycle.

2 Remove dough from pan, using lightly floured hands. Knead 5 minutes on lightly floured surface (if necessary, knead in enough additional flour to make dough easy to handle). Cover and let rest 10 minutes.

3 Move oven rack to lowest position. Heat oven to 450°F. Grease large cookie sheet or 12-inch pizza pan. In 10-inch nonstick skillet, heat oil over medium-high heat. Cook chicken in oil 3 minutes, stirring occasionally. Stir in bell pepper and onion. Cook 3 to 4 minutes, stirring occasionally, until chicken is no longer pink in center and vegetables are crisp-tender; remove from heat. Stir in salsa.

4 Pat dough into 12-inch round on cookie sheet or pat in pan; pinch edge, forming ½-inch rim. Spread chicken mixture over dough. Sprinkle with cilantro and cheese. Bake 12 to 15 minutes or until crust is golden brown and cheese is melted.

1 Serving: Calories 230 (Calories from Fat 90); Total Fat 10g (Saturated Fat 4.5g; Trans Fat 0g); Cholesterol 35mg; Sodium 510mg; Total Carbohydrate 21g (Dietary Fiber 2g); Protein 15g **Exchanges:** 1½ Starch, 1½ Very Lean Meat, 1½ Fat **Carbohydrate Choices:** 1½

bake smart The chicken fajita topping also tastes delicious on purchased bread shells and pizza crusts.

gluten-free pizza crust

prep time: **10 minutes** ✛ start to finish: **40 minutes** ✛ **6 SERVINGS**

1⅓ cups Bisquick Gluten Free mix

½ teaspoon Italian seasoning or dried basil

½ cup water

⅓ cup oil

2 eggs, beaten

suggested topping quantities

1 can (8 oz) pizza sauce

1 cup bite-size pieces favorite meat or vegetables

1½ cups shredded mozzarella cheese (6 oz)

1 Heat oven to 425°F. Grease 12-inch pizza pan. In medium bowl, stir Bisquick mix, Italian seasoning, water, oil and eggs until well combined; spread in pan.

2 Bake 15 minutes (crust will appear cracked).

3 Spread pizza sauce over crust; top with meat and cheese.

4 Bake 10 to 15 minutes longer or until cheese is melted.

1 Serving: Calories 230 (Calories from Fat 130); Total Fat 14g (Saturated Fat 2.5g; Trans Fat 0g); Cholesterol 70mg; Sodium 320mg; Total Carbohydrate 23g (Dietary Fiber 0g); Protein 3g **Exchanges:** 1½ Starch, 2½ Fat **Carbohydrate Choices:** 1½

bake smart Cooking gluten free? Always read labels to make sure that each recipe ingredient is gluten free. Products and ingredient sources can vary.

design-your-own pizza

prep time: 30 minutes ✦ start to finish: 55 minutes ✦ 16 SERVINGS

whole wheat pizza crust

- 1 package regular active or fast-acting dry yeast (2¼ teaspoons)
- 1 cup warm water (105°F to 115°F)
- 1½ cups all-purpose flour
- 1 cup whole wheat flour
- 2 tablespoons olive or vegetable oil
- ½ teaspoon salt
  - Olive or vegetable oil
  - Cornmeal

filling

- 1 lb lean (at least 80%) ground beef or ground pork, lamb or turkey
- 1 large onion or 1 medium green bell pepper, chopped (1 cup)
- 1 teaspoon Italian seasoning
- 2 cloves garlic, finely chopped
- 1 can (8 oz) pizza sauce
- 1 can (4 oz) sliced mushrooms, drained, or 1 can (4.5 oz) chopped green chiles, drained
- 2 cups shredded mozzarella, Cheddar, Monterey Jack or brick cheese (8 oz)
- ¼ cup grated Parmesan or Romano cheese

1 In medium bowl, dissolve yeast in warm water. Stir in flours, 2 tablespoons oil and the salt. Beat vigorously 20 strokes. Let rest 20 minutes. Follow directions below for thin or thick crusts.

2 For thin crusts: Move oven rack to lowest position. Heat oven to 425°F. Grease 2 cookie sheets or 12-inch pizza pans with oil. Sprinkle with cornmeal. Divide dough in half. With floured fingers, pat each half into 11-inch round on cookie sheet. Bake uncovered 10 minutes or until crust just begins to brown.

3 For thick crusts: Move oven rack to lowest position. Heat oven to 375°F. Grease 2 (8-inch) square pans with oil. Sprinkle with cornmeal. Divide dough in half. With floured fingers, pat each half in bottom of pan. Cover and let rise in warm place 30 to 45 minutes or until almost double. Bake uncovered 20 to 22 minutes or until crust just begins to brown.

4 While crusts are baking, in 10-inch skillet, cook beef, onion, Italian seasoning and garlic over medium heat 8 to 10 minutes, stirring occasionally, until beef is thoroughly cooked and onion is tender; drain. Spread pizza sauce over crusts. Sprinkle with beef mixture, mushrooms and cheeses.

5 Bake thin-crust pizzas at 425°F 10 minutes, thick-crust pizzas at 375°F 20 minutes, or until cheese is melted and pizzas are bubbly.

1 Serving: Calories 200 (Calories from Fat 80); Total Fat 9g (Saturated Fat 3.5g; Trans Fat 0g); Cholesterol 25mg; Sodium 240mg; Total Carbohydrate 18g (Dietary Fiber 2g); Protein 12g **Exchanges:** 1 Starch, 1½ Lean Meat, 1 Fat **Carbohydrate Choices:** 1

bake smart Prebaking these pizza crusts means a drier, crisper crust in the final bake.

Depending on the size of your oven, you may have to bake one pizza at a time.

grape tomato and oregano focaccia

prep time: 30 minutes ÷ start to finish: 2 hours 30 minutes ÷ 1 FOCACCIA (12 SLICES)

dough

- 1½ teaspoons regular active dry yeast
- ½ teaspoon sugar
- ¼ cup plus ⅔ cup very warm water (120°F to 130°F)
- 1 tablespoon olive oil
- 1 teaspoon table salt
- 1 tablespoon chopped fresh oregano leaves
- 2½ to 2¾ cups bread flour or all-purpose flour

toppings

- 1 tablespoon olive oil
- 1 large clove garlic, finely chopped
- 1 tablespoon chopped fresh oregano leaves
- ¼ cup shredded Asiago cheese (1 oz)
- 1 cup yellow and red grape tomatoes or cherry tomatoes, halved
- ½ teaspoon coarse (kosher or sea) salt

1 In large bowl, stir yeast, sugar and ¼ cup of the warm water until blended. Let stand 10 minutes or until yeast is dissolved and foamy. Add remaining ⅔ cup warm water, 1 tablespoon olive oil, the table salt and 1 tablespoon oregano. Stir in 2½ cups of the flour, gradually adding additional flour as necessary to make dough easy to handle.

2 Place dough on lightly floured surface. Knead 10 minutes or until dough is smooth and springy. Grease large bowl with oil. Place dough in bowl, turning dough to grease all sides. Cover bowl loosely with plastic wrap sprayed with cooking spray; let rise in warm place 45 to 60 minutes or until doubled in size. Dough is ready if indentation remains when touched.

3 Meanwhile, about 20 minutes before baking, place pizza stone or cookie sheet on oven rack. Heat oven to 425°F. Line another cookie sheet with cooking parchment paper. Gently push fist into dough to deflate. On lightly oiled surface, pat dough into 14×9-inch oval. Place on paper-lined cookie sheet. Cover loosely with plastic wrap sprayed with cooking spray; let rise 20 minutes.

4 Meanwhile, in small bowl, mix 1 tablespoon oil and garlic. With fingertips, gently make ½-inch-deep depressions about 2 inches apart in dough. Brush with garlic-oil mixture; sprinkle with 1 tablespoon oregano. Sprinkle cheese over dough; top with tomatoes. Gently press tomatoes into dough. Sprinkle with coarse salt. Slide dough and parchment paper from cookie sheet onto pizza stone.

5 Bake 18 to 20 minutes or until golden brown and crisp. Cool on cooling rack, about 20 minutes. Serve warm or cool.

1 Slice: Calories 140 (Calories from Fat 35); Total Fat 3.5g (Saturated Fat 1g; Trans Fat 0g); Cholesterol 0mg; Sodium 320mg; Total Carbohydrate 22g (Dietary Fiber 1g); Protein 4g **Exchanges:** 1½ Starch, ½ Fat **Carbohydrate Choices:** 1½

bake smart Focaccia can be adapted in many ways. Scatter olives along with the tomatoes, substitute rosemary or basil for the oregano and use a variety of cheeses, including goat cheese or blue cheese.

classic focaccia

prep time: 30 minutes ✛ start to finish: 1 hour 50 minutes ✛ 2 FOCACCIAS (12 SLICES EACH)

2½ to 3 cups all-purpose or bread flour

2 tablespoons chopped fresh or 1 tablespoon dried rosemary leaves, crumbled

1 tablespoon sugar

1 teaspoon salt

1 package regular active or fast-acting dry yeast (2¼ teaspoons)

3 tablespoons olive or vegetable oil

1 cup very warm water (120°F to 130°F)

2 tablespoons olive or vegetable oil

¼ cup grated Parmesan cheese

1 In large bowl, mix 1 cup of the flour, the rosemary, sugar, salt and yeast. Add 3 tablespoons oil and the warm water. Beat with electric mixer on medium speed 3 minutes, scraping bowl frequently. Stir in enough remaining flour until dough is soft and leaves side of bowl.

2 Place dough on lightly floured surface. Knead 5 to 8 minutes or until smooth and springy. Grease large bowl with shortening. Place dough in bowl, turning dough to grease all sides. Cover bowl loosely with plastic wrap; let rise in warm place about 30 minutes or until almost doubled in size. Dough is ready if indentation remains when touched.

3 Grease 2 cookie sheets or 12-inch pizza pans with small amount of oil or spray with cooking spray. Gently push fist into dough to deflate. Divide dough in half. Pat dough into 10-inch round on cookie sheet. Cover loosely with plastic wrap lightly sprayed with cooking spray and let rise in warm place about 30 minutes or until doubled in size.

4 Heat oven to 400°F. With fingertips, gently make ½-inch-deep depressions about 2 inches apart in dough. Carefully brush with 2 tablespoons oil; sprinkle with cheese. Bake 15 to 20 minutes or until golden brown. Serve warm or cool.

1 Slice: Calories 80 (Calories from Fat 30); Total Fat 3.5g (Saturated Fat 0.5g; Trans Fat 0g); Cholesterol 0mg; Sodium 120mg; Total Carbohydrate 12g (Dietary Fiber 0g); Protein 2g **Exchanges:** 1 Starch **Carbohydrate Choices:** 1

onion focaccia: Make dough as directed—except omit rosemary, 2 tablespoons oil and Parmesan cheese. In 10-inch skillet, heat ⅓ cup olive oil over medium heat. Stir in 4 cups thinly sliced onions and 4 cloves garlic, finely chopped. Cook uncovered 10 minutes, stirring every 3 to 4 minutes. Reduce heat to medium-low. Cook 30 to 40 minutes longer, stirring well every 5 minutes, until onions are light golden brown. Continue and bake as directed in recipe—except do not brush dough with oil; after second rising, carefully spread onion mixture over breads.

breadsticks: Make dough as directed. After kneading, cover loosely with plastic wrap; let rest 30 minutes. Grease 2 cookie sheets with shortening or cooking spray; sprinkle with cornmeal. Divide dough into 12 pieces. Roll and shape each piece into 12-inch rope, sprinkling with flour if dough is too sticky. Place ropes about ½ inch apart on cookie sheets. Brush with 2 tablespoons oil and sprinkle with grated Parmesan cheese or coarse (kosher or sea) salt if desired. Cover loosely with plastic wrap and let rise in warm place 20 minutes or until almost doubled in size. Heat oven to 425°F. Bake 10 to 12 minutes or until golden brown. **MAKES 12 BREADSTICKS**

caramelized-onion focaccia

prep time: 35 minutes ÷ start to finish: 2 hours 45 minutes ÷ 1 FOCACCIA (8 SLICES)

dough

- ¾ cup water
- 2 tablespoons olive or vegetable oil
- 2 cups bread flour
- 1 tablespoon sugar
- 1 teaspoon salt
- 1½ teaspoons bread machine yeast

onion topping

- ¼ cup butter
- 4 large onions, sliced
- ¾ cup shredded mozzarella cheese (3 oz)
- 2 tablespoons grated Parmesan cheese

1 Measure carefully, placing all dough ingredients in bread machine pan in the order recommended by the manufacturer.

2 Select Dough/Manual cycle. Do not use delay cycle.

3 Grease cookie sheet. Pat dough into 12-inch round on cookie sheet. Cover and let rise in warm place 30 minutes or until almost double.

4 Meanwhile, in 12-inch skillet, melt butter over medium heat. Cook onions in butter 25 to 30 minutes, stirring occasionally, until onions are brown and caramelized; remove from heat.

5 Heat oven to 400°F. With fingertips or handle of wooden spoon, make deep depressions in dough at 1-inch intervals. Spread onions over dough. Sprinkle with cheeses. Bake 15 to 18 minutes or until edge is golden brown. Remove from cookie sheet to cooling rack. Serve warm. Cut into wedges or squares.

1 Slice: Calories 280 (Calories from Fat 110); Total Fat 12g (Saturated Fat 6g; Trans Fat 0g); Cholesterol 20mg; Sodium 420mg; Total Carbohydrate 34g (Dietary Fiber 2g); Protein 8g **Exchanges:** 2½ Starch, 2 Fat **Carbohydrate Choices:** 2

peppered focaccia

prep time: **15 minutes** ✛ start to finish: **1 hour 45 minutes** ✛ **2 FOCACCIAS (16 SLICES EACH)**

2¾ to 3 cups all-purpose flour

2 tablespoons sugar

½ teaspoon salt

1 package regular active or fast-acting dry yeast (2¼ teaspoons)

1 cup water

¼ cup olive or vegetable oil

½ medium green bell pepper, cut into thin slices

½ medium red bell pepper, cut into thin slices

½ cup shredded mozzarella cheese (2 oz), if desired

½ teaspoon dried basil leaves

½ teaspoon dried oregano leaves

½ teaspoon garlic powder

½ teaspoon salt

1 In large bowl, mix 1½ cups of flour, the sugar, ½ teaspoon salt and the yeast. In 1-quart saucepan, heat water and 2 tablespoons of the oil until very warm (120°F to 130°F); stir into flour mixture. Beat with electric mixer on low speed about 30 seconds, scraping bowl occasionally, until batter is springy and pulls away from side of bowl. Stir in enough remaining flour to make a soft dough. Cover and let rise in warm place 1 hour or until doubled in size. (If using fast-acting yeast, omit 1-hour rise time; cover and let rest on floured surface 10 minutes.)

2 Grease 2 cookie sheets. Stir down dough; divide in half. Place each half on cookie sheet; press into 12-inch round. Brush each round with about 1 tablespoon of the remaining oil. Top each with half of the bell peppers, cheese, basil, oregano, garlic powder and ½ teaspoon salt. Let stand 10 to 12 minutes.

3 Heat oven to 425°F. Bake 12 to 15 minutes or until crust is golden brown. Cut into wedges. Serve hot.

1 Slice: Calories 80 (Calories from Fat 20); Total Fat 2.5g (Saturated Fat 0g; Trans Fat 0g); Cholesterol 0mg; Sodium 100mg; Total Carbohydrate 12g (Dietary Fiber 0g); Protein 1g **Exchanges:** ½ Starch, ½ Other Carbohydrate, ½ Fat **Carbohydrate Choices:** 1

bake smart Nix the dried herbs for a fresher option. Simply use about three times the amount of freshly chopped herbs for the dried (for example, use 1½ teaspoons chopped fresh basil instead of ½ teaspoon dried).

crusty mustard focaccia

prep time: 15 minutes ✛ start to finish: 2 hours 40 minutes ✛ 1 FOCACCIA (8 SLICES)

⅔ cup water

1 tablespoon olive or vegetable oil

2 tablespoons spicy mustard

2¼ cups bread flour

1 tablespoon sugar

1 teaspoon table salt

1½ teaspoons bread machine or fast-acting dry yeast

3 tablespoons olive or vegetable oil

Coarse (kosher or sea) salt, if desired

1 Measure carefully, placing all ingredients except 3 tablespoons oil and the coarse salt in bread machine pan in the order recommended by the manufacturer.

2 Select Dough/Manual cycle. Do not use delay cycle.

3 Remove dough from pan, using lightly floured hands. Knead 5 minutes on lightly floured surface (if necessary, knead in enough additional flour to make dough easy to handle). Cover and let rest 10 minutes.

4 Grease large cookie sheet. Roll or pat dough into 12-inch round on cookie sheet. Cover and let rise in warm place 10 minutes or until almost double.

5 Heat oven to 400°F. Prick dough with fork at 1-inch intervals or make deep depressions in dough with fingertips. Brush with 3 tablespoons oil. Sprinkle with coarse salt. Bake 15 to 18 minutes or until golden brown. Serve warm or cool.

1 Slice: Calories 210 (Calories from Fat 70); Total Fat 8g (Saturated Fat 1g; Trans Fat 0g); Cholesterol 0mg; Sodium 390mg; Total Carbohydrate 30g (Dietary Fiber 1g); Protein 5g **Exchanges:** 1½ Starch, ½ Other Carbohydrate, 1½ Fat **Carbohydrate Choices:** 2

bake smart Prepared mustard generally is made from powdered mustard, which is finely ground mustard seed, and combined with seasonings and liquid such as water, vinegar, wine or beer. Prepared spicy mustard can range from mild to sweet—use the variety that you like best.

green onion–sesame flatbreads

prep time: 40 minutes ✛ start to finish: 40 minutes ✛ 6 FLATBREADS (4 SLICES EACH)

3 cups all-purpose flour

2 tablespoons sesame seed

1½ teaspoons baking powder

1 teaspoon salt

1 tablespoon sesame oil

1 cup plus 1 to 2 tablespoons cold water

⅓ cup chopped green onions (4 medium)

½ cup vegetable oil

1 In medium bowl, mix flour, sesame seed, baking powder and salt. Stir in sesame oil and enough cold water to make a smooth, soft dough. On floured surface, knead dough 3 minutes. Divide dough into 6 equal parts; keep covered. Roll each part into 7-inch round.

2 Sprinkle each round with about 1 tablespoon of the onions. Roll each round up tightly, pinching side and ends to seal. Roll into 12-inch rope. Shape each rope to form a coil, tucking end under coil; roll into 7-inch round.

3 In 8-inch skillet, heat vegetable oil over medium heat to 375°F. Cook 1 round in oil 1 to 3 minutes, turning once, until golden brown. Drain on paper towels. Repeat with remaining rounds. Cut each round into 4 wedges. Serve warm.

1 Slice: Calories 80 (Calories from Fat 20); Total Fat 2.5g (Saturated Fat 0g; Trans Fat 0g); Cholesterol 0mg; Sodium 130mg; Total Carbohydrate 12g (Dietary Fiber 0g); Protein 2g **Exchanges:** 1 Starch **Carbohydrate Choices:** 1

bake smart This Asian bread is easy to make in advance. Just roll it out in the morning and refrigerate, covered, until ready to cook. It is traditionally used to soak up the juices of stews, soups, or gravies.

italian flatbread

prep time: **15 minutes** ÷ start to finish: **35 minutes** ÷ **1 FLATBREAD (12 SLICES)**

2 cups Original Bisquick mix

½ cup very warm water (120°F to 130°F)

2 tablespoons butter, melted

¼ cup shredded Cheddar cheese (1 oz)

¼ cup shredded Monterey Jack cheese (1 oz)

¼ cup grated Parmesan cheese

2 teaspoons parsley flakes

½ teaspoon Italian seasoning

1 Heat oven to 450°F. In large bowl, mix Bisquick and warm water until stiff dough forms. Let stand 10 minutes. Place dough on surface generously sprinkled with Bisquick mix; gently roll in Bisquick mix to coat. Shape into a ball; knead 60 times.

2 Pat dough into 11-inch square on ungreased cookie sheet. Spread butter over dough. In small bowl, mix remaining ingredients; sprinkle over dough.

3 Bake 10 to 12 minutes or until edges are light golden brown. Serve warm.

1 Slice: Calories 130 (Calories from Fat 60); Total Fat 7g (Saturated Fat 3.5g; Trans Fat 1g); Cholesterol 10mg; Sodium 320mg; Total Carbohydrate 13g (Dietary Fiber 0g); Protein 3g **Exchanges:** 1 Starch, 1½ Fat **Carbohydrate Choices:** 1

bake smart Transform this flatbread into a vegetarian pizza by adding chopped veggies, sliced olives and fresh basil.

Instead of opening two bags of shredded cheese, you can buy one of the many "pizza-style" shredded cheese blends. Use ½ cup to replace the Cheddar and Monterey Jack.

triple-cheese flatbread

prep time: 15 minutes ✛ start to finish: 40 minutes ✛ 1 FLATBREAD (16 SERVINGS)

2 cups Original Bisquick mix

½ cup very warm water (120°F to 130°F)

2 tablespoons butter, melted

¼ cup shredded Cheddar cheese (1 oz)

¼ cup shredded Monterey Jack cheese (1 oz)

¼ cup grated Parmesan cheese

½ teaspoon garlic powder

½ teaspoon Italian seasoning, if desired

1 Heat oven to 450°F. In medium bowl, stir Bisquick mix and warm water until stiff dough forms. Let stand 10 minutes.

2 On work surface sprinkled with Bisquick mix, gently roll dough in Bisquick mix to coat. Shape into a ball; knead 60 times.

3 On ungreased cookie sheet, pat or roll dough into 12-inch square. Brush butter over dough. In small bowl, mix remaining ingredients; sprinkle over dough.

4 Bake 10 to 12 minutes or until edges are golden brown. Break into pieces and serve warm.

1 Serving: Calories 90 (Calories from Fat 45); Total Fat 5g (Saturated Fat 2.5g; Trans Fat 0.5g); Cholesterol 10mg; Sodium 240mg; Total Carbohydrate 10g (Dietary Fiber 0g); Protein 3g **Exchanges:** ½ Starch, 1 Fat **Carbohydrate Choices:** ½

bake smart To make dough easier to pat onto the cookie sheet, dip your fingers into Bisquick mix.

metric conversion guide

Volume

U.S. UNITS	CANADIAN METRIC	AUSTRALIAN METRIC
¼ teaspoon	1 mL	1 ml
½ teaspoon	2 mL	2 ml
1 teaspoon	5 mL	5 ml
1 tablespoon	15 mL	20 ml
¼ cup	50 mL	60 ml
⅓ cup	75 mL	80 ml
½ cup	125 mL	125 ml
⅔ cup	150 mL	170 ml
¾ cup	175 mL	190 ml
1 cup	250 mL	250 ml
1 quart	1 liter	1 liter
1½ quarts	1.5 liters	1.5 liters
2 quarts	2 liters	2 liters
2½ quarts	2.5 liters	2.5 liters
3 quarts	3 liters	3 liters
4 quarts	4 liters	4 liters

Weight

U.S. UNITS	CANADIAN METRIC	AUSTRALIAN METRIC
1 ounce	30 grams	30 grams
2 ounces	55 grams	60 grams
3 ounces	85 grams	90 grams
4 ounces (¼ pound)	115 grams	125 grams
8 ounces (½ pound)	225 grams	225 grams
16 ounces (1 pound)	455 grams	500 grams
1 pound	455 grams	0.5 kilogram

Note: The recipes in this cookbook have not been developed or tested using metric measures. When converting recipes to metric, some variations in quality may be noted.

Measurements

INCHES	CENTIMETERS
1	2.5
2	5.0
3	7.5
4	10.0
5	12.5
6	15.0
7	17.5
8	20.5
9	23.0
10	25.5
11	28.0
12	30.5
13	33.0

Temperatures

FAHRENHEIT	CELSIUS
32°	0°
212°	100°
250°	120°
275°	140°
300°	150°
325°	160°
350°	180°
375°	190°
400°	200°
425°	220°
450°	230°
475°	240°
500°	260°

index

recipe testing and calculating nutrition information

RECIPE TESTING:

✛ Large eggs and 2% milk were used unless otherwise indicated.

✛ Fat-free, low-fat, low-sodium or lite products were not used unless indicated.

✛ No nonstick cookware and bakeware were used unless otherwise indicated. No dark-colored, black or insulated bakeware was used.

✛ When a pan is specified, a metal pan was used; a baking dish or pie plate means ovenproof glass was used.

✛ An electric hand mixer was used for mixing only when mixer speeds are specified.

CALCULATING NUTRITION:

✛ The first ingredient was used wherever a choice is given, such as ⅓ cup sour cream or plain yogurt.

✛ The first amount was used wherever a range is given, such as 3- to 3½-pound whole chicken.

✛ The first serving number was used wherever a range is given, such as 4 to 6 servings.

✛ "If desired" ingredients were not included.

✛ Only the amount of a marinade or frying oil that is absorbed was included.